Blue Moon Rising

Rising

Kentucky Women in Transition

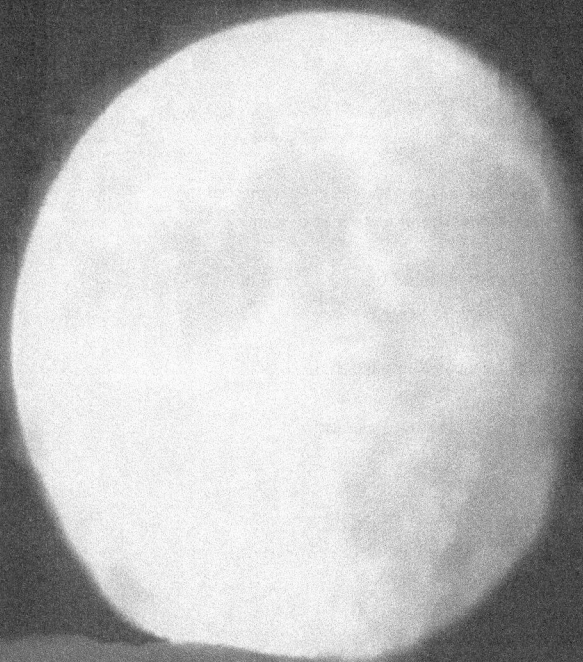

Turner Publishing Company
Paducah, Kentucky

TURNER PUBLISHING COMPANY

Library of Congress Control No. 00-112279
ISBN 978-1-56311-666-7

Turner Publishing Company Staff:
Dayna L. Williams, Editor
Shelley R. Davidson, Designer

Additional copies may be purchased
directly from the publisher.
Limited Edition.

Photos on pages 13 and 35 by Ernest Raymer.
Photos on pages 29, 45, 57, 99, 121, 141, 153 and 163
by Jennie L. Brown.
Photo on page 73 by The Ultimate, Inc.
Photo on page 93 furnished by Sheila Mitchell.
Photo on page 171 by Meyers Photographics, Inc.
Photo on page 179 furnished by Michelle Wallace.

Narrator

It's my job
to frame these paintings,
these silhouettes, these shapes
where faces should be.
It's my job
to give them a megaphone,
let them shout
or whisper at the tops of their lungs,
to punctuate these broken
sentences.
It's my job
to shore up the walls
for the weight of the collection
in this gallery
where cracks roam serrated paths
through foundations.
It's my job
to let them slice tender veins,
spill their life's blood
on these sterling canvases, then
hand them a brush;
they already know how to paint.

~Trish Lindsey Jaggers

Dedication

In memory of my mother,
Helen Dotson
and my friend,
Donna Bergandi
who never gave up on me.

Acknowledgements

This book would not have been possible without the women who shared their stories. I thank them most of all. Not only have they let us look into their lives, but they have let us see into their hearts as well. Their brave and generous acts will inspire and support other women who need and want to make their own transitions.

Additionally, I thank the following who provided me with contacts, guided me, supported my efforts or believed in me: Western Kentucky University for granting me a sabbatical leave; Elmer Gray, Phil Myers, Jane Olmsted, Kathy Edwards and Jackie Addington.

A special thanks to Trish Jaggers for letting me sort through her poetry and choose poems included in this book, and Freda Mays who made my task much easier. I am grateful to Ernie Raymer for his endless patience, his superb computer support, and for always being there at the end of the day. I was encouraged by Alice Rowe, my friend and mentor, who knew when I needed a cup of coffee. I was cheered on by Pat Carr and Angela Leone, friends and writers. And finally, I am grateful to Dayna Williams, my editor, for her sensitivity to the stories and her amazing efficiency.

About the Author

J ennie Brown was born in South Dakota and grew up in Casper, Wyoming. Before entering the University of Colorado, she worked as a bookkeeper, a secretary, a bartender, and as a municipal court clerk with a police force. After taking her degrees from the University of Colorado, she taught in Colorado, California and Seattle, Washington before moving to Kentucky in 1991. She currently teaches writing at Western Kentucky University's Community College in Bowling Green, Kentucky and is a member of the International Women's Writing Guild. She has traveled extensively, including eastern Europe and northern Africa. She recently completed a biography, *A Chance of Today*, detailing a family's life on a sheep ranch in Wyoming during the Depression and World War II.

Contents

Introduction

Holding the edge of the butcher knife against my sleeping husband's throat, I realized I had finally reached the edge of the cliff. Would he wake and send me over the edge, or would he sleep until dawn and save himself? I stared forever at the pulse in his neck, counting the beats, waiting, as I had for seven years, for him to make a decision about our future. He had planted this seed of murder in my mind the night before, throwing steak knives at the wall as he sat laughing drunkenly at my terror. I'd pressed tightly against the chair he had directed me to an hour before, and watched the movement of his hand each time he raised a knife, wondering if this time it would suddenly arc toward me as he flung it. I prayed the loud thunk of the blade, sinking into the wall, wouldn't wake the sleeping children down the hall and bring them in to demand petulantly that the noise stop. I had lived with this for so long now my mind accepted it easily; there were no flashing lights going off behind my eyes telling me that something was terribly wrong, screaming a message to my feet to take me from this insanity. My brain had taken a bit longer than my bruised body, but it, too, had eventually submitted to the truth; whatever madness occurred in the house, I was there for good.

The sound of a bird singing saved us both that morning. I came back to myself, amazed to find the knife in my hand. I slipped out of bed and returned the knife to its place in the kitchen drawer. I brewed coffee in that early dawn, sat down and thought. I knew I had to get out; one of us was going to die soon if I didn't. But seven years of abuse—living with it, learning to work around it, keeping the fights at a level so the neighbors wouldn't hear and call the police, carefully hiding the bruises—had become a web. I didn't think I could fight free of it and then, there were the children...

The story was never finished. The woman who wrote it eventually divorced her husband, entered college, and is rebuilding her life, although she still feels the heavy threat of violence. For her, it was safer to bury the rest of the story. For every Kentucky woman who tells her story, for every Kentucky woman who finds a voice, there are countless others who cannot reveal their struggle. This book honors the women who could tell their stories, and is dedicated to those who could not.

The book had its genesis during the fall semester of 1998. While teaching English at Western Kentucky University's Community College, I met two women who, through their writing, shared their unique stories with me. The first woman, Patti, wrote of her grandson's murder; the second woman, Trish, eloquently described her journey to reach her heart's desire, an education. Their courage and determination so impressed me that I decided to collect stories from other women throughout the state of Kentucky. While there is an abundance of literature about women who have become CEOs, legislators, community leaders or celebrities, it is harder to find stories of ordinary women who have achieved—and overcome— obstacles and plain "hard times." Most of these women are too involved in their struggle to find time to describe the journey. Their stories, too, must be heard.

What they accomplished would be applauded anywhere as examples of great perseverance and inner strength. These women are most extraordinary in their courage and compassion. It is not by accident so many of them have chosen, once they have achieved an education and gained power, to follow a career that benefits other people: the ministry, medicine, youth guidance, social work, college administration, teaching, criminal justice, and advocacy. One builds houses with her own hands; one designs landscapes; one writes to free others' tongues.

Their accomplishments are especially significant in Kentucky where women have lagged behind the rest of the nation in education and opportunity. In 1961, President Kennedy established a Commission on the Status of Women and requested each state to submit a report. Kentucky Governor Edward T. Breathitt established a commission to execute the order. Various committees, established by the commission, submitted their findings in a document dated May 12, 1966.

According to the education committee, "Women are especially hampered by a lack of skills and the apparent inability to seek training for a job. Some are ignorant or timid..."(Kentucky 46). The culture committee determined, "Kentucky women neither contribute as much as they could to their culture nor partake fully of the advantages available to them."(49)

Not surprisingly, the consensus of the commission was:

> Kentucky generally presents no legal barriers to the advancement of women. Women are essentially hindered by only two major factors. The first of these is the long standing, traditional role of women as conceived by men, the community, and our society in general. The second factor affecting the status of women is the view of woman in the eyes of the woman herself. To a great extent, woman has hampered her own progress in modern society by harboring and maintaining an involved and traditionally stereotyped self-image. The legal barriers to the progress and attainment of Kentucky women, with a few minor exceptions, no longer exist. It now remains only for woman to prove herself unworthy of the image that exists. If the effort involved in proving herself is too great, then woman surely must bear whatever stigma that accompanies the traditional image. The choice can only be made by Kentucky women (9-10).

As one examines the findings of the various committees, it is apparent that "woman" in Kentucky was hampered by a great deal more than maintaining the "traditionally stereotyped self-image," and she would need more than a little help to prove herself "unworthy of the image."

The "few minor exceptions" to the legal barriers to progress and equal status were neither trivial nor easily overcome. Although the committee found that "in the broad field of civil rights and political rights, Kentucky is an enlightened and progressive state," they also found that Kentucky law stipulated that property gained by joint efforts during the marriage belonged to the husband. Although a wife was not liable for her husband's debts, a husband could freely sign a note or bond, without his wife's consent, which could encumber her interest in their joint estate. Further, a divorce judgment could not divest the husband of real estate, but did not accord the same right to the wife.

Should the marriage fail, either partner could be granted a divorce on twelve different grounds, but, additionally, the husband could obtain a divorce if his wife was found guilty of "unchaste" conduct. That conduct was defined as "such lewd, lascivious behavior on her part as proves her to be unchaste, without actual proof of an act of adultery." A wife had no comparable recourse for the premarital actions of her husband (30).

Should a husband be driven to drink or infidelity by his interpretation of his wife's lewd and lascivious behavior, he was fully protected by the law. To wit,

> A wife may not obtain a divorce on the grounds of habitual drunkenness by the husband, unless the drunkenness is accompanied by a wasting of his estate without making suitable provisions for maintenance of the wife and children. Thus a husband who makes suitable financial support for his wife and children may imbibe as often and as long as he chooses...(30)

Should the wife succumb to drinking, she was only allotted one year of drunkenness, a period of which was sufficient ground for the husband to obtain a divorce.

Today, Kentucky's divorce laws are more equitable. Still, a divorced woman in Kentucky may face a tough challenge, particularly if she is a custodial parent. In Kentucky, 40 percent of the women who head families with children are considered "officially poor" (Smith-Mello 13).

These female heads of households earn less money, often receive little if any support from the absent parent, and do not receive enough public assistance to escape poverty. When they are employed, Kentucky women still earn far less than their male counterparts. Gradually, however, they are closing the salary gap by accessing higher education. It wasn't always so.

In the 1966 report, the education committee stated that the median education was 9 years for white women and 8.7 years for non-white women. Over one-fourth of the women in Kentucky had fewer than eight years of formal education. Only 29 percent of Kentucky women had graduated from high school, and only 3 percent were college graduates. Even with a community college system in Kentucky, the enrollment ratio was still only one woman to three men. Not surprisingly, the committee concluded, "Kentucky women are less educated than their national counterparts" (Kentucky 15).

That has changed: today, a significant number of women in Kentucky are attending colleges and universities; the enrollment of female undergraduates and graduates continues to outpace that of male enrollment at every state supported school in Kentucky. In 1993, women comprised 55 percent of total enrollment in state universities, and 65.5 percent at community colleges (Smith-Mello 141).

Many of the women whose stories you will read confronted the same challenges that women faced in 1960—unworkable marriages, poverty, substandard housing, little or no employment due to a lack of education or training.

As I traveled throughout the state, collecting the stories of women who overcame their circumstances, it became apparent that education was the common denominator. Through it, they gained independence, power, and self-esteem. Many bettered their circumstances, and, by extension, the lives of their children. Some said their education "saved" them.

A few of the women are still in their first year of college; others have obtained bachelors and masters degrees and are working in their chosen profession. Many intend to seek higher degrees or pursue more specialized training. All have tasted the joy of self-reliance.

The criterion for the inclusion of a woman's story in this book was that it described her particular experience in overcoming tragedy, misfortune, or a seemingly insurmountable obstacle to not only survive, but to make a positive transition in her life. The women whose stories are included in this collection have done that—and more.

For some, the challenge was an internal one: to follow a calling, to leave a calling, to quietly pursue a faith of their choosing, to follow their dream. Some faced the challenge of a life-threatening illness; others fought work place discrimination, racism, and sexual harassment. Some were homeless, some were abused as children, some survived extreme domestic violence. Several struggled with alcohol or drug addiction.

I conducted no investigation or research into the women's backgrounds, or sought to verify their facts. The narratives in this book are in the women's own words; some chose to be audio taped; others wrote their stories. The term "lifetelling" has become popular, supplanting memoir and biography, and it is an appropriate term. These women told their lives, from their prospective.

Some women chose to use their first name only; some chose a pseudonym; some chose to remain anonymous. When it was necessary, either for their own safety, the safety of family members, or to avoid embarrassment to others, they changed the names of people in their stories. In other cases, the women felt comfortable using the true names of people who supported them, loved them, or figured importantly in their lives.

I was privileged to meet these women, collect their stories, and bear witness to their courage, their determination, and the faith that sustained them. In the short year that I have known them, many of them have faced additional challenges and obstacles, sorrow and triumphs. Ultimately, that is all that "lifetelling" can really be—a few chapters out of the continuing struggle of growth and transformation all of us experience.

The governor's commission, in 1966, also recommended that "Women with talent should be encouraged to write or speak their views on political issues that concern the welfare of the family." (Kentucky 37)

They are.

Product of Illiteracy

Do you know
what it's like
to have never been
read to?
To never watch lips move
over words
like a flock of geese,
one pointed leader
guiding the rest of the arrow
into the mind,
like smoke
sucked through
an open window,
not out,
but in – in toward the
belly of the mother,
to sit like an ember
fanned bright with each
breath?
To never play in the fire,
never
know warmth?
To shiver all night
in curiosity
of what lies
beyond the black sponge
shot full of holes?

~Trish Lindsey Jaggers

Trish

Ghost-blue light from the outside street lamp fell across the pages. My eyes strained from reading yet another book, I turned to my journal. The pen made only a whisper of sound in its night flight. My mother would take the belt to me if she opened the door and saw me on my knees, book balanced on the window sill, pen in hand. She never understood, never would. I tried to tell her how I loved books, how even fairy tales spoke to me, how a story kept repeating like a melody playing over and over in my head, begging me to come back, how reading the same books again and again was like visiting a friend's house every day, and how I wrote things, words that came to me as a soft voice during the day, but she wouldn't listen or read what I wrote. She didn't know how to read.

She learned to sign her name, practicing it over and over in small scrawled shapes. Some letters were perfect – others, backward. But when she went to take the written test for her driver's license, she had to take the oral exam. She achieved a near-perfect score. Unfortunately, she never used her new license for anything but I.D. She feared driving, and she never tried to overcome her fear. She chose to avoid anything that frightened her – including reading. She remained adamant in her fear. It consumed her. It bled her, yet it dared not kill her. Fear needs a host in order to survive.

Although I didn't see it until much later, being illiterate embarrassed her, and she took great pains to hide it – hiding it from even her closest friends. She became rather good at it, too – always forgetting her glasses so someone else could read to her what needed to be read: instructions, menus, bills. She wanted me to work with her while I was in elementary school, show her some of the sounds letters made. At first, she wanted me to bring home old spelling workbooks so that I could teach her. I tried, and she wrote a little, which surprised me. She spelled every word exactly the way it sounded to her. I learned

to read it, but no one else could. Because she still couldn't read, and refused to buy any reading material, I remained in constant want of books.

I had never been read to. Just once, I wanted to fall asleep to the sound of a voice reading a story to me. On some of the TV shows I watched, parents read bedtime stories to their children. But that never happened in my house. I read to myself, and when I wasn't reading, I wrote.

I remember being most aware of voices. Whenever I wrote or read, a voice – a voice both within me and outside of me – spoke the words. Although it was my eyes that were flitting back and forth over the words, a different voice told each story, wrote each poem. I wondered if everyone heard those voices when they read? When I played on my swing – turning my seat, twisting the chain until my feet no longer touched the ground then letting it go in a mad, unchecked spin, the seat whirling around and around – I heard the voice. It told me how the wind sounded in my ears and how the chains felt cool and curled beneath my fingers. It told me the sound of rain leaving the grit of the roof, the smell of warm, wet earth beneath cool stones, the feel of damp green moss in my fingers, and it told me that I *had* to write these things.

I wanted someone to buy a pen and blank book for me, but no one ever bought books in my house. Books were for lazy people, people who had nothing to do all day but sit. I stood in front of the stationery section at the supermarket and died inside every time I was told, "No. You don't need a book to write in."

Her name was Dutch. Momma's older brother had been dating her and, on one particular evening, brought her to our house. She got down on her knees when she talked to me. "How old are you anyway?"

"Seven."

"So what do you like to do for fun?"

"Well," I said, "I ride my bike and swing on my swing. But, mostly, I like to read and write."

She told me her son liked to read, too. She said he often went to sleep with a book across his nose, and she didn't sound angry about it. I looked across the room at Mom, hoping she'd heard that I wasn't the only one who liked to read, but she was talking to her brother.

Dutch whispered, "Do you want some books? My son has a roomful."

I nodded eagerly.

The next week, Dutch came by with a large box. It smelled of old leather and musty paper, and before I looked, I knew what treasure lay inside. She said her son had outgrown many of his books. I couldn't speak, only lift onto my lap – one at a time – small, thin paperbacks, cloth-backed hard covers, and Little Golden Book after Little Golden Book.

"Thank you," I whispered, unable to breathe.

Dutch smiled. Momma simply stood with her hands on her hips and shook her head at my "silliness." Later, Momma said Dutch was probably cleaning her son's room, and since I was a garbage collector, she knew just the sucker to give them to.

Never had I ever seen so many books (except in the school library), and they were mine. All mine. I knew just what to do with my "new" books. Mom's bedroom suite came with a bookcase that she claimed was only in the way, so she'd put it in the basement, close to the washing machine. She used it for laundry supplies. I carried the books down to the basement, the one place in the house where I wouldn't disturb anyone with my reading. That basement was my castle; there, I wrote in little tablets, making up stories and poems whose words seemed to flow from the cement holding the "castle" blocks together. I plumped the cushions of a stale old chair, covered it with a sheet, and dragged the whole lot over to the bookcase which I now claimed as mine. I arranged alphabetically, and by subject, each of the precious books.

Bedtime in my house was 7:00 p.m. sharp. No exceptions. When one went to bed, one slept – no night light, no music, and absolutely no reading. I wanted to stay up late and sleep late, but the "sleep clock" revolved around what Momma thought was gospel as far as working people were concerned.

One night, I was caught reading instead of sleeping. I was so engrossed in my book that I failed to hear my mother get out of bed. She spanked me through the covers and wrenched the book from my fingers, taking it with her. I found it the next day – in the garbage. I retrieved it and hid it between my mattress and box springs. That night, when the street lamps came on, and her breathing slowed, I took out the book and turned to the window directly over my bed. Perching it on the wide maple sill, I waited for my eyes to pick out the words.

Getting new books, books that I hadn't already read from the school's small library, proved very difficult for me. I had gone without lunch many days since I discovered the Weekly Reader Book Club. Their thin newspapers came out monthly at school, and the teacher passed them out to the class. In my favorite fantasy, I found a great deal of money and ordered one of each of the books on the sheet. I could buy *Pippi Longstocking* and *Charlotte's Web* if I didn't eat my lunch for a couple of days and saved my change. Even though I was hungry, I'd rather read than eat. The kids in my class often made fun of me at lunch time; they thought I was so poor that I couldn't buy my own lunch. My collection grew. The stories were longer, more mature. The book shelf sagged.

After several months of "lunchlessness," the teacher sent Mom a note. During the bus ride home, I read and reread the note:

Dear Mrs. Lindsey,
It appears that Trish is skipping some of her meals. Is a financial problem interfering with your family's ability to pay for her lunch? We would like to meet with you if there is a difficulty so we can work together to solve the problem.

Sincerely,
Mrs. Keepers

I knew I had to read it to her. She had to sign it. So I read:

Dear Mrs. Lindsey,
It appears that Trish either skips or does not finish her meals. Is there a problem at home with getting her to eat? Maybe, if you sent her a snack on those days when the lunch menu contained foods she didn't like, she would at least have something to eat.

Sincerely,
Mrs. Keepers

I really played up the snack part. If she sent a snack, then I wouldn't be so hungry on the days I didn't eat. The lie was self-punishment. Instead of a snack, my mother packed my lunch every day for a month with egg sandwiches which I hated. I pleaded that I'd rather eat school lunches than egg sandwiches. She relented and, at last, I had a little money again. When Mrs. Keepers saw I was skipping lunch again, she asked to me to sit in during recess one afternoon.

"Why do you starve yourself?" she asked me, a look of genuine concern on her face. "Do you give your mother the letters I send?"

Though I tried, I couldn't think of a single lie. "I save the money, then buy books and tablets and pencils."

"Why don't you just ask your mother for book money?"

Tears tightening the skin on my face, I did not know how to tell her that I had to hide the ones I bought, that my mother threw away every book and writing tablet she found, that she called them "clutter" and "garbage." I did not know how to tell her Momma would take the belt to me if she knew I spent Daddy's "hard-earned money for a bunch of damned ole' books."

When Mrs. Keepers asked why Momma only signed the letters and didn't respond to them, all I knew how to say was that my mother could not read the letter – I'd been reading them to her. Still crying, I also revealed that I never told my mother what the notes really said, only that Mrs. Keepers was concerned that I didn't seem to care for the school lunches, which was partially true.

Mrs. Keepers remained quiet for some time. I begged her not to call my mother about the letters. Before excusing me to go to on outside with the others, she said, "I want to ask you one thing."

"What?"

"How did you learn to read?"

I couldn't remember when I learned to read; I just remember reading. I can't remember when I learned to write, only that my second grade teacher, Mrs. Tippin, told me I had the world's worst penmanship, and that nothing I wrote would ever be worthy of reading.

Thankfully, Mrs. Keepers never told about the books, and she continued to take my book orders. My journals became the threads of my seam, stronger than the fabric that they held. By third grade, I discovered Mead Composition Books with their black and white marbled pasteboard coverings. I felt as though I were a writing a real book. I wrote in "riddles," which made sense to me but not to anyone else.

The basement shelf worked – for a while. I assumed that keeping the books in the basement kept them out of Momma's way. One day, as I passed the washer, I noticed several of my books in the trash can.

"Why? Why? Why did you throw my books away?"

"Because you've already read most of them. What do you want to keep all that garbage for? All they are good for is to pile up and collect dust."

"In the basement? They're not hurting that old basement," I argued.

"Don't be getting smart with me, little girl," she snapped, and I dodged what I knew was coming.

During the summer break from school, I spent every free moment in the basement, but mom didn't like the fact that I spent so much time reading and writing.

"What could you have to write so much about?" she asked me more than once.

To appease her, I rode my bike, and skated some. Then I would notice the patterns on a leaf, the way the sun ran its prism fingers through the spray of a lawn sprinkler, and the voice told me what it looked like, and wouldn't let me alone, until I headed back to the basement to "cool off," and write. Momma constantly complained that I had too many books. I felt I could never have enough. I read each book three or four times. What she didn't know about was my "stash." My current journal and favorite books I kept hidden, safely tucked between the mattress and box springs in my bedroom.

One day, after coming in from riding my bike, I noticed that my room looked different; something wasn't right. The bed caught my eye My bumpy chenille bedspread and covers were tucked in at one spot as though someone had lifted the mattress and let it drop on them. I never tucked in my bedspread. Pulling up the heavy mattress by the side handles, I saw on the box springs the little square imprints from where my books had lain, and I knew Momma had found them. In the kitchen, in a little alcove where the basement and garage doors met, sat our trash can. I knew what I would find there.

For the longest time, I sat in the woods behind our house, knees drawn, pressing the tattered books and journals, now sour and clammy, into my chest. They reeked of garbage. Tears of frustrated anger starched my cheeks. *Why? Why did she hate reading so much that she didn't want me to read? She knew how it felt, didn't she? My God! What were the books hurting? Did she think she was accomplishing something by stealing my books and throwing them away? Did she think she could throw away her illiteracy so easily?*

The buckle popped on the front of my knee. I didn't feel the sting of the strap, only the sharp crack of the buckle. In her anger, she gripped the wrong end of the belt, but even that was my fault.

I howled, "You had no business touching them! They weren't hurting you!" My hands shook, my legs throbbed, and my ears roared.

"Going through my garbage! You can't leave well enough alone. You didn't need those books. You have so many now the shelf you took over in the basement is bending in the middle! And what did you mean – trying to hide books under your mattress? Sneaking around like that! What do you write in that old tablet anyway?"

Garbage. I'd heard it again and again. "Won't never amount to anything sitting around reading ... stop writing in that stupid book ... all that garbage ... just cluttering your room and piling up the basement ... !"

And, over and over again: "What do you write in there, anyway?" What I wrote were lies – things I wished were true. I was thankful she couldn't read the pages in my journal. Sometimes, I felt as though I could write anything on paper and not have to worry about my mother reading it. Other times, I felt as though she were so psychic that she knew what the black gnarling across the page meant.

I developed an obsession with writing materials. At school, I looked upon every ink pen with jealousy. Some of the kids used fancy pens, and some used plain. All I knew was that I wanted one. I had a few pencils – but those pens! One day, Elizabeth let me try her Bic Click pen. It was blue-green, with shiny silver trim. It took no effort at all; it wrote *for* me, sliding over the paper smooth as tracing my finger through the butter in my dinner plate. Never had I ever experienced such jealousy.

That weekend, I followed my parents to the grocery store, and, as usual, headed for the stationery aisle. There they hung. Not one, but two! Two Bic pens in one package – one teal and one creamy white. I raced off to find Daddy. I knew the rules. If Momma said no, then Daddy would never go against her. So I wanted to ask him first. Sometimes he said yes.

"I don't care if you get 'em," he said. "Just go ask Momma first."

My heart sank. As I approached her in an aisle, she saw me with the package. Before I could ask her, she said, "Go put those back. You don't need 'em."

When Momma said no, there was no changing her mind.

What I did next haunts me to this day, although I was only seven years old. I took the package over to the cereal aisle, parted the boxes, and fumbled with the plastic until I managed to free the pens. The pens! Two of them. I slipped both of them inside my purse and turned to walk away when a hand on my shoulder stopped me. The blood pulsed in my face, raw, stinging, and tight – like a day-old sunburn – when the manager asked me to lead him to my parents. I've relived that day a million times, how I should've run, or showed him someone else's parents, or said that I didn't have any parents. How I hated to hurt Daddy by having to open my purse and show him the ink pens concealed there.

Daddy said, "If you wanted the pens, I'd buy them for you. You didn't have to steal them."

Daddy offered to pay the man for them. The manager said that it was okay, that it was no big deal as long as I realized what I did was wrong. He didn't call the police or take me into a back room. I hadn't thought of what I was doing as stealing. Even though I really did want them, I said, "No, I don't want them." I couldn't stop crying. I hated to relinquish those pens, but I knew I could never look at them again. Today, nearly thirty years later, I can still feel the mind-screaming pain the razor strop left as Daddy whipped me. It hurt so much, I went numb.

At a K-Mart one Sunday, when I was eight, I found a treasure trove of pens – fountain pens, the type that "real" writers and true poets use. I knew I had to have one. A few of the pens were reasonable – about fifteen dollars, but some of them cost over thirty dollars. Owning one of those pens became my preoccupation. I knew it would take a long time to save the money, because I vowed never to steal again. After starving three days a week for a little over a month, I went shopping with my purse full of change. Although I was only eight years old, Mom and Dad let me wander around the store by myself and I headed for the pen counter.

The clerk asked me what it was that I wanted. I opened my purse, showing her my change. I told her I'd been saving for a fountain pen, one with the ink that flowed through a small slit to the round tip at the end. She asked me how much money I had. I told her that I had about twelve dollars. She unlocked the taupe metal sliding doors of the case. I watched as she took out a little box on the back of the lowest shelf. She opened it to reveal a silver-capped pen. The body of the pen was milk-white. It was slimmer than other fountain pens I'd seen, and for a moment I thought she'd misunderstood. Then she took off the cap. I was smitten. She said that this pen cost a little less than some of them, and that would leave me enough money to buy ink cartridges. She said a dry pen would do me no good and smiled. I could not take my eyes off of the pen and its silver nib.

At home, I sat and admired my pen, reading the instruction booklet religiously so I wouldn't ruin it. The name on the pocket clip of the pen read "Sheaffer." I looked up "Sheaffer" in the dictionary. I only found "sheaf." The dictionary defined "sheaf" as a bundle, cluster, or collection, or to bind (something) into a sheaf or sheaves. I figured since I wanted to bind words together I was a "sheafer." I still have that pen. I am still a "sheafer."

In Louisville, the neighborhood I grew up in crawled deeper and deeper into a sewer-pipe-view of the slums. So, when I was twelve, we moved to the country – the real country, with old privies and barns holding each other up, well-houses, cow shit, chicken houses, and insects everywhere. But, it was a good place. I could walk for hours without seeing anybody, find a shady place, sit, and write.

Sometimes, being adopted had its pluses, other times, minuses. The pluses were knowing just how much I was wanted. Daddy said they had a choice and he wanted a little girl. "I was hoping she would have black hair, though," he'd tease, ruffling my head-full of dark auburn hair.

The minuses were the men in the family after we moved to Kentucky. When I was in the seventh grade, Mark, one of my cousins, touched my breasts or grabbed at my ass every time I ran into him—which was usually every day because we rode the same school bus. I couldn't pass his seat without fighting him off, which only seemed to excite him more. Sitting in the front of the bus with the preschoolers got me through the school year. But being pawed at by a teen-ager was only the tassel on the corn.

"We're not really kin, not by blood," that's what another relative, Mac, told me after he slunk up behind me, wrapped one arm around my stomach, and slid his other hand under my tee-shirt and over my belly, pulling me hard against him. We were in the basement of my parent's house; I wanted to show him the drawings I kept there. I just knew he'd compliment me on my work. I was stunned – he was forty-eight-years-old and had a wife and several children. He turned my head around and kissed me hard on the mouth, sucking my lips onto his tongue. I tasted something sour, like milk gone bad, well up from the pit of my stomach. My chest contracted and it was hard to breathe. A memory clawed its way out:

Suddenly, I was back in Louisville again, excitedly running next door to show Mr. C. my new sandals. I was nine years old. I thought he was the sweetest old man. He always looked after Momma and me when Daddy had to work late and made certain that we had things from the store that we needed because Momma didn't drive. We all loved him.

Mr. C. was a big man with heart problems that made him struggle for breath and kept him uncomfortably warm and sweaty. Because he perspired all the time, he only wore once-white cotton undershirts—even in winter. That summer day, the sun puckered the air over the street in front of my house, making shiny blisters in the blacktop. I ran through the grass to avoid getting any of the tar on my new shoes. He had opened the tailgate of his old blue Ford station wagon and was sitting on it, fanning and wiping his brow.

"Hey, Sweetheart! Com'on over and sit with me a bit. No, not on the hot tailgate, here on my lap." He hoisted me up. It felt strange to sit in his lap, so I told him I really had to get back home.

"No, stay a while longer," he said as he moved beneath me.

He turned my face to look at him, "I love you, Trish. Give me a kiss."

I told him I loved him, too, and quickly kissed him on the cheek, but he turned my head back and said, "No, give me a real kiss."

Pimples of sweat swelled across his upper and lower lips. He held my head as he put his mouth on mine. No one had ever put their mouth on mine, and I recoiled. I wanted down. He kissed me again, sucking my lips in and covering a good deal of my lower face with his sweaty lips. I wanted to vomit into his mouth. I tightened my lips, breaking the enormous, wet vacuum, and twisted off his lap. My shorts were wet and stuck to my backside. I ran all the way home over the blacktop, my new sandals snapping the hot, wet blisters. I didn't tell Momma what happened until years later; she would have undoubtedly killed him.

The memory of Mr. C. still blistering, I pushed at Mac with my elbows. I didn't want to believe this was happening. *My God, he is family! He's supposed to be someone I can trust and look up to.* My eyes grew hot with the need to cry.

As I struggled to pull away, he bit at my ear and whispered, "Come on. Let a man show you what the world is all about. I can take you places you've never been before. You're the prettiest girl in the family ... such a sweet thing, such a sweet, young thing."

He forced his hand down my jeans. I threatened to scream. What he said next etched a permanent scratch into my mind.

"You got it in your blood, just like your real mom. It runs in the blood, just like freckles and dimples. I can see it in you."

Then he turned and went back upstairs, just like that. He hadn't even looked at my sketches. I felt as though he'd trespassed, that he'd entered my hiding place, found my journal, and shredded all the pages. Now I can sympathize with victims of incest, with that "ripped raw and salted" feeling that comes when someone you loved and trusted betrays you. I wrote in my journal: *Sometimes I sense that the outside of my body has betrayed me. I must look more grown up on the outside than I feel inside...*

When we first moved onto the farm, it had to be cleared of brush. That was the hardest physical labor I'd ever been subjected to. My blisters had blisters. Day after day, we took the tractor and wagon, some hoes, brush hooks, and an axe and worked until we could no longer see. We picked up rocks, cut bushes, small trees, cedars, and thistles. The thistles grew taller than I, and by the time we got to most of them, they'd already spread their seed – millions of them. I never liked cutting the cedars. What I liked most about them is that when you cut one down, you don't really kill it; it just waits, right there in the ground. Give it some time, two or three years, and a small cedar will spring up – full of defiance.

I wanted to identify with that defiance, and one day, not long after we moved to the country, I got my chance. I loved sewing, loved creating something with stitches that proved stronger than the material. Tired of the molasses pace of hand sewing, I wanted a sewing machine.

Daddy, figuring it would save money on clothes, bought me a machine – one that had a "free arm" and sewed fancy stitches. After about two weeks, I'd made Momma several loose "shift" dresses, and I was making my own "hippy-style" clothes, long, loose shirts and flowing pants, without patterns. With the addition of the sewing machine, the old desk that I kept it on, the boxes of fabric and scraps, and the boxes full of books under my bed, my tiny bedroom was soon cluttered. It did not sit well with my white-glove momma.

I walked into my bedroom one spring day to find Daddy and Momma cleaning out my room. They had pulled the boxes of books from under my bed. I asked them what they thought they were doing.

"You have too much garbage in this bedroom," Momma said.

"You can't even turn around in here," Daddy added.

"What are you doing getting my books out from under the bed?" I wanted to know.

Daddy answered, "Either you get rid of all this mess of books, or I take back that sewing machine.

"I'd rather have my books than that old sewing machine," I said, angrily.

It took him about ten minutes to unplug and gather up all the paraphernalia that came with the sewing machine. He took all of it back to the store that very afternoon. I didn't leave my room for three days, except out to pee. I lost five pounds but not a single book. The rest of that summer, I cut thistles in silence, but I never cut down another cedar tree.

I managed to fit into country life, for all its dirt and work; at least the work was personally worth something. For some reason, I never fit in at the school, though. Those kids had grown up together, gone to church together ... and me? I was instantly labeled "weird." I adopted an "I don't give a damn" attitude, which didn't help any, and ultimately gave me a bad name.

"Be careful. History often repeats itself," my father told me many times. He was talking about my birth mother. I knew the history of my mother. I knew she got pregnant at the age of fourteen, that she and my father were too young, and that she was forced to give me up for adoption. I kept saying that it was okay, that I would go to college and make something of myself. I loved books, writing, music and art. Surely there was hope for me. Daddy thought college was a legal whorehouse. "Everyone who goes there screws, drinks, and smokes dope," Daddy said. The belief that college is sinful must have been pretty strong. No one on Daddy's or Momma's side of the family had been to college. Only two or three graduated high school. I thought what an honor it must be to receive a college diploma. No wonder people were so proud when they got one. I knew there had to be a way to get the education that I craved.

With no friends at school, I wanted – needed – love and affection. Kelly was my first serious love. We dated for months before we even kissed. I matured early, and showed a disposition toward "independence" before many girls my age. However, becoming pregnant at sixteen was not the independence I sought.

In September, I discovered I was pregnant – one month after my first sexual encounter with Kelly. At first, I thought I'd taken the worst viral bug ever. I vomited every two hours – before I ate, after I ate, after I looked at food, after I smelled food, after thinking of food. My mother said I needed to go to the doctor. She knew she couldn't take me to the doctor because, of course, she didn't know how to drive. I was glad she couldn't take me.

After several days of being violently ill, without a trace of fever, something told me this was no ordinary illness. My parents were old fashioned to a paint shine. They did not believe in sex before marriage. Period. My father always said he would shoot any man who laid a hand on me. I believed him. He was a man of his word.

So the next weekend, when we left on a date, I told Kelly that we needed to get a pregnancy test kit, just to make certain. I didn't want anyone who knew me to see me buying the kit, so we had to go to a drug store in the old part of a town thirty miles from my home.

The instructions that came with the kit said I was to take the sample from my first morning urine. I set an alarm clock so that I could get up before my parents and take the test. The guide said it could be an hour or more before I got my results. My slap in the face took only ten minutes.

Kelly and I planned a November wedding – a small one. He asked Daddy for my hand. The shock was that Daddy said "yes." I had just turned seventeen years old. I felt I'd lived a lifetime. No one other than Kelly and I knew I was pregnant, although my belly swelled quickly. Normally a size four, I chose a size six wedding gown. I didn't dare take any chances. Before I got pregnant, I had a nineteen inch waist, yet by the time I was measured for my wedding gown, my waist had grown to twenty-one inches.

Marrying at seventeen, I stuck myself in a world of diapers and breast feedings before I had breasts. The economy was bad and getting worse. The major turning point of our lives came when Kelly was laid off from the first of many jobs. Someone suggested that we sign up for food stamps. I had never seen a food stamp, but my cabinets were empty. So to eat, I was forced to take my place in a row of crayon-colored seats at the Department for Social Services – a fancy name for the food stamp office. There, I lost the last ounce of my dignity.

They wanted to know the value of everything we owned – how much was our old clunker car worth, how much money we had in the bank, how much change we had saved up at home. The baby in my stomach did not count as a "dependant." I never told the case worker that we had saved some pennies. I never told her about the small collection of old coins we had. Something told me that they would not rest until they reduced me to less than I was worth. I felt I wasn't worth much to start with. I looked around at the faces of others there and comforted myself. I convinced myself that I was somehow above them, that this was only temporary, that I wasn't here for a handout as they must be. Being poor worked like a snake around my neck. Everyone felt sorry for my predicament, yet no one dared touch me, offer advice or a shoulder.

No one told me how my face would burn when I paid for my food. Spending the food stamps required me to swallow every ounce of pride remaining in me. I always waited until the stores were the least busy so I wouldn't have to stand in line in front of people paying cash for their food. I'd heard all the stigmas attached to food stamps – that people buy steaks with them, that they trade them for beer and drugs. I did none of these things, yet I was "one of them."

We received only $44.00 worth of food coupons per week. We barely had enough to eat. We bought more beans and potatoes than we did anything else. I still hate beans. Many times, our food stamps ran out before the end of the month, so by the time they came in the next month, we were out of everything. I would have a cart full of food, wait for an empty line, then check out. As if fate were mocking us, inevitably, someone always walked up behind me, saw the huge pile of groceries, and mumble under their breath when, shaking with embarrassment, I pulled out the food stamps.

I bought baking soda to brush my teeth with. I often went into a store just to buy a box of salt, the cheapest item food stamps will buy, so that I could get enough change from a dollar coupon to buy a fifty-cent bottle of dish detergent to wash our hair with, because food stamps do not pay for toothpaste and shampoo. They do not buy baby diapers. They do not buy toilet paper, soap, paper towels, aluminum foil, and laundry detergent. These things became luxuries, and forced me to get creative in order to buy such "luxuries." I understand why poor people sometimes resort to shoplifting. The only luxury I had was the time I gave to my journal. I dreamed that one day I would become a great writer. No one could steal my dreams, but they slipped into my nightmares.

An ad in the paper advertised a job opening in a local meat packing plant. It was the only "help wanted" ad. Kelly was used to factory work; he loved working with equipment. We went together to inquire about the job. The pungent smell of blood and fresh meat met us as soon as we entered the building. The company had no formal interview process. A man (a foreman?) just walked up to us in the lobby and said they really needed someone who could start right away. Excited, I grasped Kelly's arm. Kelly agreed that he could start right away and asked what his job would be.

The man said, "It's simple and requires very little experience. But you gotta do it right the first time. It's gotta be clean. With cows, you gotta shoot 'em here . . ." and he pointed to an area just above the middle of his forehead. Kelly reeled a little, and I felt his arm go stiff. He had never killed an animal in his life.

On the way home, he said, "I think I'll take the job anyway. We need the money bad."

I said, "No. You will not take a job that goes against your principles."

"The man said that I would get used to it."

"That's what worries me," I whispered.

He found a job making $4.50 per hour picking vegetables while he looked for better work. He had only a high school diploma, and I was still going to school – though I had a homebound teacher (because of the pregnancy). We were so poor that I didn't attend my graduation. I poured over the names of the graduating class in the newspaper. I never received a senior key nor a high school ring. I felt as if I'd been ripped from the flesh of my childhood – and aahh, what a raw wound.

I still didn't know Kelly's ideal interpretation of "I do." All he knew was what he'd seen displayed by the examples placed before him during his life. His mother had been kept "barefoot, pregnant, and in the kitchen." My journals grew with the frustrations of a young woman struggling for her own identity in the shadow of a man who felt she owed him something for all the work he did – one who didn't consider keeping house and taking care of a baby as work. Once, fearing that our marriage wouldn't work, I went to my mother.

"Never start anything you're not willing to finish. If you rub his back every night when he gets home, he will come to expect it. If you lie down in front of the door, he will use you for the mat. Simple as that, Trish. Simple as that. Just be careful what you start; you may have to finish it."

He had no problem with my finishing high school, but he figured that should be enough. I felt that since I had gotten myself into this predicament that I had no other choice but to lie back and be satisfied. Easier said than done. I could not let go of my dreams, but I dared not do more than dream. My husband considered himself a provider. I, willingly, had been provided for.

The birth of my son, Scott, gave me a blood link to another human being. I never knew what being adopted had meant to me until I kissed the palms of his hand – hands which looked just like mine. I relished his smell, his eyelashes, his hair, his tiny feet. "I'm related by blood to someone," I thought to myself. I spent all my time with him, making his tiny clothes, watching him discover his hands and my face, relishing this tiny person who was related to me.

Four years later, all we had was a mobile home on a spot of land that Daddy deeded to us. A mobile home! So many times in my youth I heard people talking about the kind of people who lived in trailers. On the outskirts of our neighborhood in Louisville was a trailer park. I was forbidden to play there. Now, I lived in one. Queen and king of our castle-ette. But it was new, clean, tastefully decorated – and it was ours. I worked hard to make it into a home. We had very little money, but we paid the bills, and met our needs. But it wasn't ours for long. The company Kelly worked for finally decided, "No more layoffs." It closed its doors. Kelly looked for work every day. I applied to business after business. The only businesses hiring wanted a college education or experience – preferably both.

He went back to working in agriculture, but the pay was only about $110 per week. We finally had to choose what to pay: the electric bill or the house payment. After months of not finding work and not making payments, we were told our home would be repossessed. However, the loss of his job was not my bend in the road. Losing my home was not the bend in the road. The breech came the day we moved.

In my teens, before I married, I had managed to accumulate a few good books, literary publications, craft books, magazines and such. These I took with me when I married. I turned an old stereo cabinet into a bookcase and packed it full.

Our move from the trailer came about two weeks before Thanksgiving. My father came to help us move. We were storing our things in his basement until the used trailer he'd bought for us could be delivered. I took a load of boxes to his basement while Daddy and Kelly finished packing and throwing out what we didn't need or have room for. When I came back, Daddy and Kelly had just finished loading a wagon with bags of "trash." Daddy was so anxious to help Kelly get rid of all those "old books she's always stuffing the house with," that he couldn't wait to get the tractor to the sink hole on the other side of the farm and dump them before I had a chance to protest.

Kelly didn't know what he'd done to me. I simply stood, tears threading down my cheeks, and watched as the smoke from the John Deere tractor, loaded with my precious books, disappeared over a field full of dried thistle. The next day, some men came with a large towing truck, hooked it to our mobile home, and pulled it away. All I could see were the square imprints that the foundation blocks left in the ground, matching those I found once beneath my mattress.

I missed my period. Although I was on birth control, and never made mistakes with it, I did bleed irregularly and for long lengths of time. This was the third variety of birth control pill the doctor at the clinic had prescribed. I immediately went off the pill, and we abstained from sex. I just couldn't be pregnant. I couldn't. Not that I didn't love our son, but we couldn't afford another child. Three months passed – not a spot. I knew. I cried myself to sleep at night. Why did I have to be pregnant? Just after we moved into the 12' x 65' "scrub" that someone dared call a mobile home, I miscarried.

I was suddenly overcome with the feeling that I had wished for, and therefore contributed to, the death of this child in some way. I cried for weeks. Every time we went into a store, I saw someone with an infant and was reminded of the grayish mass surrounded by scarlet swirls that took its time spiraling down my toilet.

I spent the next three weeks on my knees, trying to scrub the nastiness of the previous owners out of the bathroom, the floors, the kitchen cabinets, and the stove. Everything I touched was disgusting. I feared creatures might be hiding in the cupboards, so I washed and bleached and sprayed. Before, I'd cried from shame because I had to live in a trailer and not a house; now I cried to have it back, with its sparkling windows and walls, shiny appliances, and gleaming counters.

My marriage resulted in something I didn't expect: a newfound closeness to my mother. Maybe it's because I was a mother; that's what people tell me. I think it was because I no longer felt threatened. Once I got to know her on an adult level, I loved her. I truly loved her. But I never forgot the belt, how it felt, nor how often she struck me. We only talked about it once. She said, "I know I was a little hard on you. I didn't mean to be." That was as close as she ever came to saying she was sorry. I never heard her say the words "I'm sorry," but she never said "I love you" either – not until she got sick, not until a test left her nearly a vegetable.

She had neck problems. After years of seeking relief from the pain, she went to a surgeon who said he could help her. The proposed operation would leave her relatively pain free and able to carry out her daily routine. Before he could do the surgery, he explained, he needed to do a test – a dye procedure – that would allow him to "see" the problem more clearly.

After the dye procedure, the staff took Momma to a room and left her there – alone. Patients are supposed to be monitored and kept still to prevent the dye from traveling to the brain. Daddy went in to check on her and found her clawing the air, her eyes wide and staring. The doctor assured us that all was fine and that nothing was wrong with her. He performed surgery the next morning, right on schedule. I knew that the woman who went into the hospital never left. Instead, a stranger came home.

On February 17, 1985, nearly two years, countless psychiatric hospital stays and shock treatments later, my Momma walked into her bedroom, lifted the pistol from its holder on the wall, put it to her chest, and pulled the trigger.

The miscarriage, my mother's suicide and our utter hopelessness sent me to a state of near despair. I found joy in nothing. Not even my wonderful son could convince me that I had a reason to go on. I felt suffocated and sick. One month after the funeral, I literally couldn't breathe; I was in so much pain. The doctor confirmed pneumonia. My immune system had bottomed out. Massive doses of medication sped my recovery, but delayed my period – or so I thought. Something felt different. This time I knew for certain I was pregnant again.

The obstetrician expressed concern over the types and amounts of prescription medication I took during the first trimester. I expressed concern over the birth control pills that kept failing me. He ran a series of tests and told me that although I *was* pregnant, the pregnancy had ceased, and I would miscarry. "My God, what have I done?" I cried to myself. So low. So low. I lost my home, lost a baby, lost my mother, now this.

He continued in his cool, practiced clinical voice, "I know you don't have insurance, but things like this can sometimes take up to four weeks to run its course. I can give you a shot."

I said, "You mean, to make me miscarry?"

He said, "That's just a technicality now." He shook his head.

I sobbed into my hands. I wanted to run out of this pink and blue room, bordered with its little smiling circus bears sitting cross-legged by yellow and green tents.

The doctor looked astonished. "What's the matter with you? You act like you wanted this baby!"

Damn him! Just because I'm poor didn't mean I didn't want this child to live!

"I don't want the shot. The baby ... the baby could still be alive."

"Not in my medical opinion."

I just simply gathered my coat and purse and left. Two weeks later, while lying on the sofa resting, I felt tiny feathers fluttering in my stomach. I changed doctors. The birth of my daughter, Bridgette, completed my family. Kelly was overjoyed that we had a boy and a girl, even though many nights I felt him tossing in the bed, worrying.

I couldn't take being poor anymore. I didn't have a college degree, and my time had run out. I went to the library in search of something, anything. I checked out books on business, DOS, and computers and read and read. I faked the training portion of the interview with a temporary service and landed my first temp job. I really liked the office where I worked. I'd never seen a fax machine, so, when everyone was at lunch, I read the manual. I read the manual for the copy machine, the laminator – any piece of equipment they had – I read the manual.

I studied their filing setup and memorized five addresses a day – the region and store numbers of each of their twenty stores, which later grew to thirty-six. I knew this was only a temp job, but it was a chance for me to learn. Little did I know they were watching me. Three months later, they offered me a full-time job. I quit the temp service and became the office manager. I had a regular income, insurance, benefits – the works. For the first time in my life, I felt a sense of worth. However, what mattered most to me was going through the check-out counter and being able to pay cash for my food.

The day after the office brought in our first PC, I gave four hundred dollars for my first "computer." It was a very old IBM PS/2 word processor with laser printer—the technical way of saying "glorified typewriter." However, it functioned as a computer, and I wanted to learn as much as I could about computers, the office machines of the day. Library book after library book taught me the concepts of operating systems, computer language, and usage. It wasn't long before I showed the people in the office how to use the new PC, and not long after that, I built my own. I fell in love with this speedy new way to write. The blinking cursor just begged to be moved. I tried software program after software program until I found one that offered password protection for my "journal." For three years I wrote, delighted to, at last, have a secret place for my writing. Then I learned a very hard lesson.

One day, the PC beeped an error. I rebooted. The next message informed me of the hard disk's failure. No service person I took it to was able to salvage any data from that disk. I had no floppy backups and no printed copies of my "secure" material. I lost three years of words, poems and stories. For a time after that, I wrote nothing at all. Eventually I went back to my old fountain pen and hid my journal in the space beneath a dresser drawer, for I trusted no one, not even my husband.

Once Kelly saw the ease with which I used computers, he suggested I might want to take a computer class. The local tech school offered month-long night classes, so I applied. I fell in love with the learning process. At approximately the same time, my boss hired a controller. The man took his title very seriously. I was an object of great interest to him.

"How did you get this job?" he wanted to know. "Do you know what other people with only high school diplomas make in this area?"

At evaluation time, he stopped on the "shows a willingness to learn" section.

"Do you realize that if you lost this job that you would never find another that pays you this kind of money with the education that you have?"

Fear hit hard – fear of returning to poverty I'd left, the poverty that played audience to my little facade and waited outside in the lobby for intermission. Where once I loved my job, I grew afraid every move I made might be my last one. I needn't have worried so much.

The corporate office in California wanted to buy out the smaller partnerships to form one huge corporation. My boss agreed to sell his company, and I found myself in the unemployment line. The people in that line that had an education possessed a piece of paper that unlocked many doors. When my name was called, my representative went over the paperwork I'd completed. She told me what I'd grown accustomed to hearing.

"I'm afraid there aren't any jobs that pay this well for high school graduates."

What she said next changed the course of my life forever.

"Would you be interested in participating in a school-to-work program? We pay for a two-year college degree."

By the time I left that office, I'd made my decision, and signed more papers than I had in my entire life. When I told Kelly, he wanted to know, "What are we supposed to do in the meantime? My job is not looking good right now. How are we supposed to make it on just my income?"

I had to admit he was right. I knew I should feel guilty for asking him to be poor once again just so that I could get an education. I knew I shouldn't take any more chances, but I did it anyway. When I registered for classes at Western Kentucky University's Community College, I couldn't breathe. All I wanted to do was run to my car and drive until I found a park with a swing – and swing and swing. Although my children thought it was terrific that I was going to college, my husband and my father did not. They feared change more than I did. I feared the unknown. They feared they would no longer know me.

I parked across the street from the huge building housing the bookstore. After going in and seeing textbooks on subjects I could not pronounce, and being given a sack full of books for my classes, fear hit me. My legs shook as I walked back across the street to my car. I sat in the July heat of my closed car and shivered.

That fall was an exploration of myself. Suddenly, I wasn't afraid to say what I wanted, and sometimes, things just fell into place as though planned. At Employment Services, I was offered majors from which to choose; I didn't know one from the other, so I chose paralegal studies. My freshman English compare-and-contrast paper on occupations ended with a thesis I hadn't planned: it showed me that I was in the wrong program. My love of computers and writing could never be nurtured in the paralegal program; so, the next semester, I changed my major to office systems technologies.

After classes began that spring, one of my classes was canceled. So, two days into the semester, and still short a class for fall, my advisor asked if I'd like to take a literature class. If only she'd known. I walked into the class in mid-discussion of "An Occurrence at Owl Creek Bridge." The professor read aloud the last half of the piece. It was the first time I'd ever been read to and, by the end of the story, I was in tears. I looked around, and no one else was crying. *How could it be that the main character in the story had such a wonderful vision of utter happiness, and that it turned out to be only a vision? How come no one else realized that, as we sat there, it was possible that we were all living a dream, that we might all wake up swinging from the end of a rope?*

By the next semester I was in the creative writing class, taught by the same English professor. It was as though I'd been through a drought and, suddenly, it rained—so many sprigs sprouted from my inner desert. She pulled words from me that before had resisted the light. Her belief in my abilities enabled me to travel out of this state—for the first time in my life—to New York, to a writing conference given by the International Women's Writing Guild. In that jet, above the city of clouds, I made a pact with myself: "This will not be the last time I fly."

After I returned, my appetite was whet. I wanted the two-year degree, that piece of paper, and I wanted to be the first in my family to have a college degree, but I wanted more than just a two-year degree. No matter how much I tried to talk myself out of it, I knew I could not stop with just two years. I'd taken all the English and writing courses that the community college offered and I'd found where I belonged. I sweated with the fever of decision as I walked toward the university's English department office that cool April afternoon. I changed my major to English. I would have a writing degree.

What sickened me was having to admit that we were going to be poor a while longer. I just couldn't find the words needed to tell Kelly. Financial aid was available to help the poor attend school, so I didn't have to worry about the tuition. I did have to worry about my family due to my sudden selfishness. Many times before I started working, my children received free lunches at school. It wasn't fair to a teen-aged boy and girl to have to be poor during their school years, yet they never once complained. Instead, they gave me their love and support – told me I could do it when I didn't believe it myself.

Kelly had wanted me to get the two-year degree, but he was disappointed when I talked with him about the English degree.

"What can you do with a degree in writing?"

"Write."

"You can do that without a degree."

I found I had to prove myself. I still strive to prove myself. The first year of college, I had an essay accepted for publication in the university's annual literary magazine. The second year, they accepted one of my poems. This time, the third year, I was one of the editors for the publication (although one cannot select one's own work). Four hundred pieces were submitted for consideration. Of these, only twenty-five can be accepted. I had three pieces accepted: a poem, an essay, and a short story. The essay won the essay award—and fifty dollars.

Two of my poems were chosen for inclusion in *Writing Who We Are: Poems by Kentucky Feminists*, a book published by Western Kentucky University. Still, Kelly has not warmed to the idea of my obtaining a writing degree: "There's no money in it."

I received a postcard telling me that some of my poetry is being held for final consideration for inclusion in a national women's literary publication.

He said, "So? How much is it worth?"

"It's worth more than any check I'll ever receive," I replied.

Although he balks, his support has made it much easier for me. I come home many nights to a dinner that he's prepared after having worked all day himself. He helps with household chores and gives me space to study. He even bought me a used laptop computer so that I can "write whenever the urge hits." I knew he was beginning to understand my passion when, recently, he bought me some second-hand books.

The one person who has to remain convinced is myself. I must focus on the horizon and not the road. I want to be like both the thistle and the cedar. I want to fly like thistle down. The thistle creates its own life, flinging its downy commas through generations of weed cutters. One cannot ignore the thistle. One cannot destroy thistle. And like the cedar, rooted to a past that won't let go, I may get cut down, but there's a life pulsing deep within the scarlet wound, one that heals and sprouts back, one that stays green even when its branches sag beneath heavy casts of ice.

– Trish Lindsey Jaggers

Night Terror

Jerking from a dream
bruised from the fall
scraped raw on the way out
trying to shiver back to sleep
eyeing every shadow
suspiciously.

– Trish Lindsey Jaggers

Kathy, October 1999 –

My name is Kathy. I'm thirty-eight years old. I'll be thirty-nine in December. I have two children. My son is eighteen and my daughter is twelve. I was born in King's Daughters' Hospital, in Ashland, Kentucky, in 1960. My family lived in Hitchins at the time. In 1965, my father hung himself because my mother was going to leave him. My father was about 33 years old when he killed himself. He was really controlling over my mom. I can remember him throwing her. I can remember her running from him. That was the reason she was going to divorce him, because he was abusive to her. Now, I only live about a mile from where he hanged himself, at the farm in Hitchins. After I grew older, I'd visit the farm, because I liked being there, but it was always so hard to go back to that barn where it happened.

Three years after he killed himself, my mother remarried and my stepfather moved us to Red Fox, Kentucky. He moved us around a whole lot while he was married to my mom.

He was very abusive to both me and my mother. He whupped me many and many a time and Mama would try to get to me and tell him to quit, and he would turn on her. A lot of times I would just keep my mouth shut, not even cry, because if I cried, that was when he would really try to get to me.

Once, I went and washed his truck for him. I thought, "Well, that'll help." But I left soap on it; I didn't get it rinsed good enough. He kept a razor strap – that's what he used – in a drawer. He got really mad because I left soap on it, and he made me walk and get that razor strap, and it felt like a big old walk. So I got a whipping for it.

I had a wonderful mother – a wonderful mother. She was really creative; she made all my dresses, such pretty dresses. My stepfather was very, very abusive to her. I watched her get beat quite a few times. I tried to protect her too, but I was just little. When she tried to leave him, he poisoned her and she died. I was nine at the time. She died on December the 8th, and I turned ten on the 24th of December. It was a hard Christmas because of her death. I missed her a whole lot.

My little baby brother was eighteen months old at the time my mother was murdered. I took care of him as good as I could. He was her only child by my stepfather. I stayed with him until May of the next year, when my aunt and uncle brought me to Grayson, Kentucky to live with them. They were really good to me. While I lived with my stepfather, before they got me out, he sexually molested me, many times, and he even sold me to his friends. I was alone. There was nobody around me to really help me until my aunt got me out of it. Before they rescued me, I stayed in the hills a whole lot. I drove away my stress with nature.

My stepfather got away with poisoning my mother. It was thirty years ago; he knew a lot of people. His family was influential around Pikeville, Hazard, places like that. My aunt had a hard time even getting my mom's autopsy back. In fact, the first one that came back, months later, was for a black woman. Then they said the man that had done the autopsy on my mother left town, and that the part of the building that had the files in it burned, so there was no record of it. My aunt had to go through lawyers just to get the autopsy report. Finally, when she did get it back, it said death was due to an unknown drug in my mother's system.

After Mom died, my stepfather moved his sister in to cook for him, but I couldn't eat the food. The pancakes would be raw in the middle, and the mashed potatoes would have stuff in them to where you couldn't eat them. And I know I loved fried eggs, but he made me eat so many fried eggs I got to where I got sick on them and threw up. I was probably in my twenties before I could fry an egg. For years, if I saw an egg fried, I would be sick.

I have an older brother, eight years older than me, who left after she died. He was eighteen then. He moved to Grayson. He left really fast because he couldn't deal with my stepfather. Most of the hard times were from December (when my mother died) until May, when my aunt and uncle brought me up here to live with them.

Right before I went to live with my aunt (my step-father's sister), and uncle in Grayson, my aunt wrecked a car, and I was in the front seat. I almost went through the windshield – pieces was broke out of it but it didn't bust all the way through – and I had a concussion. It knocked my tooth out, and my ribs were cracked, and they took me to the hospital. I was supposed to stay in the hospital but my stepfather wouldn't let me stay. He brought me home and sent me to school the next day.

At school, I tried to play ball. I was at bat, and when I swung at the ball, I just went around and on down. I laid there on the ground and it hurt to breathe. When I came home that day from school, he was really mad at me because the windshield was broken in the car, where I'd hit it in the wreck. He whupped me and whupped me and whupped me and whupped me because that windshield was broken and the car was totaled!

I remember worrying about my little brother when I first came to live with my aunt and uncle. Every night, I'd lay in bed thinking about him. I knew what my little brother was going through with his father, and I would cry every night for him. I would pray and pray and pray that he would be all right. It was so hard to leave him there, but we couldn't take him because he belonged to my stepfather. And he was just a baby. At that time he was just barely two. We couldn't get him. We went to the courts to try to get my brother, but we never could get him. It all had to do with the court in that area, in Carter County, and our hands were tied.

Then, when he was five, my stepfather died. It wasn't until then my brother learned to run like other children. He was clumsy when he tried to run because he'd never been allowed out to play, to have candy, or do normal things.

One odd thing was that my mother died in the bathroom and, when my stepfather died, he died in the same spot she did. He died of a heart attack; he drank himself to death, into a heart attack. Mom was 38 years old when she died, and he was maybe 42 when he died. It was the same time of year, in December.

While I was living with my aunt and uncle, they encouraged me a whole lot through school. I became a cheerleader and I was an FHA officer. I graduated with high grades. When

I was seventeen, I married a man I loved very much, but he liked other women better. My son was three when I divorced him. I'd stayed married to him for six years.

I think I felt so low by that time, I believed everything I was told by the man I married next. He said he loved me, and I saw all these signs of how much he loved me, and I wasn't smart enough to realize they were controlling – the wrong kind of signs. But then I thought somebody loved me. I was twenty-four when I married him. We had a daughter together in 1987.

Just a few weeks after we were married, he started hitting me. I never was allowed to have any friends; I couldn't speak to anyone I'd gone to school with. I wasn't allowed to drive for years and years. He was always telling me I was going out with this man or that man, although I never even left the house. There was always something he was mad at me for. He's choked me; he's hit me; he's thrown me into things. I've had black eyes. My face has been black. He's kicked me all over; he kicked me in the back once until I peed blood. It took me a long time to get over a kidney infection, then the bladder infection from it. It was just every day. It was something that I did wrong, no matter what it was. He could be nice to me one minute, and get mad the next for no reason whatsoever.

My baby brother hadn't seen me in a long time, and when he came to visit, he said, "What's wrong with you? You're not like you were?"

And I said, "I don't even know who I am now. I don't know what's wrong with me; I just don't know me anymore." I did what my husband wanted done, thought what he wanted thought, because if I didn't it was such a struggle. It's easy to delude yourself and not even know it.

I took that treatment from him until I decided I was going to school – that was my way out. So, I started in school, and that was the first, biggest thing I had ever done. I was so scared to walk in that place, but I had a friend that started at the same time, and I think I used her as the crutch. I started school when I was thirty-five or thirty-six. I know the first day, she couldn't go to school and I went. Whew! It seemed like the biggest thing I had ever done. And being around people! I wasn't used to being around people; I wasn't used to being around anybody. It was so hard to be around people, because it had been years since I had been around even my family; I wasn't allowed to be around them very much. But, I stayed with my husband the whole time I went to school.

He told me that he would kill me every day I went to school, but I went anyhow. I'd come home, open that door and think, *Is he going to or not?*

But he didn't. Studying was hard because of him; he would get mad and rant and rave while I was trying to study. I'd get a good grade, but he never thought I worked hard for it. He'd ask, "What did you do for the teacher to get it?" It never was I had the ability to do it, it was that I used myself to get it, which was so untrue. He resented every good thing that I did in school, but I just kept going. I kept going!

When I first went, I never raised my head up. I was so scared I kept my head down, but I listened to everything. I had a hard time looking up, or looking around, or talking to anybody. I hardly talked at all. I had a writing teacher that was really good for me. My writing has helped a whole lot. After that semester, the teacher grinned and said, "Kathy, you've come a long way. You are holding your head up now." It was hard to make friends. It's still hard to make friends, but I enjoy friends a lot. So, I've made it all the way through school with high grades, and honors. I was an SI (supplemental instructor) leader for an accounting class in school, and helped other students. I joined a fraternity, the *Phi Theta Kappa*, and I have somewhere around a 3.8 grade point average.

A couple of weeks ago, it was my daughter's birthday, and we had her a birthday party. We was up to the firehouse, our house is close to it, and my husband came to the birthday party, when it was almost over. He was drinking – he's an alcoholic. He was throwing a fit to get her things and get them in a car, and she was crying, and we went home, which was maybe five minutes away. He cussed and cussed and cussed me out. I just walked from room to room, just trying to ignore him. My son was laying down; he had to go to work the next day, and he lay there with his eyes closed. And then a friend of mine called me, and my ex-husband told me to get off the phone so he could talk to me. I said,"You've been cussing me for an hour. I'm not getting off the phone. What else can you talk to me about?" So, he unplugged the phone, and my friend didn't hang up, so when he plugged it back in, she was still on there. It made him mad, and he told me two or three more times to get off the phone, but I just kept on talking and ignoring him. He grabbed me by the hair of the head and dragged me onto the floor, and that's when my son jumped up off the couch and told him, "Never again. You're not doing it anymore."

That was on a Friday. We left the house, but on Monday I went and filed for divorce. He is out of the house, but right now I'm going through a tough time, because I'm scared. I went into the hospital Monday night, from anxiety, being scared of him. He came to the house Monday night. My son and his friend were there, and my son was asleep, but he woke up and saw my husband. He had a gun or a knife with him, holding it behind him. It was concealed, so my son just saw a little bit of it; he couldn't really tell what it was, but that it was some kind of weapon. My husband went through the house looking for me. No one told him I was in the hospital. He even went through my car. I am going to the state police here in just a little bit, tonight, to see what I can do, since he came to the house with a weapon. I'll try to get a restraining order on him.

I'll have my degree in December. It's a two-year degree in accounting technology. If I go back to school after that, it's going to be learning to work with handicapped children. That's what I want to do so bad. I'd love to work with handicapped children.

I'm beginning another life. I'm very happy about that. I'm excited about finally being able to have my own opinion. For a while, I didn't know who I was. I knew who my husband was, but I didn't know who I was anymore. I lost me. I'll never lose me again. I know that.

My kids are wonderful. I love them both very much. They're what has got me through a whole lot. I'm getting ready to start working when I finish my degree. I worked over the summer at the National Rubber Plant. I worked as an intern in the accounting department, and I liked that really well. I got a very good recommendation. I'll probably work for a while, then go back to school. I would like to work with kids. My battle now is getting through the divorce and getting past him. I've got good things to look forward to.

February 2000 –

Now I am getting my divorce. I got my degree from the community college in December 1999, and I am working days as a substitute teacher, mostly at a high school. I get along good with the students and don't have any trouble with them. I am also working part time on the farm, which is hard work, but I need the money to pay the lawyer for my divorce.

I had to finish school early in December, because I was diagnosed with cancer. I had to have a complete hysterectomy. I studied hard and finished my classes. I had come so far; this wasn't going to hold me back. I am looking forward to the graduation ceremony in May.

There's times my younger brother will call me, but he goes really deep within himself sometimes. He hurts a whole lot from his early life. Seems like we don't have to talk during that time, but he wants me with him. I'll just sit and hold his hand or hold on to him – just hold him. There aren't many words between us. I know what he is feeling, and he knows that. He doesn't have to tell me. It's really hard for him to talk about it. He keeps it all bottled up in him. But, he does really good. He works every day, but you can see the effects. He's got a coldness to him, within him. I feel sorry for him. I don't have the coldness that he's got, but he lived in it a lot longer than I did.

April 2000 –

My divorce is supposed to be final this month, and I can't wait until the last chains are cut. Now, I have the pleasure of walking into my home knowing that it has peace and love. There is no fear of laughing or talking left. I am free to feel and say with my own mind and heart. It is worth everything that I did to get out of the horrible nightmare that I was in. I have good people around me now, people that I know won't hurt me. I have learned to trust in them somewhat, but I'm still afraid to completely open up to anyone. Maybe someday.

I would advise any woman who is in the situation I was in to take all the courage she has and if she doesn't have an education, get an education. It gives her a way to get out of it. Before I got an education, I was thinking, *How can I get away with my two kids. I don't have any money.* When I lived with him, my husband would work two or three months, then not work. He hardly worked at all, and I did everything I could to just keep food on the table for my kids. Then he realized, I guess, that he was not capable of keeping food on the table and that's when he let me go to work. I worked probably two years before I started school. I worked on a farm to make the bills and put food on the table. I dug ditches, built fences, cut brush, painted – whatever I was told to do, I did it. That's the only thing he would let me do – work on a farm for his uncle. I worked on the farm and it was terribly hard work. But one of the main reasons that got me through that was I thought, *Well, since I'm going to have to fight like a man, I'm going to have to work like a man.* Now, I have pretty good muscles.

It's impossible for a woman to try to get away with nothing – no money – if she has kids. I thought, *I can sleep under a park bench, but my kids can't. I can go without food for a day or two, but my kids can't.* So that kept me there with him. I guess that's pretty much what happens. Education is a way out. A way you can go out and get a job. I guess that's why I did so good in school, because it was my survival. It was my way out, and I worked really hard at it. Whenever things would get tough, I just kept thinking, *This is my way out; this is my only way out.* The thought just kept pushing me and pushing me, because I realized if I didn't keep going, I was stuck there. Now, if I have to leave, if I can't live in this area, I can take my degree and go elsewhere. I can take my kids. I can have a life with them. So, I would advise any woman to get an education. I know it's hard; it's hard to go to school when you are under so much pressure. It's really hard to concentrate. It's hard to keep your mind on what you need to do, but you just have to keep pushing and pushing. You just can't give up and say, "I can't do it because he is screaming tonight," or "He's dumped an ashtray on the floor, or he's...," you know.

It was survival. And I wasn't going to let him take it away from me, no matter what. He wasn't going to take it. I'm still at the point that I haven't talked to a lot of people. I'm not sure why the abuse happens. I can't figure it out. Sometimes I felt like I was in a "twilight zone" and everybody was just like that, around me. I'd hear about this woman down the road, or this woman over here being abused. I don't know why there is so much of it (abuse). I don't know if it's this area, or if it's really all over the place, but it's really strong in this area. Seems like Kentucky has never come out of it. There's a lot of women in my shoes. I do know that.

November 2000 –

I have attained my career goal and it is a dream come true. I am working with handicapped children through an organization called Community Presence.
– Kathy (full name withheld)

Sheep Mongers

There are wolves in the dark –
seeking acceptance
also,
in a world of prey,
where those who could deliver
cower
under the cover of night.

– Trish Lindsey Jaggers

Patti, Spring 1999 –

On May 28, 1998 I received a frantic telephone call from my daughter Stephani. I will never forget as long as I live that horrifying phone call.

"Mom, there's been an accident with James," Stephani cried.

I felt myself go numb. James was Stephani's first born. Unmarried at the time, she lived with us throughout her pregnancy; her dad and I stuck by her side right through the delivery. James made his appearance into the world on June 11, 1994 at 6:11 p.m. I was there to cut the cord, I was the first to hold him, and I was the first to let her know we had a healthy baby boy.

"What happened, Honey?" I asked her as calmly as I could muster.

"Steven was watching the kids. Braunlyn was in the swing in the living room, and James had been outside playing. Steven said James came in the house with poop in his pants, so Steven took him into the bathroom, took his clothes off and put him in the tub for a bath. When he went back into the living room to check on the baby, he heard a splash, but didn't think anything about it," Stephani stated.

"Stephani, Honey, did he go back and check on James?" I replied

"Yes, he said when he went back; James was under the water!" Stephani could hardly speak for her weeping. Tears streamed down my face, but I tried not to let my voice shake. Stephani was weeping.

"What did Steven do next?" I asked her.

"He took James out of the tub, laid him on the bed and called me at work," Stephani said.

"Why did he call you? Why didn't he call an ambulance, and then call you?" I asked her, the alarm rising in my voice.

"He panicked, Mom," she said.

I said to her, "Steven is a fireman; he is supposed to know how to handle an emergency situation."

"The ambulance is here, I'll call you as soon as I can," Stephani said.

"Okay, Honey," I replied, my voice heavy.

Oh, God, the nightmare is coming true, I thought. Just a few weeks before, Stephani and her new husband of six months, Steven, had visited us in Auburn, Kentucky, where I, my husband Carl, and our two sons, Bryan and Carl III, were living. We had planned a joyous occasion to celebrate Bryan's twenty-second birthday. Stephani and Steven had arrived from Pennsylvania on May 1, with our two grandchildren, Lonny James, age three, and Braunlyn Kaylea, age four months old.

On May 2, James was in the living room with his grandfather, Pappy, and his Uncle Bryan. James asked Pappy if he wanted to see what his new dad did to him. Carl had responded with "Sure, Buddy." James pulled his right arm out of his long-sleeved shirt, and showed Carl the black, blue, and green bruises that began at his shoulder and extended down to his wrist.

Not wanting to panic James, Carl said, "Buddy, why don't you show that to your grand-mother, Nunny, okay?" James agreed. I was in the kitchen doing dishes.

Carl called to me, "Hey, Nunny! Can you come in here? James has something to show you." I dried my hands, walked into the living room, and sat down on the couch.

"What's up, my little man?" I lovingly said to James. James asked me the same question he had previously asked Pappy.

"Sure," I replied to him. I was dumbfounded when he showed me the bruises.

I asked him, "Honey, which dad did this to you?"

"Steve," James said.

I looked over at Carl and asked where Stephani and Steven had gone. He said they had gone for a walk. My anger was welling up fast and furious, but for my grandson's sake I tried to remain calm and get to the bottom of the atrocity.

"James, Honey, would you like to take a walk with Nunny? We'll go down to the park."

I knew he would. James loved the park and delighted in playing in the sandbox, in climbing up the steps of the slide, then sliding down with his arms straight out, waiting for me to catch him at the bottom. We walked and talked. Calmly I asked him what had happened that caused his dad to do that to him and when it happened.

He said, "It was a couple weeks' ago, Nunny, I accidentally peed in my pants, and my dad beat me."

I asked, "Where was Mommy when this happened to you?"

James replied, "She was at work at Giant Eagle."

After we played in the park, and we're on our way back to the house, I promised my grandson I would make sure it never happened to him again. Stephani and Steven were back from their walk, and I asked Stephani to come into the bedroom with me where she and I could have a private talk.

"Steph, James showed his Pappy, Uncle Bryan and me the bruises on his right arm. Were you aware of them?"

"Yes, I saw them the following morning when I got James up for a bath. I asked him what happened and he told me," she said, repeating the same story he told me earlier.

"Did you approach Steven with this?" I asked her.

"Yes, I called him at work when I saw them. He said he lost his temper with James; he swore he'd never do it again," Steph replied.

"Steph, it sounds to me like he has a problem with James. You need to get him some help. The next time it might be worse; he's bigger than James and could seriously injure him or kill him," I said to her.

"Mom, Steven said he was sorry; he won't do it again," Steph said, defending him.

"Do me a favor then, okay?" I asked, "Don't leave him alone with the kids, find some-one else to watch them, or quit your job and stay home. The babies need you to protect them." Stephani agreed, just to shut me up.

At the dinner table that evening, May 2, I was the first to approach the subject with Steven.

"Steven, you haven't been a part of this family very long, but haven't we treated you as one of our own?" I asked him.

"Yes, Mom, you've all been really good to me since Steph and I married. Why?" Steven asked me.

"We entrusted the care of our most precious family to you, and I am curious why you would carelessly injure the people we love," I said.

Steven broke down in tears, "I am so sorry! I swear it will never happen again. . . I didn't mean it to happen." I am a caring person, but I had no pity for this twenty-one-year old boy sitting across from me.

Carl waited patiently for me to finish my lecture, then chimed in, "Steven, I am warning you, if you ever strike out at our grandson, our granddaughter, or our daughter in anger, the way you did to James, I will come after you, do you understand?"

"Yes, Dad, I understand, and I promise you both, I will never let this happen again," Steven replied.

While we waited for Stephani to call back, Carl and I quickly packed an overnight bag with clothes and a few toiletries, and put the bags in the car, just in case we had to leave in a hurry. At 9:30 p.m. the telephone rang.

Stephani's voice rose hysterically, "Mom, the air ambulance brought James to Conamaugh Hospital here in Johnstown. I rode in the ambulance with James all the way. I keep talking to him. Mom, his eyes are open, but he is not responding! I need you and Dad here!" she cried.

"We're on our way, Honey, just keep your faith," I said to her calmly.

My mind went back to the day several weeks before when I talked to Stephani in the bedroom. I'd told Stephani her dad and I wanted James to stay the rest of the summer with us.

She'd said, "I have a party planned for his birthday, all the invitations are out already, maybe you all could come get him the week after and bring him back before you start school in August."

"Okay, we'll do that, then we can have a second party here for him," I said.

On Sunday, May 3, when they backed out of our driveway to head back to their home in Pennsylvania, tears flooded my eyes and dripped down my cheeks. I felt powerless and heavy-hearted. A voice inside me kept saying, "Stop them. Bring James back. It's going to happen again."

Now, I was afraid it had. Before we left, I called my best friend, Marion, to let her know where we were going. When she answered, I recounted what Stephani had told me. At that point, I was beyond clear thinking, but I knew, in the pit of my stomach, that it was not an accident, and stated as much to Marion.

"Now, Missy," she said, using her pet name for me, "calm down until you get there and get all the facts. You don't know for sure that it wasn't an accident."

Carl and I left for Johnstown.

"I just know this wasn't an accident," I said to Carl, "Not with the incident over James a couple of weeks ago."

"Baby, I hope you're wrong. I hope this was an accident – you know how wild James can be at times. He could have been jumping up and down in the tub. Maybe the mat slipped out from under him. We just won't know until we get there," Carl said, trying to reassure me.

Still, I couldn't get the nagging feeling out of my mind. I cried the whole trip; at times Carl had to pull over to calm me down. I kept hearing my last words to James, "I promise you, Honey, this will never happen to you again."

We took the shortest route possible to Johnstown: through Lexington, into West Virginia, into Maryland, and finally into Pennsylvania. We arrived at Conamaugh Hospital at nine-thirty, Friday morning, May 29, exactly twelve hours after we'd gotten the telephone call. We asked the lady at the front desk to page Stephani and Steven. We waited for what seemed an eternity. Finally the elevator doors opened and Stephani ran into her dad's and my arms at the same time. In tears, she told us the doctors said the outlook was grim. James had fluid on his brain from the fall and he was in a coma. However, there was no water in his lungs from being under water in the tub. Right then, Carl and I knew it was not a bathtub accident.

We went directly to the intensive care unit and into the room where James lay. Cautiously, I tiptoed around all the wires, tubes, and monitors. His little eyes were partially opened. I stroked his soft, sandy blond hair.

As I leaned over him, I kissed his cheek and whispered in his ear, "James, Honey, Nunny and Pappy are here. Wake up, and we will take you back to Kentucky with us."

Carl was standing at the foot of James' bed, tears streaming down his face. Steph and Steven had stepped out of the room. I looked closely at James' face, arms and legs. The head nurse came into the room.

"Did you see these bruises on my grandson's face?" I asked her, "This is a hand print, and these are fresh bruises on his legs and arms as well."

"Yes, we have seen them," she replied.

I glanced over to Carl, "Honey, shut the door please, I think it's time we had a talk with the staff."

After retelling the May 2 events to the staff, we were informed that there would be an investigation into James' injuries. The doctor told us they were taking James up to the next floor to run a brain scan on him. They had been monitoring his brain waves since he arrived, and up to that point, there was no activity at all. I was trying hard to concentrate on what the doctor was saying, but my eyes were on my grandson. Glancing up at the clock, I saw it was 1:30 p.m. The staff was filing out of the room as Carl and I took a few steps over to the bed. This time we both leaned over James. Carl was on one side, and I was on the other. We needed to spend that precious time with him before they come back for him.

"James, Pappy and Nunny are here for you, Honey. James, squeeze my fingers if you can hear me," I spoke into his ear. Maybe I imagined it, but I still believe he was able to slightly squeeze my fingers.

As I caressed his tiny hands, and kissed his forehead, my mind drifted back to the first of the month, the Saturday James was visiting. He and I had decided to make brownies. I poured the dry mix into a bowl, put the egg in, added the rest of the ingredients. I pulled a chair up to the edge of the counter, handed James a wooden spoon, and let him mix the chocolate goo and pour it into the pan. While he was mixing, I sneaked into the living room to grab the camera. I raced back into the kitchen just in time to see James stick the empty bowl over his face, enabling him to lick out the remaining mixture. I snapped the picture just as he pulled the bowl from his face. What a sight he was! James was such a ham for the camera.

"Mrs. Henry?" The nurse was saying to me, "We are going to take James upstairs now. Why don't you all go get something to drink, and relax until we come back? It will be about an hour."

Carl coaxed me out of the room into the waiting area. Stephani and Steven walked up and asked us to go out on the fifth floor terrace with them. Outside, sitting on a bench, was James' biological father. With him was James' paternal grandmother. Carl and I walked over and embraced them both. Not much was said, the eye contact said what our mouths could not.

"Mom, could you come here for a moment?" Stephani requested.

I walked over to her, and put my arms around her. "What, Honey? What can I do for you?"

"Mom, will you go over and put your arm around Steven; he thinks you all hate him for what's happened," Steph said as she turned and pointed to the bench by the wall.

Numbly I walked over and sat by Steven, who had hung his head and was crying. Placing my arm around his shoulders, I pulled him close to me, and whispered, "Steven, we don't hate you; we just want to know the truth of what happened that caused James to be here."

Suddenly the damn broke, Steven sat upright, and threw his arms around me, almost smothering me.

"Mom, I swear I didn't mean to hit him that hard; he made me so mad when he peed in his pants that I threw him into the bathtub. I only hit him one time on the butt," he cried.

I broke from his grip and backed away from him.

"Steven! Why didn't you say this before? Does the doctor know this? Does Stephani?" I yelled at him.

He shook his head no. At the far door, the receptionist was signaling to us to follow her. Like an assembly line we followed. She told us the doctor wanted us all upstairs for a meeting. My heart sank to my feet. I knew we were about to hear something that was going to change us all forever.

"We did a brain scan on James to find out if there was any activity at all," the doctor stated, "and I want to extend my deepest regrets to you all."

At 2:29 p.m. on May 29, 1998, they pronounced James brain dead. Stephani decided to donate James' organs, so another family wouldn't have to go through this tragedy. The grief was overwhelming at that point. Lonny (James' real dad), his mother Kathy, Stephani, Steven, Carl and I all gathered in James' room to say our goodbyes. One by one we sat in a chair, and held for the last time our beloved grandson.

Stephani and Steven were the last in the room with James. Carl and I had gone out to speak with the doctor. We requested an autopsy. The doctor said he had already contacted the coroner and ordered one. He gave us his telephone number, and told us to call him in two weeks, when he would have the results. When Stephani came out of James' room, we told her we were going to her Grandma Miller's (Carl's mother).

"Stephani, Honey, give me a call later and let me know where you are going to stay, okay?" I requested.

At my mother-in-law's house, I went straight into her waiting arms and we both cried. When I regained my composure I sat down and tuned out all the conversation around me. I had to think about how I was going to flush out my grandson's killer. The telephone interrupted my thought. It was Stephani.

"Hi, Hon, did you get home all right?" I asked her.

"Mom, will you call Ott Funeral Home in Irwin and make the arrangements for me, please?"

Tears began to fall again. "Yes, Stephani, I will do it for you," I said, my voice shaking.

After making the arrangements, I called my two sons and told them to come to Pennsylvania. Carl was asleep, and I was exhausted.

I remembered when Braunlyn was ready to come into the world in January. James was looking forward to a little sister. With Stephani's help, he'd call me and inform me the baby had moved inside his mom's stomach.

"Nunny, I am gonna have a baby sister," he would say excitedly.

He loved her dearly and, when she arrived on January 28, 1998, he told me she had all her fingers and toes. Stephani let James help name her, hence her middle name Kaylea. When I asked him what he was going to do with his baby sister he replied, "I'm gonna protect her from all bad stuff, Nunny." We were so proud of him.

The viewing was held on May 30, 1998, at two o'clock in the afternoon. The first hour was a private viewing for the family only. Stephani had decided on an open casket, and there were things she felt James should take with him. The room was full of beautiful flower arrangements; the casket was pearl white with gold trim. James wore the long-sleeved, striped shirt and tan dress pants his mom bought him the Christmas before.

I watched Steven's face, every opportunity I got, for signs of remorse. Tears fell from his eyes, but they were fake. There was no redness around his eyes or nose from the wiping away of tears. He looked at me on more than one occasion, as if he were aware that I knew his horrible secret. And he was right – I knew!

On June 2, we put James to rest in Union Cemetery in Irwin. Beyond the cemetery was an elementary school where children played out on the playground as we said our last goodbye. Now, it was time for me to put my plan into action for the sake of my grandson, his mom, and our granddaughter.

The following morning, I called Stephani and asked her to follow us home to Auburn.

"The weekend will give you all time to relax and contemplate," I said.

"Sounds good, Mom, but we have some final business with the funeral director before we leave for Kentucky," she replied, "We will drive up Thursday morning, okay?"

"Honey, can your Dad and I have Braunlyn with us on the trip?" I asked.

"Sure, when are you and Dad planning on leaving?"

"About noon today," I said, "that way you and Steven can have a relaxing ride."

She met us at the gas station in Irwin, gave us the baby, the clothes and supplies we would need, and last minute instructions. She kissed me, her dad, and Braunlyn, and we were on our way.

Thursday morning after getting the baby fed, bathed, and dressed, I got out all of James' pictures I could find – from his birth up until the last pictures I'd taken of him two weeks before his death. I knew Stephani and Steven would be arriving sometime around noon, so I had a lot of work to do. I began putting all the pictures into frames and hanging them on the walls of the living room.

Carl was puzzled by my behavior, and asked me, "Babe, why are you doing that now, don't you think it's a little soon?"

"No, I am going to call Steven's bluff, Carl. I know he killed James, and I am going to help his conscience along. If he doesn't act suspicious, then I'll take them down after they leave, but you mark my word, he is going to slip up this weekend," I said.

Next, I called my friend Marion and explained my plan to her. I asked her to come over on Saturday, so she could meet the kids, then stay for supper. Friday came and I watched the way Steven behaved. He was nervous, and followed Stephani everywhere she went. Carl and I spoke lovingly of the funny things that James used to do, and Stephani said she liked the pictures of James all over the walls. I made it a point to take Steven by the arm and walk him over to the new frame I had just gotten. It had the "Footprints" story on it, and pictures of James in the small open places meant for such items

"How do you like it, Steven?" I asked him.

"It's. . . uh. . . nice, Mom," he said.

I wanted to reach up and grab him by the neck and choke the breath right out of him. He pulled away from my grasp, and went to sit on the couch.

"That's the exact spot where James last sat," I stated casually.

Steph was sitting in the rocker with Braunlyn, telling her how much her big brother loved her. Steven got up and walked out the front door. I knew I was getting to him. Carl and our two sons had begun to pay close attention to Steven's behavior as well. The rest of the day, Steven avoided my eyes. That night I prayed, and I told James I wouldn't let him down again.

Saturday came. Stephani was busy with the baby, and I was putting my menu together for the evening. Steven was downstairs in the bedroom most of the morning. Carl and our sons were outside. Marion arrived about four o'clock. She was tickled pink to meet the kids and see the baby for the first time. She had never gotten the chance to meet James, and expressed her regret. At supper that evening, Stephani began the conversation.

"Mom, the hospital called in the police to investigate James' death. They said they think he was abused, and a detective came to ask us questions."

Marion said to her, "Stephani, you know they are only doing their job. They have to be sure because there is so much child abuse going on these days."

Stephani replied, "Yeah, I understand that, but can't they wait until we are done grieving before they start asking questions?"

I stepped in and said, "Honey, they are not trying to be careless about your feelings; they are just doing what they have to do."

Carl said, "If there was no foul play, they will know, and the investigation will be over."

Out of the blue Steven stood up from the chair, folded his arms in a crisscross fashion and yelled, "If those S.O.B.s come to my door again, I am going to tell them where to go!"

Stephani's jaw dropped open, and her eyes sprang wide open as if someone had slapped her in the face.

Marion looked at Steven and said, "Oh yeah, you do that and they will know for sure you have something to hide."

Carl pointed his finger at Steven, who was really agitated at this point, "You act like you do have something to hide. Is there something you're not telling us?"

"No," Steven yelled at Carl, "I just get tired of everyone asking about what happened. It's over. Can't it be forgotten?"

Stephani was dumbfounded and said to him, "What do you mean forget it? My son is dead, and you want to forget it?"

Steven knew he had said the wrong thing, and told us all he didn't mean what he said. But, I knew he did.

As Marion was leaving, she told me I was right about Steven, he was acting funny. She, too, thought Steven caused James' death.

Stephani and Steven left on Sunday morning for the journey back to Pennsylvania. Steven said he had to be at work Monday morning. He said his goodbyes to both boys, shook Carl's hand, gave me a casual hug, and got into the car. Stephani and I embraced for a few minutes, and I whispered in her ear, "Call me if you need me, Honey."

Then she hugged her dad, and he whispered, "We love you, baby girl."

Aloud she said, "I love you all." Then they were gone. I sat on the front porch and cried with Carl's arms around me.

The telephone rang on Monday morning at about ten o'clock. Stephani was on the other end, frantic. She said, "Mom, Steven was arrested at work a little while ago; the detectives just called me. They asked him some questions, and he confessed to killing James."

She began sobbing and could hardly speak. I did my best to calm her down, but at the same time my heart was rejoicing. He told the detectives he couldn't stand the nightmares anymore; he'd been having them since he killed James.

What a relief, I thought, *We finally got to him.*

"Honey, calm down. I need to call your Dad at work and let him know what's going on; then I will call you right back, okay?" I said to her.

"Okay, Mom," was all she said.

I called Carl and told him, and he, too, was relieved. I called Marion and told her. She and I cried on the phone together.

"Your plan worked," she cried.

"Yes," I answered, "I was starting to wonder if I was doing the right thing or not."

Steven is still in jail awaiting his trial for murder. Stephani is receiving counseling. She not only lost her beloved son, but her husband as well. Her whole world was shattered in the blink of an eye. Carl and our sons are trying to deal with their grief on their own. I, too, have sought professional counseling.

To assist Stephani, and to be present at the trial, we left our home in Kentucky and moved to Pennsylvania in December 1998. The trial was originally scheduled for February 1999, but a long string of continuances has kept postponing it. Each new trial date, and then postponement, is a fresh reminder that my grandson's murderer is still unpunished, albeit in prison.

Spring 2000 –

The move from Kentucky was not only strenuous emotionally but financially as well. My husband and I had to deplete our savings to rent a moving van to pack and transport all our belongings. The things we had no room for were sold or given away. The worse part was when I had to say goodbye to my mentor and friend from college, Jennie, and leave my best friend, Marion.

I transferred all my credits from Western Kentucky University's Community College to Westmoreland County Community College in Youngwood, Pennsylvania. When we initially arrived in Pennsylvania, we settled in with my father-in-law. I was not thrilled with the idea of attending a strange college where I knew no one and no one knew me. The upcoming trial and hearings had forced me to inform those in authority of the circumstances of my transfer to their college, and the possibility of my having to miss class from time to time for the hearings. Because the murder of our grandson was still fresh in the minds of the local people, I was met with sympathy and shock.

Living with this nightmare, hoping that some morning I will wake up and my beloved grandson James will still be here with us, has at times been more than I can bear. I live "one day at a time," smiling on the outside, but always crying on the inside. Our family has struggled to prepare emotionally for each of the preliminary hearings, only to have them postponed on the scheduled day.

As we wait for the trial of the man who murdered our grandson, we have met many times with the district attorney, meetings at which all concerned parties must attend: me; Stephani; Kathy, James' paternal grandmother and Lonny, James' real father. Those of us who are directly affected by the murder of the once smiling, laughing three year old, must sit in a conference room with the district attorney, a woman from Victim's Services, and a tape recorder. There are tissue boxes stationed at each end of the table where Stephani, Kathy, and I are sitting.

Many new developments have surfaced: the charges have moved from second-degree murder, to first-degree murder, to premeditated murder. Each time, the trial is moved further into the future. We learn that Steven has told other inmates of his plan to murder James. We learn that these inmates are in for life with no chance of parole, and have come forth with the information because the crime was so heinous. I never think of him as Steven anymore – to me, he is "the monster."

We must listen to a recording made by one of those inmates who heard Steven tell how he enjoyed killing our grandson. We must listen to each gory detail of how he accomplished it, and in which room he committed this horrendous act. Tears spill down my cheeks and wrenching sobs escape from my daughter. My heart aches as much for her as it does for myself. We all sit in astonishment as the tape plays. *How could someone do this to an innocent child?* My mind cannot comprehend it.

The district attorney requests our permission to ask the judge for the death penalty. The tape recording proves this killing was premeditated. We now know that Steven, who we once thought was a wonderful, caring person, meticulously and methodically planned to kill James. My mind can't comprehend this information. Over and over in my head, all I can think of is how terrified James must have been, and that there was no one there to protect him.

I try to compose myself enough to understand what the district attorney is saying. In a couple of months we will have yet another hearing, only this time it will be a pre-trial motion. The "monster" will walk into the courtroom in shackles and handcuffs, and once again I will stare him down with no expression on my face, like all the times before. We are not allowed to show any emotion when he enters or exits the courtroom, because if we do, his attorney will be able to use it against our side. It sounds like a childish game, but it's all too real.

On March 14, 2000, at 9:00 a.m., a motion hearing took place in front of His Honor, Judge Blahovec. A major decision was made in His Honor's chamber: the decision to no longer hold the motions in an open courtroom. The press was always there, and Judge Blahovec did not want the paper to make a mockery of the hearings. If that happened, we would need to have a change of venue (location). None of us wanted to travel any farther than we already do now. My daughter and I no longer have to go to court until the actual trial begins. As of now, the district attorney is praying for June of this year. June 3 will mark two years that our grandson has been in the ground.

In Kentucky, my degree goal was a paralegal degree. I changed that to criminal justice. I decided that I could no longer help my grandson, but somewhere down the path of my life, and through my education, I could help some other child. I could perhaps prevent them from suffering through what James endured. So, with life experience in hand, and determination to stop the "bad guys," I threw myself into the criminal justice program. My professors were very understanding. I became the best overall student in each of my classes. I made the dean's list in my first semester. I soaked up information like a sponge. I am still soaking up information and have remained on the dean's list. I have five more classes to complete, and, at the end of fall semester, 2000, I will graduate with my associates degree in criminal justice.

That will not be the end of my college career however. Several months ago, I decided to go for my four-year degree in administration of justice and will study at Penn State University to be a criminal profiler. My determination to stop the killing of innocent children, like my grandson, is still the driving factor.

In the meantime, my story will continue until justice is served. I will continue to write my poetry to relieve stress and remember the good times with our grandson James. His memory will live on through my writing.

I am forty-four years old, and I feel like I've seen more tragedy than most experience in a lifetime. I lost my father to a heart attack when I was six and a half years old. I had been his pride and joy, and I was distraught when my mom told me, "Daddy has gone to heaven to be with God." My father was my protector, my security, and my friend. With his death, my mother became both father and mother to me. Through the years, my mother and I grew to be more than mother and daughter: we were the best of friends. Then I lost her in October 1990.

One month and one day after James was murdered, his uncle, Mark, was killed. It was Mark's twenty-fourth birthday. He adored James and, still distracted by grief, stepped out in front of an oncoming truck and was killed instantly. They are buried side by side with matching tombstones. Sometimes I feel as though Death follows me around like a black cloud, hanging over my head, but I have faith we will all make it through this, and time will heal the wound. Eventually, James can rest in peace.

– *Patti Lynn Henry*

People

The seed of life, abundant
As those tucked into
a flower.
For every day, every hour,
The seed grows into
a wondrous flower,
One must see
Individuality
in a seedling.
No two are the same.

–Patti Lynn Henry

Christin and Diane

Christin and her mother, Diane, share this story. Although it is Christin who battled cancer, both women shared the heartache, and both women were changed forever by Christin's experience. The bond between mother and daughter speaks to both women's resilience and courage.

CHRISTIN: My name is Christin Garrard. I was born February 25, 1977, in Evansville, Indiana. I've lived in Poole, Kentucky all my life; it's a very small town, about a half mile long. It's just a main street. The biggest thing we have is a caution light; everybody makes fun of that. My dad was born in Poole, and he's not one to move out of Poole, so we live there to this day. I still live with my mom and dad. I'm in college right now, currently taking classes through Western Kentucky University's off-campus classes in Owensboro.

I was diagnosed with cancer when I was four years old. It was a malignant tumor behind my left eye. The treatment lasted for two years. I think the most important thing is that my whole family is very Christian-oriented, and our faith is based on God and the Bible, on His word. At the time I was born, my parents became very strong Christians in a charismatic, nondenominational church. When the cancer was discovered, my parents sought answers from God. My problem basically began with a little redness in my left eye. Mom contacted our pediatrician and he said it was probably just an eye infection and prescribed some eye drops. At the time, mom thought, "This isn't right. It's not an infection; there's more to it." She had a sense, from God, that it was something more serious.

DIANE: We first noticed it when her eye began to water and I phoned the doctor about it. We thought she had a cold and it was effecting her eye, like children often have a cold settle in their eyes. The

doctor prescribed some drops over the phone, but it didn't get any better and it seemed as if there was some swelling going on above her eye, so I called him for an appointment. When he saw her that day, he got very quiet on me. He came back in the room and said "Diane, I think there is something behind her eye, pushing it, causing that swelling." I asked what he meant. He said, "Well, I don't like to use the word 'tumor,' but everything I've seen looks like that. I may be wrong." This was a family pediatrician we had trusted for years and I didn't really think that he was wrong, but I wanted to believe that he was. That same day, he sent me to an eye specialist in Henderson, Kentucky. I went to my mother's, called my husband, and we met at the doctor's office. The unique thing about this was that God, from the very beginning, let me know that she was going to be okay. I had no idea what I was facing. But when we went into that eye doctor's office, I picked up one of those little books they have in doctor's offices that have all those Bible stories in them. I remember Christin wanting me to read it to her while we were waiting. The story I read was the one she had opened the page to; it was about when the disciples came to Jesus and asked him about this person who was sick and whether or not he was going to die. The thing that stands out in my mind was Jesus's response to him that the illness was "not unto death."

I didn't realize at the time how much that was going to speak to me in the weeks ahead. The doctor said he didn't think it was a tumor, only a clogged sinus cavity. He set her up for a CT scan to be done in Evansville two weeks from that date. That was as soon as they could get us in. I went home and again had a strong sense that this wasn't right – we couldn't wait two weeks. Again, it was as if God directed us. A good friend called and said she'd heard there was something wrong with Christin's eye. She said, "You know, my dad's a member of the Lion's club and he can get you into the eye institute in Louisville. In fact, Diane, I think I can arrange it where you all can go up there on Friday." It was a Wednesday, so I said, "Let's do that."

We went and they spent five or six hours examining her. They just kept bringing doctors in, and then decided to do an ultrasound. They pretty much verified it was some type of growth and it was growing rapidly, because, at this point, Christin could not close her eye. It protruded so much that her eye was almost laying on her cheek. It is astounding that she even has her eye today. They said she needed to go into the hospital for a biopsy. The soonest they could do that was Monday, so we came home with her over the weekend. When you mention growths or tumors and such to people, they react by assuming the worst. Christin picked up bits and pieces of what people were saying – bits about death and such. When Christin got up in the morning, I was sitting there rocking her because her eye was just awful, in terms of how bad the swelling was, and I remember her telling me, "Mama, you don't need to worry because I'm not going to die." I asked her how she knew and she said, "Jesus was in my room last night, and he told me I wasn't going to die." I thought, *All right. We're all a little stressed here.* But she was insistent. It seemed that over and over again, God gave us that type of revelation to let us know it wasn't going to take her life.

On Monday, we went to Norton's Children's Hospital; they admitted her and did a bi-opsy right away. The next day they said it was definitely malignant; the type of cancer was *rhabdomyosarcoma*. They said that the tumor was in the third stage, going into the fourth stage, which was not good because, that meant the cancer was probably throughout her body. The percentage of survival in this type of cancer was typically about six percent. That was pretty hard to hear. But again, we had a group of supportive people who prayed with us that God was going to intervene, and I really believe He did at that point.

The results of the first spinal tap they performed, to determine if there were other tu-mors, came back showing suspicious cells. The doctor came in and said, "This indicates to us, with that tumor behind her left eye, the chances are very likely that she has cancerous cells in her brain as well." Then he said, "Let us do one more just to be sure, because it wasn't a really good sample." So they did it again and they came back the next day. I never will forget this, a large, strong-looking nurse, the last person I'd expect to break down and cry, walked into the room and said, "The test that came back showed nothing. There are no other tumors." She started to cry and we all thanked God. Christin had no real concept of what was going on; she was just lying over there with all her stuffed animals and her balloons. Her only mission was to get to the playroom and paint. She was spared much because she was so young.

At that point in her life, Christin was already immersed in God's love. She'd tell people, "I love Jesus," and things like that. She was making a poster to hang up in her room that said "Jesus Loves Me." The nurses were all amazed by her spunk. Even though they started radical chemotherapy on her there in the hospital, she never let it get her down. She was given three different very strong drugs intravenously. After the biopsy, they sewed her eye shut because, if the swelling didn't go down, they didn't want her eye to come out. It was an awful sight. They couldn't operate; they couldn't remove the tumor. This happened in 1981, and about three years before that, when this type of thing showed up, they would typically go in and remove the eye and most of the area around the eye, but they'd discovered surgery that radical was not necessary. They found that just leaving the tumor and treating it with chemotherapy and radiation was more successful. Thank God for that.

We brought her home for Christmas. She began two years of chemotherapy in December. Then, during the month of February, we went to Louisville and lived with a friend, my roommate from college, during the week so that Christin could get her radiation there. She was four when the tumor was discovered, and five that next February. They told us, going into the radiation, we'd crossed the hurdle. The swelling went down which meant the tumor was shrinking. They told us when they did radiation it would be aimed directly into her eye. They said that normally radiation causes a lot of aggravation to the tissue and, most often, they have to remove the eye because it becomes so painful for the patient. But, in order to make sure the tumor is gone, or shrunk by radiation, we'd have to continue the treatments.

Again, I thought, *God, we are this far along; let's not lose her eye.* I went home and sought God in prayer, and it is amazing how God used different things – stories from the Bible – to speak to me about what he was going to do and how he was going to do it. He directed me to Shadrach, Meshach, and Abednego. I read it and it was as if He said, "If they could walk through that fiery furnace they were placed into, and come out without a smell of smoke on their clothes, do you not believe I can take Christin through radiation without her losing her eye?" I said, "You know, God, if you can do that (take them through the fiery furnace), I think this will be minor for you."

So again, the medical people were astounded at Christin's progress. She never once had any irritation or negative response to that radiation. Later on she had a little bit of dryness, and we dealt with that with drops, but going through the treatment she did not have a problem and she came through it with her eye. Anytime we go to any eye doctor, and we have done so throughout the years, they're amazed that she has her eye. They said it should have at least clouded or looked dysfunctional, and we would have wanted to have it removed, but that has not happened. And she has beautiful eyes. It's like God's hand has been on her from the very beginning. She can tell you more about the last years, how God has helped her. The ordeal never did anything but strengthen Christin. She was just a little fighter from the very beginning. She never agreed to letting them stick her with a needle without screaming. The amazement of it all was the child was never sick a day in her life until this – never had a cold, sore throat, anything. It just blew us away whenever that happened.

They told us that the chemotherapy would tend to make her joints stiff, so they suggested we put her in dancing. I entered her in some dance classes while I was in Louisville. Well, she started in doing dance, with her little bald head, and she's never stopped dancing. She danced all the way through school and then high school.

She went to kindergarten with the Heparin lock in her arm so her treatments could be done. I would take her five days a week for her treatments at St. Mary's Hospital in Evansville, one week out of the month. I'd take her for treatment, but she'd want to go back to school. She'd have me drop her off right after the chemotherapy. She just never wanted to miss school.

CHRISTIN: I remember crying when my mom would drive up to take me to the treatment. I didn't want to leave school. It was a big interruption. I loved school.

DIANE: It was very inconvenient to her life to have to take chemo, but the nurses at St. Mary's all fell in love with her. St. Mary's was like a home away from home. A lot of times her blood count would drop so significantly low that she would have to be in isolation, but she came through it all.

When she went into radiation, they did a CT scan – they didn't have MRIs at that time – and they told us the tumor had shrunk to the point it did not look like there was very much there, but they advised us, very strongly, to go ahead with the radiation so it wouldn't return. That was where the confusion came in, because I felt almost assured the tumor was gone, because the eye had gone back into place and her stitches had come out. But, we felt like we needed to go ahead with radiation. Then they did a CT scan following the radiation treatment and I remember getting a phone call on the results of that and, again, the nurse cried over the phone with me. She said, "It's not there! It's gone." So at the end of February 1982, the tests were not showing any tumor at all. Still, they insisted that, with the type of cancer it was, we continue chemo for two years.

Our biggest battle was with the chemo because it would just break her down. She lost so much weight; she got shingles which spread up the side of her neck, her ears and one side of her head. She was in the hospital with a temperature of 105 for about two weeks and it was just a real nightmare.

But, in spite of that, she was the flower girl in her aunt's wedding and wore a hat. I made her all these little bonnets that matched her outfits so she could go to school, because she had no hair. Her head was as bald as a cucumber. No eyebrows, no eyelashes.

CHRISTIN: Of course, I never used to like to wear them. They would always bug my head and itch. As soon as I had the chance, I'd take that sucker off. I remember to this day, through kindergarten and first grade, anywhere we'd go out in public, people's eyes were just automatically glued to me because I was bald. The comments I would get. "Oh, look at that boy." That just totally set me off when they started teasing me about how I looked like a boy just because I was bald. Even adults would make comments like that, in public, in the mall, anywhere we went. "Oh, my gosh, look at that kid." It was like they'd never seen a kid that was bald before and they had no idea. People stare at anyone who's different. It was hard, looking different, even in junior high school.

DIANE: This was in the early 1980s, and I think it is better today, I really do. Anyway, we were there on the floor in St. Mary's where they treated all the little cancer patients, and, of course you get to know people. I saw three children, toddlers, fight the disease and not win it. During the two years Christin was there, we went to the funeral for one little boy who had leukemia. Another little girl had the identical thing Christin had and the staff told us how fortunate we were that Christin's tumor was behind her eye. I thought, *How is that fortunate, just tell me?*

They said, "Mrs. Garrard, you don't realize that, because it was behind her eye, it showed up almost immediately." The other little girl had it in her stomach area first, then it metastasized, and by the time they found it, she was blind, then she died. I've always told Christin God's hand was on her from day one. Christin can talk more about what it was like. As the mother, I pretty much carried Christin through, but her character got her through it too.

Then we began noticing differences in Christin's appearance. That's when Christin's story comes in, because when you talk about overcoming obstacles, that was it. Every year we went back for bone scans and CT scans to make sure everything was normal. On one occasion, the doctor said, "Mrs. Garrard, Christin will probably, at some point in her life, want to have plastic surgery because her face is not going to grow on that left side." It was from the radiation. They did not use any type of safety shields like they do now. The radiation that was given to her left eye spilled over into the area of the left side of her face. That caused all the bone structure on the left side of her face not to grow. Her face on that side stayed the same size as when she was a four year old, so when she went through her growth, puberty, her face did not grow. Her sinus cavities, her left eye socket, all stayed the size they were when she was age four. Not only that, but we also found out that her permanent teeth had no root structure to them at all. They told me that, in years ahead, Christin would lose a lot of her teeth because there were no roots to hold them in: they, too, had been destroyed by radiation.

They saved her eye but there was a whole new set of problems to deal with. They'd look at me and say, "But aren't they (the problems) just trite in relation to her life." And I would look at them and say, "You're not her mother. You don't have to live with the pain she suffers." She'd won the war, but she had a battle ahead of her. When she went through puberty with all the other little girls, and later when everybody started dating and having the best time of their lives, it was very difficult. Even my own family members – God love them; they can hurt you the most – would say things to me like, "Diane, don't you think maybe you ought to take Christin and see if there's something they can do. Maybe they can make it look a little less noticeable."

CHRISTIN: I talked to my mother about it and we did see a plastic surgeon. It was the summer before I entered high school and I was fifteen years old. I'd never thought of plastic surgery as an option. When it came up, I thought, *What do you mean, plastic surgery?* I thought it was only the Hollywood people who did it. Mom told me about a plastic surgeon that did reconstructive work on patients with similar conditions. He was out of Nashville. We went to see him and, when he heard the details, he was shocked that I was even sitting there, that I'd survived. He told me my options. He was a very, very generous man and he asked what it was that I wanted. I said, "I want my left side of my face to look like the right side. I'm tired of people looking at me, staring at me, and asking the constant question, 'What happened?'"

It still comes up today. People ask me what happened to my face. And, of all careers for me to choose, I've decided to work with kids as an elementary teacher. I think kids are the most honest and truthful. They just come out and bluntly ask me, "What happened to your eye?" Or "What happened to your face?" At first, it totally upset me and made me want to go hide in a corner and cry. Until recently, about a semester ago, I asked myself, "What am I thinking? Why do I want to be an elementary teacher?"

I totally didn't know how to handle it, so I discussed it with my pastor's wife, who is an elementary teacher herself. She helped me a lot, and prayed with me, and told me kids are just curious, and they don't know how their questions affect people. They don't know what others are feeling, or if the questions are going to hurt them or not. I've pretty much overcome that big question, the one I hate, "What happened?" I just tell them I've had surgery. I don't want to get into detail and tell them I had cancer and so forth, not little kids, because they don't understand that. Even after I give them the little answer about surgery, they just keep going. "Why? Why? Why?"

DIANE: Christin has never shied away from doing what her heart's desire is, despite the obstacles. She wanted to be on the dance team in high school and I mean she wanted to be on the front row of the dance team. She didn't want to hide. It's never been a question of limiting herself.

CHRISTIN: I don't limit myself. There's no reason I should. I think growing up in a Christian environment, and having God as my counselor and advisor and leader through life, have shown me that I don't have to limit myself because of what Satan has tried to steal from me. It's just his way of trying to get me down and prevent me from living my life the way God would want me to.

When I was seven, and through with the chemotherapy, I grew my hair back and got rid of that hat. Yeah, buddy! Before my hair fell out, it was really light brown, but it came back very dark. I thought, *Whoa!* I wore a hair bow in it, every chance I got, to get past that "Look at that boy" comment. At seven, I didn't notice the changes in my face.

DIANE: That was later. She was very late in going through puberty. She was always petite, very small. People were amazed at her age. We even went to a growth doctor because we were concerned about that and he said, "I really don't think Christin is going to have that much problem, but she's two years behind everybody." It's as if chemo stopped her growth for two years. She was always going to be behind in growth, so it wasn't until she was about fifteen that we really started noticing her face.

CHRISTIN: I noticed it in junior high, in the seventh grade, when they took school pictures. In school pictures, they make you sit and look at the camera directly, straight forward. I saw, in those seventh grade pictures, that the left side of my face was smaller. That's the first time I noticed a difference. By about eighth grade, I started sitting sort of diagonally, looking sideways at the photographer. I always asked the photographer, "Can I sit slanted so the left side of my face really doesn't show that much?"

In elementary school I was blessed with an excellent environment. It was a small school and the principal, the teachers, and even the students, were all very conscientious, and they all knew me. They understood my situation. Even during junior high, I don't remember a lot of people asking me questions, and if they did, other people would tell them. So, as far as classmates, I didn't have a problem with people asking me, "What happened?" I would have a personal friendship with someone, and they might get comfortable and feel they could ask, and I didn't mind telling them. But when the question just comes out the blue, in a different environment, I don't choose to tell them. If they don't even know me, I wonder why it matters to them.

So, in junior high I started noticing my face was not symmetrical. That's when mom told me about the plastic surgeon. I had discussed it with mom, asked her why my face looked so different. Asked her what the deal was. She explained it to me and told me about the plastic surgeon and asked me if I was interested. She didn't push it on me and say, "I want you to get this done." She totally left it up to me. She just told me my options. I said, "Yeah, we should at least check it out." So we took the trip to Nashville to a plastic surgeon and he told us the procedure he would do to make my left side of my face look like the right side of my face. He told me he couldn't get it exact, but he could try. He said it would consist of a bone graft and a tissue graft, taking bone from my skull and grafting it to my cheekbone and eye socket. Then he would do a tissue graft from my stomach and apply that to my cheek area. The soft tissue hadn't grown, so he said he needed to add some stuff in there to make it look like it had. He said it would require three surgeries: one a bone graft; one a tissue graft, and then a touch-up.

It totally scared me. I said, "What do you mean, taking bone from my skull and tissue from my stomach?" I thought, *Whoa!* We went home and we thought about it. I don't know if I prayed and asked, sought God, or just kind of went out on my own, but I'm sure mom prayed before she would allow it to happen. But, we decided to go through with it, so we began the reconstructive surgeries. The first one was the tissue from my stomach and that was the worst; it was the surgery that required the most recuperation. It was a little bikini incision, like I'd had a caesarean. I was in the hospital for a week.

He put the tissue from my stomach on the left side of my face. He wasn't going to make incisions that were very obvious, so he did an incision around my ear. You couldn't even tell it was there. Like a face lift. That's how he described it. That was during a summer break because I didn't want to miss school. I didn't want any of this to effect my education and graduation from high school. Next was bone grafting and we did that during Christmas break, after Christmas. We weren't doing it before and ruining the Christmas holiday. He took bone from my skull and put in on my cheek and around my eye socket. He said the bone from my skull was used because the skull bone would grow back, which was something I didn't know. I'd asked him if it was going to leave a hole in my head! There are layers of bone in the skull and it grows back. I thought, *Okay, that's cool.* He also used some artificial bone. That surgery was tough because it was an eight-hour surgery and it took more energy out of me. Then, the following spring, we did the touch-up surgery. It wasn't until after that surgery, in the fall, that I had complications.

My body started recognizing the artificial materials he'd used to fill in around the soft tissue area, and I developed an infection on my cheek. My body was rejecting the artificial material, so he had to go in and remove some of it. A lot of the surgery that he did, that had helped so much, had to be undone.

DIANE: That was the overall low point. Because it was coming along very well up to then and we thought we had the answer.

CHRISTIN: Yeah, and it was looking really good. I thought, *Wow!* It was really odd for me because my face is almost like my identity, and with him doing those surgeries, the left side of my face got bigger and it was a total shock to me. It wasn't the me that I was used to seeing in the mirror my whole life. When the swelling went down, the left side was still a little bigger than the right side of my face, because the surgeon said he put extra material in there, beyond what would be corrective, because sometimes some of it would deteriorate and be absorbed by the body. We started noticing a change after the complications of the infection.

The plastic surgeon said, "Let's do another surgery and replace the artificial bone that I took out, with your real bone this time." So we did another bone surgery and that's when he realigned my jaw because my jaw bite wasn't straight; it was lifted up on the left side. He cut my jaw and lowered it and even put screws in to hold it in place (this was during another Christmas break) and I had arch braces on my teeth to hold my jaw in place. That was the most horrible of all the surgeries. I was like a zombie, it drained me so much. I felt like I was in a coma, which I wasn't, but I just lay in the hospital bed, waiting to get my energy back.

All this went on from the time I was fifteen until I was about seventeen. It was a three-year process, seven surgeries in three years, plus all the complications that kept showing up. He even did another surgery where he took more tissue from my stomach and put it on my face, because the work he'd done had deteriorated. We had never expected so many surgeries.

DIANE: They tell you that radiated tissue is very hard to deal with and they can't be sure how it will react. It doesn't react the way that normal tissue does. It didn't have a good blood supply. The doctor really didn't know what to expect. I think it was at that point that we decided to take a break.

CHRISTIN: I came to the conclusion that I was trying to make myself look perfect according to the way society thinks a person should look. That's what I was trying to go for, but all these complications kept coming up. I think that's when God got hold of me and I realized that it was God's will for me to go through all the reconstructive surgery – well, maybe not all of them – but I think it helped me a lot with my self-esteem and the way I looked. I didn't just think, *Wow, I'm beautiful,* but I felt better. Then I realized that it didn't matter the way I looked. Actually, I'd known that my whole life, but, in high school, I'd started thinking I didn't have a boyfriend because of the way I looked. I wondered why I didn't go out on a lot of dates like everyone else and thought it was because of the way I looked. I didn't look beautiful. But I finally concluded that was just Satan feeding me lies. I finally came to the point, after all the surgeries, that it didn't matter how I looked on the outside. I got tired of going through all those surgeries, one after another, after another. I decided to put the plastic surgery on hold for a while. The surgeon had wanted so badly to make it happen. He was very compassionate and he wanted, as much as I did, to make it work. He just kept looking for more answers and coming up with more ideas, but I said, "We're going to sit back and see."

DIANE: I think what really happened during that time period was she fell in love with herself for who she was, because Christin has such a beautiful spirit about her. She really does, and people have always said that about her. I knew that about her, but I think she had to see that for herself before she could finally be comfortable with who she was and how she looked. I think her involvement during that time period, with a group of Christian friends, people who see people for who they are, not what they look like, helped. That's when she started going to the youth group and started surrounding herself with people that supported her for her gifts, for her talents, for her humor, for all that she is other than her looks. That was when she became comfortable. I always told Christin, "You just haven't met anybody yet that recognizes your beauty. Christin, you're a beautiful person."

You can put a beautiful face on somebody, but if they're not at peace and don't love themselves, it is hard for them to love others. That was what I really saw happening to Christin during that time when she didn't feel good about herself. Here was this surgeon, trying to create this "right" look, yet on the inside she had all these hurts and anger. There was a lot of anger there that she'd never allowed herself to express. Before, she wouldn't let herself cry; she was trying to hold it all in. Eventually, we had a lot of tears. Finally, she allowed herself to get rid of that after I told her it was okay to be mád.

I felt so bad for Christin because it was horrendous what she went through. I don't think she has any idea of the extent of those surgeries because she was knocked out with morphine. I was so disheartened when it didn't turn out to be what she wanted. But, in the end, I think maybe it did, because she saw through all that and knew what God creates is beautiful and, no matter how she looks outwardly, someone, someday, is going to recognize her beauty. And, of course, that has happened. She has met a wonderful young man that thinks she is the most beautiful woman in the world. He was obviously sent by God, for her life, and they are just the most beautiful couple. People see that in them.

CHRISTIN: When all those reconstructive surgeries were going on, I was in high school. We put an end to the surgeries when I graduated from high school. The number one question then was, what was I going to do with myself? Where was I going to college? What career was I going to choose? Golly, I searched that question for two years, I believe. I knew I had to go to college.

I didn't know then I didn't have to hurry up and decide. It was God's timing, he would let me know what to do, so I turned to God and asked him what he wanted me to do. After all, He saved my life, what more could I do than live my life for Him? I started seeking what God wanted me to do with my life, what career He wanted me to choose. I went away to a Christian college in Oklahoma.

I knew nobody out there, but the youth group in my church has a youth camp in the summer. From that I discovered Destiny College, which was for high school graduates trying to figure out what their God-given destiny was. God has a purpose for each and every one of our lives, so I went to this college, figuring God would let me know what it was He wanted me to do. I was only in Oklahoma for six months, but it was a healing process for me. While I was at Destiny College, trying to find out what God wanted me to do, a complication came up with my eye.

My left eye had been declared legally blind since I was six years old; I could see light out of it, but it was just a big old blur. There was nothing they could do to correct it; the treatments I had when I was a child resulted in a really scratched cornea. They could do a cornea transplant, but that's too risky. They advised me not to do that because of the effects of the radiation on my eye. After the reconstructive surgeries, an eye doctor in Nashville discovered my eye was dry, and the radiation had damaged the tear duct.

In second grade, after the chemotherapy, I had to wear a contact in my eye. So, from second grade until tenth grade, I wore a contact in my left eye to keep it moist. When we started the reconstructive surgeries, an eye doctor said they could plug off the tear duct, because the tears were draining out of the tear duct, and by plugging it off, the tears would stay in my eye. So, that was a real Godsend, because I got rid of the contact.

But, the surgeries took a toll on my eye. So, when I was out in Oklahoma, I had a complication; some tissue showed up underneath my eyelid. That really scared me because I thought it was a tumor. It was a little piece of tissue which I could see it if I pulled down my eyelid. I was out in Oklahoma and my family was back in Kentucky. I did have good, Christian friends there in Oklahoma and one lady, who was the motherly type, tried to help me and we went to doctors there to see what it was, because we had no clue. It was so odd. Oklahoma has this big eye center and I told the doctor all the history, but he didn't know what it was. That's when Mom and Dad made a trip out to Oklahoma and said, "You're coming back home." I didn't want to leave, because I loved that environment: a Christian college where I could take education classes and tie God into that and use our Bible as a text. I was also discovering my talents and using them. I was singing and playing the piano.

The college also had an elementary school across the field. They had us college students substitute teach for their teachers when they had their meeting day. Little did I know that it was my calling. I didn't realize until I came back from Oklahoma that God wanted me to be an elementary teacher. It was there I realized how much I enjoyed working with kids in the school system.

Although God showed me what I was meant to do, I'd been looking for something different. I loved children, but I thought I was supposed to pursue a music career because I loved music, especially Christian music, and that's where I had talent. I played piano and trumpet, and I loved dancing. Dancing was my life; I was dancing all the time. But when I came back, I knew I wanted to be a teacher.

The eye complication wasn't anything drastic; it was scar tissue which had started to grow and built up on itself in an effort to heal. All they did was simply cut it out. But when the doctor cut it out, that was drastic because he didn't put me to sleep and I'm used to being put to sleep when things happen to my eye. After cutting the scar tissue out, the eye doctors were recommending that maybe I needed to have my eyelid clipped shut a little bit on the outside corner because of the moisture problem; they couldn't do anything else to provide more tear ducts to my eye, and what is there isn't enough to keep the eye moist. They said, "Of course, it will be noticeable." At one point, they even suggested removing my eye and having a glass eye put in. I said, "There's no way. I know there is a greater Power that can fix this. God can heal this."

Now, my eye gets irritated every once in a while. Right now, I'm putting ointment in at night and taping it shut. When the muscles are relaxed at night, it doesn't close all the way, so it dries out. That cause redness, irritation, and even makes it sore, like somebody punched me in the eye. So I'm using the ointment and taping it shut and believing in God for another miracle to heal my tear ducts and even the eyesight. I know nothing is impossible for God. We're strong Christians and believe in God for healing, even for my eye. In spite of the effects all of the procedures had on my eye, I know He can restore it.

It's so neat what recently happened. When I cry, I only cry out of my right eye because the tear ducts in my left eye don't produce tears. I was at the altar of our church, for prayer, and I was crying. When I got back to my seat, I noticed tears coming out of my left eye. I thought, *Oh, thank You, Jesus.*

Lately, I'm having dental work done. The radiation did effect my teeth and teeth have fallen out on the left upper side. Now, I'm going through the procedure of dental implants. I'm having to have braces put on the bottom to accommodate the teeth on top. But eventually it's all going to be finished. Complete. I believe God is still healing my face. I've had prophecies from preachers and speakers and close friends even, who say God is going to heal my eye. He is healing my eye, and I believe that He is going to even restore my eyesight. Doctors can't give me the answers now; they've done all they can, so it's up to God. Every day I get more confirmation that God is healing me.

When I was going through the procedures, my face was constantly changing. I kept waiting for it to be complete but it never got there. I finally realized that if it was going to, it would only be through God. I don't think I would ever do any more reconstructive surgery. No. Not unless God told me to because, toward the end, I realized I needed to start seeking God and learning if He wanted me to do it. At that point, I knew I didn't need to go any further. The doctors had done what they could and it was up to God from then on.

One other important thing: when I was born, my mother named me Christin Joy. If you reverse the spelling, and separate the Christin, it's Joy in Christ. I've tried to live up to that in my life and reflect the joy that Christ has and let the joy of Christ shine through me.

– Christin Garrard and Diane Garrard

Unique

Originals throw away
The carbon papers
Of the self-righteous.

– Trish Lindsey Jaggers

Suzanne

My name is Suzanne Bonnette. I am forty-eight, and just starting my life. I was born in Brandenburg, Kentucky, a small rural town approximately fifty miles south west of Louisville, right on the banks of the Ohio river. I'm divorced, and I have two children and three grandchildren. In 1951, a chemical plant was started in a small, rural community in Kentucky – they put it in the middle of nowhere – and basically they made plastics. After my father graduated from college, he taught for a while, then took a job at the chemical plant because of the higher pay scale. They moved there, but there was always a big divide in the town; either you were from there, or you were one of "those plant kids." I was always one of the plant kids. It was very stratified, very class driven. My father served in WWII and lost a kidney. Because of that he was not able to be "career military," but, since we lived close to the military base at Ft. Knox, he still felt connected.

We had a lot of family secrets. I was reared in a very abusive household; my father was an alcoholic. The drinking Mom did was never mentioned, but she more or less drank to drink with Dad. There was a lot of physical abuse. Her behavior was basically just hysteria. The first, distinct, memory I have is Mom locking herself in the bedroom and screaming at the top of her lungs. I was maybe five years old at the time. That was the first time she was put in the mental hospital. She was diagnosed as paranoid-schizophrenic. Of course, today, I know my mother was not a schizophrenic; my mother was a victim of my father's abuse. He was very controlling, and we did well at keeping our deep, dark family secrets.

When my mother was going to the mental hospitals, they used thorazine and shock treatment. She had low self-esteem and thought she was stupid, but she'd put my father through college when he came out of World War II. She worked for a newspaper; she was not a stupid woman. But, throughout the marriage, she was a victim. At the time, people didn't recognize victimization.

To the community he was a straight-backed guy, a "martyr" who took care of his mentally ill wife. He was very involved in the community, early on, and so we led a double life. What we looked like to the public was not what was happening. It became very confusing to me as a child. My brother was not born until I was nine years old. For many, many years it was just me, and I have a patchy memory of much of my childhood, a lot of blank spots. There was a lot of physical abuse and he sexually abused both me and my mother.

Drugs, as well as alcohol, were involved. I say today my father was a junkie – a middle-class junkie. When he was thirty-five, he had his first heart attack. After that, he'd get angina pains. The liquor store closed at twelve o'clock on Saturday night and, about one a.m., he'd start having chest pains. That was still in the days when the doctor made house calls. The doctor would come and shoot him full of morphine or demerol, knocking him out for the rest of the weekend. I've seen times when the doctor would come, shoot him full of drugs, then he and the doctor would sit at the kitchen table and drink.

Between my father and mother was rage, and there was constant turmoil in our household. I was reared to believe it was all my mother's fault; that Mom was the bad person.

Dad would say, "You've got to get up out of bed and control your mother; I can't."

He dominated us both. There were periods he locked her in the basement. He'd take her to the mental hospital, then blame it all on her.

When my mother was sent to the mental institution, I became the replacement. I was expected to take care of things, at five years old! There was a baby sitter who came into the home, but it was my father who controlled me. When my mother was home, and as she got worse, she started acting out very violently. She frightened me. Once I woke up with a phone cord around my neck; another time with the garbage can in my room on fire. She became very jealous of me. A lot of her hatred was directed toward me, and she blamed me for a lot.

They didn't want me to begin with, that was very clear. When Mom got pregnant with me she got very ill, and Dad wanted a son. When he had a daughter, it was the end of the world. I was not a wanted child, so when my brother was born, to them he was going to be the fantastic son. He became the perfect son, and I became the bad one. There was a time my brother fell off a tricycle and broke his arm. My mother tried to break my arm because she said I should have been watching him.

She was probably more physically abusive then than my father. Today, I realize she had no capacity of her own. She did as she was told, and, when it didn't work, she reacted. I believe she had a severe case of post-traumatic stress from the abuse she took from my father. She had no support from her mother. Then too, she was kept isolated. He moved her from her home in Arkansas to Kentucky, and isolation is a strong factor in abuse.

I was always the one, later, who had to take Dad to the hospital. I was always the one who had to call the doctor. By the time I was fifteen, I did the grocery shopping and I took care of my brother. During the periods when Mom was home, everything was supposed to be okay. But in all this time, no one said Dad had a drinking problem: it was a "heart condition." He was the martyr; he was the one who struggled so hard – he went to work every day.

When he began putting her in the mental hospital, his sexual abuse of me started. Other people talk about what they remember, but I don't have any firm memories; I remember scenes. I remember at five years old, sitting on my father's lap, being molested and throwing up on him. I was sexually abused the entire time I was growing up. I actually grew up thinking that I was meant to be a sexual object, to be used by men as they pleased. That was a woman's role. My father was also abusing Mom horribly, sexually, in front of me. There are memories I still have a hard time verbalizing because, if I verbalize them, it takes them out of the realm of being memories and puts them into the realm of reality. The abuse was horrendous. Women, in my home, were strictly for men's pleasure. We did as men said, or we got beat, or they locked us away.

By the time I reached twelve or thirteen years of age, I was acting out. I was really becoming a "bad kid." I was involved in drugs and alcohol, but for me that was normal. I remember when I was twelve years old, and started my period, I was given thorazine for the cramps. I was very sexually active, with no discrimination about it, because I thought that was what my role was. I was a runaway. I think one of the worse memories I have is that, every time the cops would pick me up and bring me home, nobody ever asked me why I ran away. I was just a "bad kid."

Some of my friends from that time are still my staunch supporters. One of them, Jeep, and I have memories of being virtually reared in the parking lot of this beer joint. His dad and my dad would be in the liquor store, and we'd sit in the car and every now and then they would bring out a beef jerky or a cola. As time went on, the acting out got worse, along with the confusion. I liked school and always had a secret dream to go to college, but I knew that was not in the picture for me. I'd been told that enough. I was told I was stupid and that I would never go to college.

When I got old enough to really fight back, the sexual abuse stopped. Once I reached my teen years, the abuse changed from sexual to verbal and physical. At that point, I became a "whore" to them and the physical abuse escalated. So, too, did the physical abuse that was perpetrated on my mother. Dad would just beat her to a pulp. Then he would tell me I had to control my mother if I wanted to prevent it. I was caught in the middle. There was even a period of time when I fell into blaming Mom. It became very confusing and conflicting to me. Both my parents made suicide attempts.

We led two lives – the one others saw and the real one inside our home. Dad was making a very good income, but we were living at a dirt poor level, even though we lived in the "right" neighborhood. I had to do all the "right" middle class stuff: ballet lessons, baton lessons and all that, yet I couldn't bring my friends home. We kept a very closed house.

Growing up, school and books became my life saver. I read everything; books were my escape. To this day, I read *Alice in Wonderland* every year on my birthday. I feel like Alice – I've fallen down that rabbit hole many times. I was a good student, but my grades weren't what they could have been because there was always family interference. I was taken out of school to watch my baby brother, to take my mother to a mental hospital, to rescue my father from a "heart attack."

I tried to participate. I played in the school band, a very "learned" effort because I am not musically talented. I always knew there had to be something different, that somewhere life had to be better, but then I'd think, *I was born bad; I'm just a bad person.*

So, by the time I was sixteen, I set out to show the world how bad I could be and did a pretty good job of it. I got real bad. Coming out of all the horrendous abuse that went on in our family, I was a fighter. They had laid that pattern for me, and I had to be a fighter to survive in that atmosphere.

When I was thirteen, I was in a pretty serious car wreck. I was dating a sixteen-year-old, and we were in a stolen car and about killed ourselves. It may sound really strange, but the time in the hospital was a very good time for me because I was actually getting nurtured. My mother was lost at that point from the alcohol, drugs, shock treatments. I remember picking her up from the mental hospital, and she didn't even know who I was because of the shock treatment.

It was a chaotic, horrendous lifestyle. I'm not what you'd term a religious person, but some Higher Power was definitely on my side to have gotten me through that.

By the time I was sixteen I had pretty much decided I was a sexual object to be used by men and this led to a series of really severe incidents. I had tried going to church and ended up getting molested by a youth minister. When I was not quite seventeen, I was brutally raped by two men. There was a girl my age who had been in a mental hospital with my mom. She set me up on a double date with her. I thought it would be okay because I knew my date's brother very well, but the other girl left me alone with the two men, who were in their middle-to-late twenties. We'd all been drinking wine and doing acid. The two men proceeded to rape me, very brutally, that night. It was a very violent rape, involving coke bottles and foreign objects. I suffered severe blood loss and bled out of both ears. At one point, I got away from the two men, at a local bar, and ran up to a state trooper and cried, "You've got to help me," but the two men came up and said, "Look, she's with us. She's had too much to drink. Let us take her home." The cop let them take me home! I never told my parents about that rape; I told them I'd been in a car wreck that night. They didn't question me. Of course, there were times when I could be gone for a whole weekend, and it was never questioned. At this point, I was the bad kid, the bad person, the runaway. I was actively involved in drugs, alcohol, men – into the whole scene.

At home, the physical abuse, both that which was directed toward me and that which I witnessed, escalated, and it had it's effect on me. My father beat me, but I was never supposed to upset the routine because Dad might have a heart attack, and Mom would go crazy and have to go to the nut house. That was the big family control. It was not uncommon for me to drive my dad to the hospital in the middle of the night, when he believed he was having a heart attack. I spent most of my Saturday nights sitting in the emergency ward of the VA hospital so dad could get his shots. Guilt was a factor because I always thought, *What if he is really having a heart attack this time and he dies?*

When I left home, my brother got really upset with me and we didn't speak for years. I could never understand why, until just recently when we've had the opportunity to sit down and talk. I learned that he was angry with me for all those years I left him there. He'd lived with the same threats I had: if he did anything wrong, someone was going to kill themselves or have a heart attack – always something major. It was just continuous. We never had any idea of what sitting down to a normal family meal was like. At our house it was all about pleasing Dad and making sure he got his fix.

I ended up pregnant when I was seventeen years old. Since we lived near Ft. Knox, my father knew people on the base and brought GIs to the house. There I was, a sixteen-year-old who'd come to believe she was a whore – the pregnancy was inevitable. During my pregnancy, I was sent to live at Catholic Charities. We were told every day what bad people we were. But, even though I was in a home for unwed mothers, I was receiving nurturing. A lot of the people thought the abuse was really bad there, but compared to what I came out of, it was nurturing. My family didn't come to see me. I was a disgrace to my father; I was ruining his public image. Strangely, during that period my mother was very strong. I remember I was six months along before I had the nerve to tell my parents I was pregnant. I was baby sitting, and called Mom from there to tell her first. She said, "Well, you know, it's not going to be good with your Dad, but I want you to know I love you." That sticks in my mind so much. Mom was supposed to be the crazy one, Mama was supposed to be the bad one, but Mama's the one who stood in there with me. She helped with the arrangements. Dad wanted me to get an abortion, but she got me into the home. She wrote me letters, but told me not to let my dad know that she was putting five dollars in them for me. She was very supportive. I put the baby up for adoption, and I didn't feel bad about the decision. The last thing in the world I wanted then was a child. After I got out of the home, I stayed with friends of Mom and Dad's for a couple of weeks, and then I went home.

An aunt and uncle had taken custody of my brother for the summer, but they left me with my parents. I had a really hard time with that. I thought, *He must be perfect ... he must be right ... he must be the good one because they took care of him and no one cared about me.* I didn't last long at home, but I did graduate from high school.

It was the 1960s, and I was very involved in sex, drugs, and rock-n-roll. I was ripe for the protesting that went on in the sixties. I hated anything that had anything to do with the military. I went to Louisville. I was looking for either the hippies or the bikers, and I found the bikers, or, more accurately, they found me. Another girl went with me, and she was going to stay in Louisville, but I was just out to party for a while. After I had the baby and got out of school, I lived this really wild, party life. I was with a different man every night, whoever would pat me on the head – I was like a lost dog – and take me home. I stayed really strung out on drugs and alcohol. After all the sexual abuse, the molestation, the rape, I was really wide open for the 60s rebellion and I hit it wide open! I was into acid, made it to Woodstock, and got wonderful support from a lot of other people who were lost too. A lot of people may have trouble with this next part of my story because I have a very deep, loving affection for the biker gang, The Outlaws, and the biker who became my "old man" in that organization.

The Outlaws, at that time, were a national group. In the1960s, the Hell's Angels controlled everything west of the Mississippi, and The Outlaws everything east of the Mississippi. I was picked up off a street corner by a biker, J.T., and he took me to the club house in Louisville. They fed me; they bathed me; they clothed me.

J.T. asked me. "Are you here to party or do you want to stay?"

I said I guessed I was there to stay, I didn't have anywhere else to go.

He said, "Well, you know Outlaw's old ladies work."

I said I had a high school education. I learned really quick what type of work they were referring to, and it didn't need a high school diploma. It was stripping and prostitution. He asked if I wanted to stay and be somebody's old lady, and I said I did. He had an old lady, and he sent me home that next day with her, and she gave me clothes. Even though her old man had been the one who picked me up, she and I got to be best friends. He said Lindsey, who was president of The Outlaws at the time, would be coming in off the road, and he needed an old lady.

I was sitting on the steps of the club house when Lindsey and another guy, Marshall, pulled up. Lindsey looked at me and said, "You're looking for an old man?" I said, "Yes." He told me to get on the back of his motorcycle, and he took me home. He spent two weeks just totally romancing me. Although it was like stories you hear of how young girls are exploited, I think at that time they probably saved my life, because they took me in off the streets. No telling where I would have ended up at that point.

Lindsey took me to the zoo; he took me to the ice cream parlor; he bought me clothes. It wasn't even a sexual thing. I was seventeen; he was over thirty-five. Then one day he told me I needed to think about going to work, and he explained that I would be a prostitute. At that point, I had a sexual relationship with him, but he was very loving to me. He was my knight in shining armor.

I never felt exploited. I didn't feel like I was forced into anything. I always had the attitude that it was what my father reared me to do, so I did it well. Lindsey was aware of where I had come from and the abuse I had experienced. He never put me in the streets. I always worked in a house; I always worked pretty much in safe surroundings, in Louisville. My first trick was down at the old Brown Hotel. It lasted about two nights, and I got so scared. Lindsey wouldn't send me back. Next I worked for a lady called S. who ran a house. Then I worked for a lady, called M., on Jefferson Street.

I think this is where a lot of people might get confused because I don't have horrendous, scathing memories of this life of prostitution. I have wonderful, warm, family memories because, all at once, I had people who were nurturing me, people who cared about me. I had never really experienced that before. Even though I was in a very volatile, criminal organization (at that time The Outlaws were considered one of the largest criminal organizations in the United States), Lindsey kept me very separate from the Outlaw business.

Lindsey had a degree in marine biology. He was very well educated. His job was to run the club, however, and he didn't work at his profession. He was a wonderful man who had his own reasons for living his life in the biker community. Every day wasn't rosy, but my memories are not terrible. Eventually, sex between us died out, but my fondness for him had nothing to do with sex. Lindsey became a substitute father. It was the protective arm around me all the time which became important.

I was kept very strict. I didn't go to many of the parties. If I did, I wore my patch, which indicated I was the property of The Outlaws, and I stayed close to him. I handed over every dime I made to Lindsey, but I never wanted for anything either. There was no physical abuse whatsoever. I don't know what the whole dynamic that resulted from that is, but I bonded really strongly with Lindsey and he took care of me. If he was involved with other women, I never knew about it. He always told me there would come a time when I would leave him, that I would want that house with the white picket fence and two kids.

I would argue with him, "Oh, no, I'll never leave you."

But eventually I did. I ended up leaving for the dream of the house with the white picket fence. Still, I always stayed close to Lindsey. He was always there in the background, and I loved him until the day he died, two years ago. I was able to maintain more dignity and respect with him than I ever could in the world that was supposed to be "normal."

There were times I worked "lockup." We would go out and stay in a place for two weeks and just turn tricks twenty-four hours a day. I wouldn't even want to think about being involved in it today. It's a horrible profession, very degrading, very oppressive. When I was in the profession, though, we didn't have any AIDS; we didn't even have herpes. The houses I worked for sent us to the "clap" clinic once a week to get tested; we were given a pink slip. We were working with the police. We knew when we were going to get busted, and who was going to go to jail and who wasn't. Of course my first experience in jail scared me to death.

I made my money by being "daddy's little girl" with older men, and I acted out a whole lot. I was very good at it, and I made good money at it. Once or twice, I attempted working in the bars, but I'd end up getting drunk and it just didn't work. I was still so young and, even though I was living in a very violent, criminal world, I was put in very sheltered, protected areas of that world. I know that a lot of it was because I was a money-maker, and that allowed me a lot of protection, but at the time I didn't view it that way. I viewed it as people caring for me.

I finally ended up in the hospital with peritonitis. I'd never had any post-natal care after having the baby and developed an infection that was neglected. I went to University Hospital and the doctor asked me what my profession was. I told him I was a prostitute. He immediately assumed I had gonorrhea and gave me a dose of penicillin. Well, I didn't have gonorrhea. I had a severe yeast infection, and the penicillin didn't help it, so the infection just blew all the way up and went into peritonitis. Lindsey ended up fighting with the Baptist Hospital to get me admitted there. So here I had all these so called "bad people" in our society fighting to save my life, sitting by my bed day and night, right there, hanging in with me. Again, I was very grateful; I would have done anything they asked. Outside of the prostitution, and my slipping out the back door with guns when the police raided, they never involved me in anything. I know there was a lot of stuff that went on, but I was kept very far from it. I thank Lindsey for those five years. I loved him. I would have done anything for the man.

Every Sunday we got up and had our Sunday run (group motorcycle ride). We all went out and rode, then after the Sunday run they would have the meeting, in which the women did not participate. Of course, we were all considered "cunts" which, today, I wouldn't find a very appropriate term, but at the time it was different. Then, after the meeting, Lindsey always took me to the mid-city mall here in Louisville; there was a Kresge's store that was open on Sunday afternoons. He'd buy me a new outfit and a new book to read, then take me to the ice cream parlor. Sunday night, we always went to the drive-in theater. It was a set pattern. I never had to work on Sunday – that was our day.

I was on this marvelous trip in a whole new subculture. I was involved in this whole wonderful scene that was everything that my father hated. I was right there in the middle of it. My parents knew what I had been doing. I saw to it that they did. I pulled up in front of my father's office with a whole pack of Outlaws one day. It was just orneriness.

Lindsey used to tell me, "If it weren't for men like your father, I could never find girls to go to work."

But, I reached a point where I could not deal with the prostitution anymore. I was getting older; I was twenty-four. The prostitution was getting to me. I decided I did want the house with the white picket fence and the two kids.

I didn't think I could stay with Lindsey and the club and drop the prostitution; I was very indoctrinated into the club ways, and knew Lindsey was never going to leave the club. He'd die an Outlaw. If I left the club, I had to leave Lindsey.

Then, I broke the ultimate rule of prostitution: I married a trick. Of course, Lindsey immediately blackballed me from prostitution, which was another way of saving me. But, I entered into a whole new nightmare world.

Once again, I was trying to live up to the values of the dominant, mainstream society. The man I married eventually lost a leg, previously injured in Vietnam when he stepped on a booby trap, but he still had his leg when I met him, around 1973 or '74. He had been in and out of the VA hospital. He was a customer at the house where I was working. I thought he was my knight in shining armor; he thought he was saving me from the horrible world of prostitution and bikers.

I had a very long talk with Lindsey and he told me I was making a mistake, that I would get into more trouble. I wasn't mature enough to understand that if I'd told Lindsey I didn't want to be a prostitute anymore, we could have worked something out. We would have probably been together until the day he died. I learned that the one love of your life may be the one you walk out on, and I loved Lindsey. He was probably the only man who has ever shown me any real love and affection.

But, I left and married Bobby and discovered he was alcoholic. It was a horribly abusive marriage. He was five or six years older than me. The marriage was a joke from day one, because he came from a fairly comfortable family and, basically, he brought home this little whore to shock his family. I saw to it he did this quite well. He did it deliberately, and didn't try to hide the fact that he had picked me up out of the gutter. He wanted them to know because that was going to make him a good person. Me? I wanted that house, the one with the white picket fence. But our marriage? He married a whore. He wanted a whore, so I became his whore.

When I had been working in the "lockups" as a prostitute, I abused alcohol and drugs. For a while, working in a "lockup," I did heroin. When Lindsey found out – he was totally anti-drugs – I had to get off it. But, when I married Bobby, the drugs and alcohol dominated again because we both did them. It took me awhile to get pregnant, but I did get pregnant, after a year of trying, and I thought everything was going to be okay. I had married a war hero, which was going to make my father happy. Bobby drew a 100 percent disability pay, his parents gave us a 42-plus acre farm, and I was going to have his kids, so that meant I was doing things the right way, the way society says they're supposed to be.

It didn't work. The sexual dysfunction was incredible. He married me for what I was, a whore, and he intended to use me for that. There were always other women. I remember waking up after we had all been drinking, and he was with this other woman, laying in bed right next to me. This was a constant. I was supposed to accept that because I was a whore. So, I became that whore and played it very well. We ended up selling the farm and bought a house in Jeffersonville. Then we made the fatal mistake. We sold that and bought the house right next door to my mom and dad. Bobby and Father became wonderful drinking buddies.

It turned into a nightmare at that point, but by then I had two children, a son and a daughter. I loved my children. God knows I loved my children. But I couldn't make anything else work; it was all falling to pieces around my ears. I was in bad shape then due to drugs and alcohol. According to my husband, we had an "open marriage," so there was a lot of sexual activity going on, even down to orgies. I couldn't deal with the scene. Even the girl who was supposed to be my best friend was sleeping with my husband. Once again, I internalized everything. I thought it was all my fault. I ended up drinking myself into a detox center. They literally dragged me into the emergency room at Ft. Knox Hospital. I was in a total fetal position; my hair hadn't been combed for days. I was in bad shape.

Bobby served me with divorce papers while I was in the detox center, and he got custody of my kids. After a period of going in and out of detox, I began living in the streets. My life was virtually over. The bigger and meaner a man was, the harder he beat me, the more I was going to be right there with him. I ended up in Birmingham, Alabama, at one point, not too sure how I got there. I lived as a street prostitute, trying to get enough money to get back to Kentucky. I no longer had the luxury and protection I had with The Outlaws. I had lost all that. I was in and out of jail. It was jail – detox, jail – detox, jail – detox. In those days, when they picked a person up drunk, they put them in detox.

God knows, I loved my kids and I wanted my kids so bad, but when my ex-husband brought them to see me, it was always when I was in detox or when I was in jail. That hurt me even more than not seeing them. In the meantime, he was living with another woman, and he was sexually and physically abusing both her kids and my kids: both my son and daughter. I wanted my kids back but I didn't know what to do. I'd gotten caught up with a really abusive man who'd almost physically killed me. We lived together on the streets. We spiked men's drinks. We stole guns. He stole pot. During the period of time I lived in the streets, I weighed about 95 pounds. People asked me what was my drug of choice. I didn't have a drug of choice. I'd take whatever I could get my hands on. I was sitting around in the back alleys with the winos.

Then, I ended up in jail for first-degree armed robbery and assault, and did four months. It happened because the man I was with was pimping me out on the street, and there was a fight with another pimp. That's when I finally got the nerve to call Lindsey, and tell him what I'd fallen into. He helped me get a paid lawyer, and all the charges against me were dropped.

After he got me out of jail, he left the door open to come back to him, but there was no way I could because I felt I had totally failed. He said, "Your only choice now is to come back to me, or go back home to live with your parents." I opted to go back to my parents and was able to get visitation rights with my children. I took training, and got a job working as a nurse's aide.

It was 1979, I was 28 years old, and I was worn out. If anyone had shot me at that point, I don't think I would have even fought for my life. I was worn out – beat up. The marriage to Bobby had been worse than anything any motorcycle club could ever do to a human being. Plus, he had the kids, he had the money and he had the power. I was "the drunk." I was the "drug addict."

I was the one who woke up in the morning, never knowing what man I would wake up with. I'd never really slept with a man just because I chose to sleep with him. Even Lindsey fell into that category. The only time I'd ever slept with a man was because they paid for it, because I felt obligated in some way, or because I was too afraid to say "no." That's still true today. I've never been with a man because I chose to; as a matter of fact, almost four and a half years ago I totally quit dating. I had to for my own survival.

But, even when I was working as a nurse's aide, I was still drinking and doing drugs. I couldn't understand, when I visited my kids, why they weren't returning the love to me that I felt for them. Of course, I now realize I'd abandoned them. I had no idea what to do with children then. I couldn't fight for them, for custody, when I didn't know how to fight for my own life.

There are times in my life, the time between my first and second marriages, which are really fogged up. I think partly it is denial because I have a hard time admitting how badly I abused my own children. Even though it wasn't physical, it was emotionally devastating to them. And the drugs and alcohol made me lose time.

When I went to work at a hospital, I met my Randy, and that was when I really sold my soul to the Devil. I took another nightmare ride, this time into hell, which I never want to experience again.

Once again, I thought I'd found my knight in shining armor. He was going to come into my life, take over, get my kids back, and our life was going to be beautiful. Of course, we met on a drug deal; both of us were very drug addicted. He was just out of the penitentiary, for bank robbery. He wanted to get to know the biker scene, and I had a very interesting position in the biker world at that point, because everybody in the biker world knew about Lindsey's and my relationship. Lindsey had another old lady by then, but we still saw each other. Everybody knew about our relationship, so none of the other bikers would ever really date me because of a promise I had made to Lindsey, that I would never "patch" to another Outlaw. I was very safe sitting in a biker bar. Nobody was going to bother me there, but nobody was going to take me out either because of my tie to Lindsey.

I met Randy in a bar. We were both very drug involved. The first night we met we were shooting speed. I walked him into the biker world, which was what he wanted. He wanted to be this big biker. When I met him, he had on a pair of corduroy pants and a JC Penney's shirt. Within three weeks he had on the blue jeans, a Harley-Davidson tee-shirt, and was riding a Sportster. I was the stepping stone.

But I still had my dream: I wanted to be a wife and a mother again. I'd had my tubes tied, and there weren't going to be any more kids, but I wanted custody of mine. And, Randy was going to save everything. He was going to make it wonderful. We got married. I got my children back for a while. Several small incidents occurred when Randy was physically violent toward me. I found out he was very controlling. He controlled through the drugs, but more than that, he controlled me through my children. He knew that was where my whole world centered.

We lived off and on in Louisville. Randy was in industrial construction, and he always worked. We traveled all over the country, though he also had several local jobs. But, once again, sexually, I was the whore. Sex became very sick, but I was determined to make my marriage work this time. I convinced myself everything was going to be okay. Then, I made another fatal mistake. We bought a house in Brandenburg because I still had a tie to my father. Randy ended up losing his job, then got in trouble with the law again. He was always in trouble with the law. I defended him, saying the charges were impossible. When I look back, I see that he was very into rapist sex, very much into the handcuffs and the tying down. He would convince me it was just a game we were playing, but today I see that it wasn't all a game to him. He was very brutal. Yet, I was trying to present a normal life to my kids.

Things fell apart with Randy and me, except, this time I went totally straight, totally off the drugs and alcohol, and I got caught in the world of AA (Alcoholics Anonymous), which, although I don't want to be offensive to AA, was one of the worse things that ever happened to me. I had no idea of how to function as a singular individual. I could not function unless there was total control. I did what I was told, and I did it well. I was told I needed to leave my husband, and yes, I probably did, but that was because I was involved with another man in AA. A good old thirteenth step. I divorced Randy and my kids went back to their dad. At that time, the facts of their father's sexual abuse hadn't come out. We knew there were bad things going on, but not how bad.

When my son was visiting with me, he told me his father was sexually abusing both of his stepdaughters. Alarmed, I got back together with Randy because he was there again and ready to help me make it all better. I kidnapped my children, with Randy's help, and we went to live in Ohio while I went to court to get custody. In court, I charged Bobby with child molesting. They gave me custody of my daughter, but they weren't going to give me custody of my son. He wasn't going to get any protection at all, yet he was the one who turned his father in for the molestation. They were going to send him back to live with that man.

One incident that happened between Randy and me, when we were in Ohio, sticks out in my mind. It was while I was battling to deal with the information concerning Bobby's molestation of his stepdaughters. I found out that my children had experienced severe physical, emotional, and sexual abuse – things like being made to sit on their hands on milk crates for hours on end. Horror stories. I'd been in court all day, in Kentucky, and had come back to Ohio that night. I was tired and stressed from the stories that had come out in court. Randy told me he wanted to have sex, and I told him I didn't feel like sex, after hearing everything I'd heard that day. That was the first time he really became violent with me.

"How dare you accuse me of being like that filthy child molester?" he demanded.

I didn't know, at that point, that I'd married another child molester, but, in essence, he was. I later found out from my daughter that he had already molested her. Of course I didn't see it – didn't want to see it. But that was when he first really became physical to the point it scared me.

Before I got custody of my kids again, he and I lived on the road, traveling all over the country so he could work. I would be in Oklahoma and I would drive to Kentucky to spend a weekend with my kids. I never missed a visitation day, regardless of where I was living. I never missed the opportunity to telephone them.

Randy and I were together and I had my kids; but then, it just got bad again and I divorced him for the second time. I found myself a single mother with two kids. This was around 1982 or 1983. I worked stripping tobacco and picking strawberries. I still had all that crazy AA stuff going on, but I had severe problems with the men in AA. Especially after they heard my story. There are a lot of sick individuals in AA. If I had to stay in AA today, I'd be drunk. There were a lot of sexual issues, a lot of sick sexual issues. This was while everyone was telling me AA was great, and they were going to make it better. But again I was caught up in feeling like I was a sexual object and that was what I was always going to be.

One of the interesting dynamics in my life, from the way I was reared, was that I always had to have drama in my life. Everything had to be dramatic. Randy provided a lot of drama. I remarried Randy for the third time, and my son ran away from home. He was about ten years old, in the fifth grade. The missionaries from the Mormon church found him, brought him home, and asked if they could spend some time with us. My son became very attached to them. He had been continually seeking a male figure in his life. At that time, I was grateful for anything. When my son went to take the instructions, I ended up joining too. I was still looking for "family" I guess. Suddenly there was another whole set of messages coming at me. Of course, it really upset everybody in my family. "Mormons!?" But the Mormon Church ultimately helped me survive Georgia.

About that time, Randy said he was going to Georgia because he had work down there, and I could go with him or not. So we went to Georgia, all of us. Randy was in full control of me at that point; he controlled me through alcohol and drugs. Our fights were starting to get violent again. But I never saw myself the way I really was. I'd see these commercials about domestic violence on television, and I'd see a poor woman sitting there, in a corner, being beat up. I didn't identify with that at all because I fought back, so I thought I was different. I thought I was just a tough lady. We moved to Georgia and it was a trip to hell.

Financially, our lives were starting to get good. He became vice-president of an industrial company. We bought land, bought a trailer, put it on the land, and began building our own house. Everybody just thought Randy was the greatest. I went to church, the Mormon Church. It looked good on the surface, but in reality my kids were falling apart. They were literally falling apart.

I was steadily getting fatter and fatter and fatter. The sexual abuse I was experiencing from Randy at this point had gotten terrible. He'd convinced me I was stupid, that I couldn't survive without him. He said we wouldn't have any problems if it wasn't for my horrible kids. He took my son out and took him to prostitutes and did drugs with him. My son was only twelve years old. He told my son not to tell me. He had our entire family polarized. He would bring my son home, and my son would be drunk. He would tell my son he wouldn't get any more alcohol or drugs if he told me what was happening. Then Randy would say to me, "Look at that drunken son of yours. You need to do something with him." I would be very upset, but I had no idea Randy was behind it. Of course, I was using, too, but I thought that was different.

This opened up a period when my children went in and out of Charter, which is a behavioral center and mental hospital. My son was twelve, and my daughter was nineteen months younger. By then, Randy was physically and sexually abusing my daughter. There were times my daughter gave me indications that Randy was molesting her, but I didn't want to hear it. It wasn't going to happen to me again. I'd think, "I go to church. People like Randy. He is a vice-president. Everything is going to be okay."

The physical abuse escalated. It seemed if I didn't have one kid locked up in the mental hospital, I had the other one locked up. All the blame was being put on Bobby, their natural father. One day, at Charter, my daughter told me Randy was molesting her, but the psychiatrist at Charter and the social workers in Georgia didn't believe it.

They told me, no, that wasn't what was happening. "She is using transference; that was what her natural father did to her."

I think I knew in my heart that it was true, but it was easier to believe a lie. She has no memory of even being with her natural father. I think he may have abused her, but I don't know. I know he did abuse my son.

All at once I was thrown back exactly to where I had been at fifteen years old, living with my mom and dad. I was in the same kind of marriage. I weighed 300 pounds. If I wasn't getting drugs from the street, I was getting Prozac and Xanax from the doctor. But, I went to church every Sunday and that was supposed to make it better. In a way it did. If it hadn't been for the support of some of the people in that church, I honestly don't think I could have survived. The abuse was becoming more and more blatant and the trip to hell was progressing.

My daughter had a friend spending the night with her. They were sleeping on the couch. We were still in the trailer, in the process of building the house. Randy was a gun fanatic. He had guns all over the house and he slept with two .45s, one on each end of the bed. He was a sportsman, or so he said. I woke up. Randy was standing in the kitchen, masturbating, watching the two girls. They were asleep. I couldn't believe it. I picked up a .45 and I was going to shoot him. He wrestled the gun away from me and threw me out the back door. My daughter doesn't even know what happened. She heard us fighting, but it was nothing for my kids to wake up and hear us fighting. We ended up, Randy and I, over in the house we were building. He had the gun. He'd tied me to one of the railings with my hands behind my back. He'd taken the gun and put it between my legs, inserted in my vagina, and he was standing there, just pulling the trigger, and I didn't know if it was loaded or not. The gun wasn't. Of course, when it was over, he said, "Oh, I never want to do anything like this again to destroy my family."

At that point, I had just totally given up. I went to bed. I started taking pills. He started working out of town. My son was in Atlanta, in a treatment center for drugs and alcohol. At that point I don't think I wanted to live, but I don't think I wanted to die. I was just existing. I had no comprehension of my world. My daughter was falling apart in front of my face.

I got a phone call telling me Randy was in jail. I had to get out of bed. I had to finally get up out of the bed and find out why Randy was in jail. He was in jail for stalking teen-age girls.

My son was in still in Atlanta, and I sent my daughter to my parents in Kentucky. I went to South Carolina, where Randy had gotten arrested. I believed him when he told me it was a setup, that he hadn't done it. It was easier for me to believe it was a setup than to believe he was guilty. But the police had tapes where one of these girls – he'd picked a very prominent family in South Carolina – recorded his voice. The police wanted me to listen to the tapes and identify his voice.

At that point, I'd been around the world and back again: I'd been a prostitute, rode with one of the largest criminal organizations in the United States; I'd lived in the streets; I'd been through things most people don't even read about. But I'd never, in my life, heard anything as disgusting, as horrifying, as what I heard on those tapes, what the man I was married to said to these teen-age girls.

I went back to our lawyer's office and I told him I needed a drink. He fixed us a scotch. I went back to my motel room. I didn't want to die. I just wanted the pain to go away, but I overdosed. I was using crank at the time. I was also drinking whiskey, eating Valium. I had a whole array of drugs. I have very little conscious memory of the next two days. I just tried to ease the pain. When I came to, I was sitting in a parking lot looking at a big cross.

I thought, *Wow, this isn't where I need to be.*

I went back to my lawyer and told him, "I'm dying."

I was in bad shape. He got me put in a halfway house in Columbia, South Carolina. I told Randy I would stick with him through the trial. I still wanted to believe he was innocent, even though I knew better. In the middle of the trial, his mother became very ill. While he was in jail, I was driving from South Carolina to Cincinnati to sit with his mother. She died not ever knowing he had been arrested. She died of cancer, and I went to Randy and told him his mother had died of cancer. He never shed a tear.

He just asked, "What can we do to get me out of this?" I buried his mother for him. He didn't go to the funeral.

The court date came and what I remember the most was having to walk down the aisle of that courtroom, knowing it was one evil man standing there. People were looking at me and shaking their heads. I was a total outcast in that town in South Carolina, yet I was still his wife and I was still going to do what I thought a wife should do. I never will forget the way the people stared at me, like I was some kind of poor, hideous creature. I guess I was, pretty much.

He was sentenced to ten years for illegal use of the telephone. By then, I had been told by a psychologist that he was a true psychopath. I know it today. I heard the tapes. I know what happened in South Carolina; he knows what happened in South Carolina. Those two teen-age girls know what happened in South Carolina. He can lie and say anything he wants, but I know what happened.

I look back on our marriage and I see where incidents like that were happening all the time. When we would have to leave a town, he'd say, "Oh, the cops are after me because I was peeing in the back street," or something like that. Now I see all the horrible, horrible, horrible, horrible sexual things. Today I see what they did to my children.

In 1990 I came back to Kentucky and I was luckier than a lot of women in a domestic violence situation, I had a lot of space between me and my husband and the control was broken.

Six years ago my father died. He had his final heart attack. He drove almost fifteen miles to where I lived to tell me I needed to take him to the hospital, and said he thought he was having a heart attack. I didn't take it very seriously. I remembered when I had realized the truth about his health problem. It was after I divorced Bobby and had two kids. One night, I received a call from the hospital telling me they were admitting my father and needed me there. So I drove to Elizabethtown, to the hospital, and he was throwing a fit.

He told me, "Tell them to give me my shot; that's all I need. Just give me my shot and my pain will go away."

Meanwhile, he fell off the table and busted his head. It was really a nightmare.

I remember the doctor coming in and saying, "Do you think your father might have an alcohol problem?"

At that point, I just collapsed, laughing. "He has an alcohol problem; he's a junkie. Give him a shot and send him home with me."

I think the whole dynamics really hit me then, what was going on.

So I didn't take it very seriously when he came over and asked me to take him to the hospital.

I said, "Okay, get in, and I'll take you over there."

I got him over there and they put him in the cardiac care unit. I told the nurse I was going to go home and I would be back the next day.

She said, "If I were you, I wouldn't leave. He's not going to make it this time."

Eventually, the alcohol just ate up his heart tissue. I remember one time when he had had a major heart attack, and I went to see him, he was sitting in bed and sharing a bottle of whiskey with a friend. It was constant. He didn't quit drinking until the very end. He was remorseful, but he was ready to die. He died without ever saying he was sorry. Even then, Dad ruled.

Still, his death was a total shock to me. I really never expected it was actually going to happen. I had a very difficult time at my father's funeral. In public, I was always "Daddy's little girl," and he took me everywhere. Everyone thought that my "mean, vicious, crazy" mom couldn't take care of me. Little did they know how much of a "Daddy's little girl" I was!

At the funeral, everybody in town thought, "Oh, she's just having a hard time because she's always been her daddy's little girl." But I was struggling with a feeling of freedom, not grief. At forty-two, his death made me feel free, not horrible.

I started back to school in 1992. It took me time to build a better life. I was involved in two abusive relationships after Randy went to prison and I divorced him for the third time. Once, I moved in with a guy because I was a welfare mother with two dysfunctional teen-agers, full of hate, full of rage. That was over quickly.

The second one was when my son was in jail and my daughter married. It, too, was a very sexually abusive relationship. I was already going to Elizabethtown Community College. I had some wonderful professors who really stood behind me. They saw something in me I wasn't able to see myself. At that time, I wound up in the hospital from living in a trailer with no heat. I was still doing drugs and drinking and trying to go to school.

Two people who had been my supportive friends for years, Jeep and Donna Kay, forced me to choose between my friendship with them or staying with the man. And they didn't give me a week to make up my mind. They said I was coming home with them, I was going to stay in school, and I was going to keep doing what I was doing positively. They said if I went back to the man, I would never see them again. It takes quite some friends to stand up and tell somebody something like that. I went with them. It's pretty much been all uphill since then.

That was in 1994, just before I started college at Spalding. I got a two-year degree at Elizabethtown Community College. Then I went to Spalding, in Louisville, for three years. I earned a bachelor's degree in social work, then a master's degree in social work in May 1999. I graduated Magna Cum Laude, at the top of my class. I've won a lot of awards. I'm Phi Beta Kappa. I've won the Most Outstanding Social Work Award at Spalding. I'm in the Pinnacle Society, an adult learner's honor society. I've served on the board of directors for Community Action in the county.

Now I live in Frankfort, alone. I haven't even dated for the last four and a half years. I have a small apartment, a car, and it's all mine. My work is important to me. I am a community activist – a community organizer for Community Farm Alliance. I think part of the reason I got into activism was all those years of all that abuse. I realized it wasn't all my fault.

I started looking at the dynamics of oppression. I think that is why I became such a strong activist, because we live in the richest, freest country in the world. We should not live in a society where the dynamics are so ripe for that much oppression, as in my life, to occur in anybody's life. And I believe there is such a thing as social and economic justice in this world. Right now, I'm fighting for small farmers who are losing their farms.

When I came to Spalding, I was virtually living in my car, sleeping on people's couches – I had no home. People don't understand that when a woman decides to be non-male dependent, and has never had any education, so to speak, she has nowhere to go. When I divorced both of my husbands, I got nothing. I lost everything. So, I started with nothing, and I've got very little right now, except I have my life today. I know who I am. I'm a very happy person. I don't have to wallow in the guilt anymore. I enjoy life. Spalding gave me so much more than an education. I had to find peace within myself. I no longer battle drugs. I have no desire to get out of control. I can drink, but I know my limits, set them very strictly and I can adhere to them. Now there is no pain to destroy. My alcoholism wasn't a disease. It was a symptom. I still have a lot of challenges in my life, but today, I cope. I don't have to hide.

I'd been taught to hate my mother, so I've had to totally rebuild a relationship with her. We really have to struggle together, today, as a family. My mother is a pretty tough lady. She stayed married to my father all those years. Her whole life centered around making sure he had the right foods, making sure that his life was good, at whatever sacrifice it took for her. Even to this day, she still worries that maybe he died because she didn't cook right for him. Mom was fighting for her own life; she had no clue of what to do with two children in the middle of all that. Today, I don't feel a lot of hate because I find that controls me. When I start hating my father, then he is controlling me again.

I would say to other women, don't feel guilty when you find out you are having the time of your life in recovery. Don't let that guilt pull you back down where you were. I've battled that. I'm having a ball. I loved going to college. I absolutely loved it. When I was doing my master's degree, I worked on it through the week and in weekend classes. I did my placement, with Jobs for Justice, in the morning, then I worked their front desk in the afternoons. In the evenings, I ran the information desk at Spalding. At night I went home and did homework. People asked how I kept up with that schedule. Nobody ever really understood that I was having the time of my life. It was an answer to a dream. It was a dream come true. I did it. I achieved it. People say, "Well, you've had such a hard life, how can you feel good?" But my message is that everyone deserves a good life; they deserve every inch of it. If it feels good, don't feel guilty. It's okay to recover, to get well, to feel better.

I hope, ten years from now, when my oldest granddaughter is sixteen and my youngest grandson is ten, they never have experienced any of the abuse that I or my children had to endure. And, if anything does happen, they have a grandmother that will come to them and do whatever is in her power to help them. I want them to know they do not have to live that way. I had nobody to go to; my children had nobody to go to. I want my grandchildren to know they've got their Nanny to come to, and Nanny is enough of a fighter to do whatever it takes.

I also hope to get some of the oppressive laws changed so women, worldwide, do not have to experience the economic and societal injustice that puts them in a position they cannot get out of, because they are tied to a man who makes ten dollars an hour, and they can only get five dollars an hour, and can't support their children. I want see that changed.

– Suzanne Bonnette

In the spring of 2000, Suzanne took a new job. She is still an advocate for justice, but this time as a victim advocate with a domestic violence program. Her experience and compassion will be invaluable. Suzanne has changed the names of some individuals to protect herself and her family. She has used the true names of those individuals whose support, love, and faith have helped her through life, and her transition.

Cracks

Pausing at the edge,
gathering courage
to admit
defeat
or accept fate –
One will have its way.
Water
finds the smallest
crack through which
to seep
in the most dense
of dams.

– Trish Lindsey Jaggers

Martie

My name is Mary Martie Ruxer-Boyken. I was born in Kentucky. I was one of five children. My father had an eighth grade education. My mother graduated from high school and had a scholarship to go to college, but opted to get married instead. They were married for seven years and couldn't have children. They wanted them so bad, prayed on it – and finally put in their papers to adopt. They went away on a vacation to Mammoth Cave and when they came back, she was pregnant. She had to have a Caesarean with the first, a boy, born in May 1953, and literally died on the table. The doctor brought her back and told her she couldn't risk having any more babies. Well, she was a good Christian and she said, "No, God has blessed me with this baby and I'm not stopping until He tells me no." The doctor told her the same thing when her next child, another boy, was born in April 1954, and she again said "No." I was her third child, born in August 1955. She waited a little while, and then gave birth to my two younger sisters. Altogether, she had five Caesarean sections, which was unheard of back then.

At the age of four, I had double pneumonia and almost died. At the age of eight, I was sexually abused by my step-grandfather. It was a repressed memory for years, and I was in my twenties when it came out, when I felt I could deal with it. I was afraid. He'd told me that, if I ever told on him, no one would believe me, and he and my grandmother wouldn't be allowed to come back, ever. I was eight or nine years old, and I really loved my grandmother.

I believe in angelic whisperings, that we have guardian angels that help us through things. I strongly believe in angels. When my grandmother died, she came back to visit. I was in the eighth grade. I remember we had bunk beds in our room. I slept on a roll-away bed and there was a chair in the corner. I looked up and there she sat. I was scared, and I remember clasping my hands over me and

praying. The next morning, I woke up and I still had my hands clasped, but someone had covered me up. I asked my mother if she had covered me, but she said no. I knew my grandmother had been there and it was just her way of saying goodbye and checking on me. There have been several instances since then that have convinced me of the presence of angels.

I had a lot of responsibility because both my parents worked. I did the cooking – my best dish was oven-fried chicken. I helped to make sure my brothers and sisters did what they were supposed to do. I felt like I was kind of a second mom. I was used to being independent and doing things for myself. We all did well in school. I wasn't the best student, but I did okay. Even at that age, I was working. I was baby sitting by the time I was eleven years old, and the lady next door hated to iron, so I took in ironing from her. We didn't have a lot of money, even though my mother worked at General Electric, because Dad was self-employed and he didn't always have a stable income. Mother was always the strong one. I think that's where I get my strength, from my grandmother, my great-grandmother – all were strong. My sisters are strong women also. There was a tradition of strong women in my family on my mother's side. Mother was the leader in the house. She kept us all on track. She paid the bills. She had the best job. She wanted us to all go to college, but my two brothers went into the service when they graduated high school. I went to a business college. I attended the college and was employed there as well, as a night receptionist. When I graduated, they sent me out for an interview on a bookkeeping job and I got it. I had my own office, and I learned the job, although I had no bookkeeping experience. At one time, before I had my children, I worked four different jobs. I was a single person then, and I wanted things in life.

Although I am Baptist now, I was brought up in the Catholic religion, where you're not supposed to have sex before you're married, and I didn't until I was twenty-one. Plus, before I was twenty-one, I'd had two different guys try to rape me, force sex on me, and it was very devastating. I decided I would wait for marriage, but I found I didn't want to get married. I enjoyed my life the way that it was. Finally, at twenty-one I opted to have sex. When I was twenty-five, I became pregnant and had a miscarriage. When I went to the hospital for them to do the D and C, they found out I was in the first stages of cancer. Had I not had the miscarriage, I wouldn't have known. They treated the cervical cancer and removed the cancerous tissue and I've had no problems since then. They told me it was really a miracle that I'd even gotten pregnant because my uterus was tilted and my cycle was abnormal, only occurring about four times a year. So then, even though I knew I would want children, I just gave up. I thought, *God doesn't want me to have children; I might as well forget it.*

When I was twenty-eight years old, I went to the doctor. I had been dating a guy seriously. I wasn't the type that just slept around. I was in a serious relationship. We had been dating and we'd broken up. I went to the doctor because I'd lost weight, just a regular visit. They always did a routine pregnancy test before they gave me a prescription to start my cycle. I was sitting there waiting for the results, and when it came back, I said to the nurse, "Well, it's negative. Can I go now?" She said, "Oh, no, Hon, it's positive." I started crying. I walked out and went down the hall and just kept walking up and down the hall. I went back in and asked them again, thinking "There is no way I can be pregnant." The doctor told me I was four months pregnant. I thought then, *God has sent me a blessing.* I was so thrilled. I told my parents and they were very supportive.

I worked at Kroger and Long John Silver's at the time I had my first little boy. I'd gone to Kroger in October of 1981. Both jobs were part time – it was hard to get full time – so I had no insurance when I got pregnant. I had to go down and sign up for a medical card, which I hated, because I had always worked, sometimes four jobs, just to make sure I was independent. To me it was the worst thing to have to do, break down and ask for that card, but I knew I had to for the baby. I worked up to three days before he was born. He was born on June 13, 1984. He was the best baby, calm and laid back. I went back to work as soon as they would let me.

It was 1990 before I got on full-time with Kroger. I lived on my own, made it on my own. It was tough. I wasn't making much money, but I got on a program that helped pay for the day care and I had my mother's support when I worked on Sundays.

I got back together with my son's father, and we continued to see each other. I didn't want to marry him. He ran around, and I didn't want to be in a marriage like that, even though we loved each other. I was taking birth control pills and I'd arranged to have my tubes tied because I knew, as a single parent, it was very hard with even one child. Well, God decided differently. We had just moved from an apartment into a house, and I was painting. I got really dizzy. I had fans blowing and all the windows open for good ventilation, but I got dizzy. I lay down on the floor and while I was laying there, I thought *I haven't had a cycle for a while.* I was still on the pill, and taking it faithfully, but the doctor forgot to tell me that if a person is taking antibiotics or certain medication, it will knock the pill out. That's the only thing they could figure out happened.

I got a pregnancy test and it showed I was pregnant. I thought, *God, there's no way.* I shook the sample again and it went back to showing pregnant. For two days I shook it and finally realized it wasn't going to change. I was four months pregnant again. I said, "God's decided I need this second child." But, I told the doctor, "I love children and there's no way I would do anything else. I will have this baby because it is meant to be, but I want you to cut, tie, whatever you have to do, to my tubes, because the pill apparently isn't going to work, and I don't need any more children. It's hard enough with one. It's going to be harder with two." The father helped some, but he never really gave me child support. He'd buy them stuff once in a while, give me twenty dollars every once in a while, but that was it. I never lived with him.

In 1989, I decided that the relationship just had to end. About six months later, one of the girls I was working with at Kroger told me her parents had divorced, and she wanted her father to start dating again. He'd come into the store a couple times and I'd talked to him and cut up with him. She asked me if I'd double with her and her date and go out with him, just to help get his confidence up. Well, we doubled, went out, and it was so sweet because he was the perfect gentleman. He walked me to the door – just really good. I told him I was only going out with him as a friend. On our fourth date, he walked me to the door and kissed me, then took off running.

I thought, *What in the world?*

He called me after I got home, and I asked him why he ran.

He said, "You were just so beautiful, and I wanted to kiss you, but I was afraid you'd smack me."

A year and a half later we got married. I think God sends you what you need, when you need it. God sent him to me because eight months later, my illness struck. And he was there for me. He's a mechanic and has a business, a garage, called Boyken's Garage in Mosleyville. He works on combines and diesels and all that. He's really good at what he does.

I think what doesn't kill you, actually makes you stronger. All the things that happened when I was younger might have been what gave me the strength to get through my illness.

Now I'm forty-four, and I'm a survivor of Guillain-Barre' syndrome.* This is the way they explained it to me. They think the cause of it is an allergic reaction to a virus. What it did was attack my body. They said most people die when it goes as far as mine went. I was thirty-six years old when it happened, in 1992. I'd had the flu, starting in about November. It would get better, then it would get worse, then it would get better. I finally broke down and went to the doctor.

I was working at Kroger, where I'd worked for thirteen years. I was working the night shift, and I'd gone into work that night, knowing I had a bad cold, or flu, but I had been given a prescription for antibiotics. The doctor's office ordered X-rays. I didn't know I had double pneumonia, so I went on into work that night, thinking I had the antibiotics, and as long as I took them, I'd get better. When the boss came in, I was sweating profusely. He said I was white as a ghost. I looked at him and told him, "I feel like I could go sit in that corner and die." I barely made it to my car. I had to sit there for thirty minutes and rest before I could drive myself home. When I got home, my husband said, "This is it. You're going to the doctor."

The doctor wanted to put me in the hospital immediately, but I had two little boys at the time, one going on five, one about seven. They had never been away from me because I was a single parent – I'd just remarried in June of 1991. I told the doctor I had to go home and take care of my children. I didn't want them to be afraid. So we went home and took my boys to my mother's house. I kissed them, told them I loved them, and explained to them I had to go to the hospital, but I probably wouldn't be there very long. My husband took me to the hospital. There, they treated me for the double pneumonia. They didn't know anything else was wrong with me at that time. That was on a Friday night. On Sunday, Gary, a friend of mine from Kroger came into the room to see me; my husband and children had already been there and had gone home. My friend came in, and while I was laying in the bed, I got a tingling sensation that started at my feet and came all the way up. At that time I thought I was going to die. I didn't know what was wrong, but I knew it was bad. I was very afraid. I looked at Gary and I said, "Get the nurse and leave." I didn't want him to see me die. I just knew at that moment I was going to die.

The next thing I remember was waking up and a nurse stood over me. Bobby, my husband, stood behind her. I opened my eyes and it was like I'd just been asleep for the night and they were waking me up the next morning. It wasn't until later that I found out I had been in a coma for almost three weeks, and had almost died. Three weeks before, everything had just shut down. When I woke up in ICU, I should have been terrified. I had tubes coming in and out of me, and I couldn't move. All I could do was barely move my head. I couldn't move my arms or legs. I couldn't move the rest of my body. You would think I'd be terrified, but I'm a Christian and I knew that God had me in His hands.

I went into the hospital on March 20, 1992. I refer to that as almost the last day of my life. It could have well been if I hadn't had such excellent doctors, family support, and prayer. A lot of people don't believe in the power of prayer, but I truly believe that was one of the things that helped me through. My husband never accepted the fact that I might not make it; he had faith.

I also believe I had a near death experience. My father and mother, who have both passed on, were there with me. When I came to, my father was sitting at the end of the bed. I looked at him and I said, "Dad, when am I going to get my garlic steak?" He started crying. I thought, *Why is he crying?* We used to go to my great-grandmother's on Sunday and have garlic steak. He'd always called me "Big Girl" because I'm kind of large. When I was in the coma, he came to me and said, "Now, Big Girl, when you wake up, we're going to have garlic steak." He said, "As soon as you get better, however much garlic steak you want, we will have it." He told me this while I was in my coma, and he started crying because he had the realization that I actually heard everything he said.

I saw myself in a place that was very calm and peaceful. There were two ladies there who'd lived in our neighborhood before they passed away. I'd grown up around them, and they'd died a year or two before, but they were there with me. They were telling me, "Don't worry. It's not your time. Everything's going to be okay." So when I woke up, I was very calm and peaceful because I knew I was going to be okay. I truly believe I had a near-death experience. I believe one of the reasons God let me come back is for my children.

After I regained consciousness, I got nervous with the different things they were doing to me, because when they found out I couldn't move from my neck down, they called in more specialists. I had been on life support, I still had a tube down my throat, and I couldn't talk.

All these people were coming in and I couldn't communicate with them. That was so frustrating because everyone was trying to talk to me and I was trying to find out what was going on. The only way I could communicate was by blinking my eyes: once for "yes," and twice for "no." I knew sign language, but I couldn't even use my hands to do sign language. Once the tubes were all taken out of my throat, I had my speech, but that was all.

They didn't know what was wrong with me until they finally called in a neurologist. He came in, two big orderlies lifted me up, and they held my arms up above my head and the doctor took fluid from my spine. As soon as he did that, and tested it, he knew what it was. That's when they told me what I had. For the three previous weeks, while I was in a coma, they hadn't known what was going on; they had just treated me for the double pneumonia. When I went into the coma, they called my family and told them I would not live through the night. I was put on a respirator. I had to have thirteen pints of blood. I have scars all over my body because the veins in my arms completely shut down. They had to go into my chest and put a shunt into the artery that went directly into my heart to give me blood and do the IVs. My kidneys shut down, and they put me on kidney dialysis. They said that the kidney dialysis was actually what helped to save my life. When I got better, I did a lot of research on Guillain-Barre' to see what the treatment was. If they catch it the first stages, they do plasma exchange which cleans out the blood and helps a person get a quick return. It was the kidney dialysis that cleaned out my blood and helped save me.

They needed to do CAT scans, but I am severely claustrophobic. They said they could see in my eyes that I was frightened, but they didn't know what to do. I was just all to pieces because I couldn't stand it. My sister was there and she knew I was claustrophobic, so she convinced them to let her go in with me. They were going to tie my arms up because I couldn't lift and hold my arms up. She convinced them to let her put on the lead suit, and she went with me, inside the room where they put me in the machine. They put me in only up to my neck and didn't go any farther. She stood there and talked to me to keep me calm and held my arms up while they did the test.

Because of my claustrophobia, when I was paralyzed, essentially trapped in my own body, I was terrified. The nurses would come in and tuck the covers tightly around me, and I could not stand that. It was the worst thing they could do. My husband came in one time and sat on my bed, and he'd forgotten about how I felt. When he sat down, it pulled the covers even tighter and I started hyper-ventilating.

It was really devastating to me, when I came out of the coma, to realize that I was paralyzed. I hated it when the nursing staff had to do things for me, turn me over and so forth, because I had always been an independent person. I'd been a single parent to my two boys before my husband and I got married, and I'd worked full-time to take care of them. I was used to doing for myself and for others. People still refer to me as "Mom" because I'm always trying to help people. So, when they were coming in and doing all that, it was terrible. At that stage, I couldn't even scratch my nose. My sister would always come in and do it for me. I was so frustrated. For example, when I was in ICU, they'd give me a button to push if I needed a nurse, but I couldn't push the button. We figured out that I could barely wiggle my left wrist, so they taped a bell in my hand, so I could wiggle my wrist and they would hear the bell. Most times they would forget to put the bell back in my hand. I couldn't reach over and get the bell if I wanted a drink of water. I'd lay in the bed and listen, and when I'd hear one of the nurses come down the hall, if I didn't have my bell, I'd lay there and, instead of screaming, go "ding, ding" so they'd hear me. I didn't like to ask for too much help, and I didn't want to be a burden.

In order to get feeling back in my body, I knew I would have to work on it myself. I'd lay there and focus on one area, at that time my left thumb, and I'd concentrate with all my might to try and get that thumb to move. Even in the middle of the night, when I couldn't sleep, I'd lay there and focus and work on that thumb. I remember one night, after I'd worked on my thumb all day, I went to sleep and I dreamed I had that little button caller in my hand and, when I pushed it, I concentrated so hard it broke and crumbled in my hand. The next day, when a nurse came in, I had practiced, and concentrated, and focused on it so much that I actually pushed the call button. This little male nurse was dancing up and down the hall hollering, "Oh, she did it! She did it!" He was so thrilled.

The doctor said this disease supposedly eats at the nerves where the messages go to your brain and tell your body what to do. Usually, you don't really have to think about movement. You just do it. Well, I had to think about every little thing and focus to get it all going again. It took awhile.

I talked to my boys on the phone, but I didn't let them come until I was out of ICU. It was Easter time, and I'm the type of mother who always buys early and has everything ready. When they told me how long I'd been out, and that Easter was the next week, I cried, because I thought *How in the world am I going to get that stuff to my babies?*

Luckily, I had a stepdaughter, Betty, and she took care of that for me. She came and cared for my family while I was in the hospital. I didn't see the boys until a month after I went in. It was so hard for them, because I couldn't put my arms around them, but they came up and they hugged me.

I was in the Daviess County hospital for two months, then I had to go through rehabilitation for two months. I had to stay in a rehab unit at Mercy Hospital until they thought I was able to go home. Then I had outpatient therapy. They even checked my home to make sure I had the equipment there I needed. It was almost four months, from the day I went to the hospital until I was home again, right before July 4. The first time I went home was totally devastating to me because I went to sit on the couch, and my legs wouldn't hold me. I'd gotten back some upper body strength, but my legs felt like they had forty pound weights on each leg. I had what they called "foot drop." So they had to put braces on both my feet. For me to walk from the middle of the room to the door way was like contemplating walking twenty miles under normal circumstances. It took every bit of effort for me to take just one step. I learned to not look at the whole picture. If I had to look from here to there, I would think, *I can't do it.* I had to concentrate on each little step – not just the walking but the physically lifting of my foot and putting it down. I had to focus on taking one step at a time. It was so overwhelming to think about going that far (to the door) and knowing how exhausted I would be, that I would only think of the one step, then the next one.

Kroger wouldn't let me come back. They said I couldn't handle the job. The risk management people came down and made me walk. I couldn't stand easily, but I'd worked it all out in my head in rehabilitation. Before my illness, I worked in the bakery and the deli. I did party trays, made pizzas and did various bakery jobs.

In rehab, I was so optimistic. They worked with me and helped me to make sure I could still decorate cakes, even do the roses. I went into great detail telling Kroger management how I could still perform my duties, because there were a lot of things I could do from a stool. We had carts back there that you could put stuff on and push around, so I could manage since I had the braces on my feet. I'd worked it out so I could do everything, but then they slapped me in the face. One week the manager would say, "Yes, you can come back," Then he'd say, "They're not going to let you." It was just back and forth. In the meantime, I was waiting to go back to work, and wanting to. Right before Christmas they refused me.

They said I walked "too cautiously." That's why they wouldn't allow me to come back to work. That crushed me. I became depressed. I slept a lot because when I was asleep I could still walk and run and do all the things I used to with my kids – roll on the grass, play. It was wonderful. In your dreams everything in life can be how you want it to be. When they wouldn't let me come back to work, I got to the point that I contemplated killing myself. It was so hard because I knew I could do the work, but I could not get that through to them. I went through a year of fighting with them, trying to go back to work.

One of the presidents of Kroger saw me in my wheelchair and said, "Bring her back; she's a good worker."

I was, too. Before I got sick, I worked 48-60 hours a week: whenever they needed me, I was there.

He said, "Let her sit in a wheelchair and hand out coupons."

I told them, "Fine, as long as I've got something to do."

I could have worked in the office. I had the business experience and had graduated from the business college. They didn't want me!

On top of losing my job, my health insurance had run out at $100,000, and the hospital bills totaled over $200,000. Fortunately, a scholarship fund took care of $50,000. I wrote to the rest of the doctors. Some forgave the bills and the others agreed to let us make small payments monthly. It was so rough. One prescription alone cost over $300. At the time I contemplated killing myself, it was just before Christmas and we were out of money.

I thought, *Well, I still have my life insurance. If I kill myself, at least my family will have something to live on. If Kroger doesn't let me go back to work, who's going to hire me? No one.* If I could have gotten to the gun, I'd have blown my brains out. Finally the realization hit that I couldn't desert my boys and husband.

Kroger had no legal grounds. I had to file a lawsuit against them. I don't like to do stuff like that, but I won my case. It was an Equal Opportunity Employment violation. The small settlement I got went to pay off the doctors and the medical bills. I had the opportunity, because I won, to go back to work. But I knew if I went back to work there it wouldn't be any good. Not because of the people I worked with, because they all loved me and all said they would work around my disability.

It took me a long time to get out of the depression. I was sent to the Opportunity Center by the Department of Vocational Rehabilitation. They did all this testing to see where I stood, to make sure I had the mental capacity to succeed if they invested money in me. At that time I knew I had mobility problems, but I didn't know I had memory loss also. They asked me who was the sixteenth president. I had no idea. I should have known that. I had to really dig deep to answer their questions, and some of that memory wasn't there. I did okay on the tests, but not as well as I should have, so I started doing things to stimulate my brain. I did crossword puzzles which helped.

At that time, it's like God led me to the community college. I'd graduated from high school. I had gone to the business college and gotten a a clerk-typist degree from there, but I decided to go back to school, because I wanted to get back to work. It was terrible for me to stay home. I loved my family, but I had always worked, ever since I was a young child. I started college at Owensboro Community College in August 1994, and became employed there. I really feel God sent me there.

When I returned to college, I still had to use my wheelchair and crutches. The first day, after classes, I was totally exhausted. I went out to my car, sat there for an hour and cried. I thought there was no way I could do it. But, I decided I had to go back to my method of breaking it down into a process, one step at a time. I figured out ways to get from class to class, sometimes pushing my wheelchair with a backpack in it, sometimes using it to sit in, whatever worked. Things fell into place.

I became president of student government and president of Phi Beta Kappa. I got really involved with the school and got to be on the search committee when they hired a new president. I got to be on a lot of different committees and on the college's advisory board. I learned so much, and it was so beneficial to me. Now, I have two degrees from the community college. I have a business management degree and an associate of arts degree. I graduated with high distinction in both of them, which to me was a big accomplishment. ** A major joy was when I graduated and I walked across that stage without my cane.

I am finishing my bachelor's degree at Western Kentucky University now. I will graduate on December 16, 2000 with a bachelor's degree in business management.

At Owensboro Community College, I worked full-time in the Financial Aid office. I was a Title IV processor, and although I loved my job, I've recently moved on to a new challenge, and a new job. Before, when I wasn't working, I'd take up to 19 hours a semester. I am a worker and I'm used to work. That's what helped me get better after my illness.

I'm thinking about going on for my master's degree. I love college; it's moving forward. I don't want to ever stand still or take a step back. I want to continually move forward.

One thing that makes my heart dance now is my boys. Although my illness was hard on them, I think it's also been good for them. They have learned from my struggle. They have learned to give from their heart and find the joy of giving. To see that in them is great.

After I came home from the hospital, I'd do my exercises, and my boys would climb up in the bed with me and help me. Timmy, the little one, would get behind me and push me so I could sit up. Then Steven, the oldest one, would get in front of me and lift my legs for me. I'd tell them I was tired and couldn't do anymore.

They'd say, "Oh, no, Mama. You have to do at least one or two more. We'll help you."

My right foot came back the fastest. I was determined to drive again so I would sit in the living room, and the boys would hold their hands next to my foot. I would act like I was pushing the gas pedal and the brake, to help me build the foot back up. They knew that was what I really wanted, to drive again, so it was a team effort. They became a big part of my rehab.

When I first went home, I could walk some with crutches, but I was still using my wheelchair. The kitchen in our house has a two inch step-up, and I couldn't make that. So, in order to cook, I would have to wheel to the dining room table and my boys would bring the ingredients to me and I would fix them. Then they'd take the food to the stove, put it in the oven, and my husband would come in from the garage and take it out.

My husband was wonderful. We had our own business, by the house, so he was always close by. He set up a speaker, so, if I needed him, I could call him down at the garage. It was really a family effort. We still all work together. My oldest son is fifteen now, and stands six feet, one-inch tall. No matter where we go, he gets out of the car and puts his arm out for me.

I continue to do daily exercises. A year after I left the hospital, I still could not lift my left foot by myself. They say that usually, after a year, if you don't get the feeling back, it's gone. I said, "No." When I was in the hospital, they told me the best I could hope for would be to be in a wheelchair for the rest of my life. I said, "No." Every morning, it's hard getting out of bed. I still have mobility problems. I have degenerative arthritis. I fell a couple of years ago, and they found out I'm in the first stages of osteoporosis. I have a defect in my spine, I think it's called Pars defect. Also, I'm diabetic and have to watch my blood sugar. My legs go numb, so I have to be cautious. When I get tired, my left foot drags. I did have braces on both of my feet, but I threw them away because I knew if I kept wearing them I would never get better.

Also, I have to really concentrate on what I'm reading. I have to focus. I have a lot of trouble with my short term memory, and, in order for something to stick, and for me to do good in my classes, I need repetition. I have to keep going over and over the material and force it into long term memory. In my classes, if they give me papers to take home or projects I can focus on, and work on, I do really well. But, I've failed I don't know how many tests. The one "C" I got in college was in my business class. On all the papers I turned in, I did excellent, but when it came to the test, the wording threw me off. And the time limit! I've learned to ask for extra time, and I've learned to ask to be off by myself so I can concentrate. So far, other than that one "C," I've been able to maintain "A" and "B" grades.

Everyone is faced with challenges daily, it's just according to how you take them. It's best not to look at them negatively. You need something to look forward to, a goal, something to strive for. Because if you don't, you'll just dwindle away.

– Martie Ruxer-Boyken

* Guillain-Barre' syndrome is a rare illness that effects the peripheral nerves of the body. It is an acute, usually rapidly progressive form of inflammatory poly-neuropathy. It can cause paralysis and weakness. It can occur at any age and to both sexes The cause of Guillain-Barre syndrome is not known, although an autoimmune basis is probable. It is generally believed the body is attacked by it's own defense system and the nerve insulation is damaged. Different events seem to trigger it: viral infections, aftermath of surgery, insect stings, and various injections (during the winter of 1976-77, a number people who had been vaccinated for swine flu fell ill with Guillain-Barre syndrome). Some cases are mild; some very severe, even causing death. Severe acute polyneuropathy is a medical emergency. Considerable improvement over a period of months is usual, but about a third of adult sufferers still have residual weakness three years later.

**Martie is being modest. Her resume lists 18 awards or special recognitions and indicates she was a member of no less than 16 organizations. She has an equally long list of community involvement endeavors and has been the focus of several newspaper articles, lauding her for her courage and persistence. Her grade point average is a 3.58

Sealed Silence

Strangely, the grass grows more slowly on this
Plot of ground, now my mother's home.
Martyred
Roses, stiffened by hidden harnesses,
Cling to the small space of white bone-
Hard earth
Washed dry from tears of useless begging
On knees worn to callouses
By Hours.
Forgiveness cannot come from trudging
To place on this sealed silence
My Flowers.

– Trish Lindsey Jaggers

Cheyenne

One of the earliest and certainly the most vivid memories I have of childhood is of my father drunk. I remember thinking he was funny at first, dancing around the floor and singing at the top of his lungs, and then, for whatever reason, he became angry. I heard a loud crash in the kitchen and then everything was havoc. Furniture flew, dishes broke, and my mother herded us seven kids out of the house. We were in our nightclothes and barefoot. The snow was up to my knees. We ran to a city park, which was about two blocks away and hid behind a building. We were all huddled in a row, and my mother said, "Stay still and be quiet, maybe he'll think we are bushes." I was around five years old at the time, and I remember thinking, *I'm going to die, right here in this snowdrift, with no shoes and no coat, I'm going to die.*

Although this is my earliest memory, it isn't the only one like it. This was a pretty regular event in my childhood and even on up into my adulthood. We would run from him on Saturday, and visit the used furniture store on Sunday. My father, like most alcoholics, would always be sorry and embarrassed afterward, but it never seemed enough to make him stop. If he ended up in trouble, it was always someone else's fault. We left our home and moved to Kentucky when I was eight years old. We thought that if we could be near family, then my dad might straighten up. Things did get better. His drinking and rampages didn't stop, but at least they became less frequent.

I am number seven out of ten kids in a close, yet conflictive, family. We were farmers, and my teen years consisted of getting up at 5:00 a.m. to go to the tobacco field, coming home at 7:00 a.m. and getting ready for school, getting home at 4:00 p.m. to have supper, and going back to the field from 5:00 p.m. until after dark. Homework was done late at night, because education wasn't a big priority in my family. My father went through the third grade, and my mother never went to school at all. She couldn't read or write, and could barely sign her name. I remember when I was about ten years old, telling her that I could teach her how to read and she would just say, "I've done without it this long, I don't need it now." I knew she often used her illiteracy as a crutch. I suppose that was why I always tried to learn everything I could.

Life was difficult for us. We never did the things that all the other kids did, like going to the movies or shopping. We wore hand-me-downs, which were always just out of style or way out of style. This wasn't always a bad thing, because I always felt like I was getting something new even if it did pass through several kids before me. Other kids had a field day with us though, making fun of the clothes we wore, or of the fact that we had no inside bathroom or running water. I suppose that is one reason why my brothers, sisters and I were always so close. The younger ones of us would fuss and fight and quickly become friends again. I was always closer to my older siblings, because I always felt I could be free and let go with them. I always thought that I had to take care of the younger kids and keep them out of mom and dad's way, so I never really played with them much. When we did play together, I was always the teacher or the mom. Where most kids were playing house, we played a game called orphanage home, and I was always the lady who ran the home. They were always the terrible, rebellious kids.

My older sister would always play with us; she was six years older than I, and could handle us very well. We would go on long walks and play hide and seek. She would help us build a playhouse under the limbs of an old willow tree we had in our yard. She became my best friend; we would do everything together. Even after she got married, they would come home every weekend and stay with us. One night my younger sister and I stayed at her house and helped her clean out an old silo that was in her yard. Her husband and I found an old patchwork quilt that I proudly took to her, and she and I cleaned it and hung it out to dry.

When it was time to haul a load of junk to the dump, my brother-in-law asked if I wanted to tag along, so I did. We had unloaded the truck and started home when he asked me a question I would have never expected in a million years. He said, "Do you know anything about sex?" I was twelve years old and didn't know anything, but still I was leery enough to scoot farther away from him, and closer to the door. When I didn't answer, he said, "You are a pretty little girl, and it won't be long before the boys start to notice that you are developing into a young woman." He reached over and squeezed my breast. I slapped his hand away and moved closer to the door. I was wearing shorts; he grabbed my leg and stretched his fingers until he was touching my privates. I went into a panic and began to cry, at which point he stopped the truck and grabbed me. He said, "Don't cry, I just want you to know what to do when the time comes because I care about you." I cried harder and asked him to please leave me alone. He held me back against the seat and continued to touch me at which point I began to scream, "I'm going to tell Dad and he will kill you!" This made him stop and he became very apologetic, saying that he had lost his head and was high from smoking marijuana earlier. I didn't stop crying. He said, "This would kill your sister; you would really hurt her by telling her what happened here." I said I wouldn't say anything if he took me back to the house and left me alone.

We got to the house and I must have had a terrified look on my face because my sister took me to another room and asked what was wrong. I said nothing at first, then she said, "Did he hurt you?" I burst out crying and told her the whole story. She went into a rage and we left and went to my parent's house.

After they got my sister calmed down, they called me into the room. I could tell right away from the look on my mother's face that it was me that she was angry with, and not him. She said I should have known better than to go off with him by myself. Maybe I should have, but I trusted him with my life. He was my family, like my brother. He had been with our family for two years, and I never thought in my life that I would ever have any reason to fear him. But fear is exactly what I had, for years to come: fear of my father, brothers, uncles, any man who was in the same breathing space that I was in.

My sister stayed with us for about two months, then he came back crying, blaming his actions on drugs. Since she was having trouble being back under my parent's rule, she went back home to him. On weekends when they came to visit, I would always leave the house and go to the willow tree, or lock myself in my playhouse because I never wanted to be in the same space he was in. A couple weeks after she went back, she came to the willow tree with the quilt I had found. She said, "You found this, and I want you to have it." I took the quilt, with knots in my stomach, and smiled and said, "Thank you," but inside I was raging, because all it reminded me of was what had happened the day we found it. I knew she was trying to make peace. She apologized for what had happened, said he wasn't himself, and that she loved him. I listened quietly and stared at the ground the whole time. When she had finished, I told her that I understood, although I didn't, but that I could never forgive him for what he had done. He'd made me fear all men, and I couldn't forgive him. She said she understood, hugged me and left. I stared at the quilt for a long time, then went to a clearing in the yard and set it on fire. As I watched it burn, I felt myself harden a bit.

Life was an emotional roller coaster from that point. My mother blamed me for what happened, and for the turmoil in my sister's life; she never ceased to remind me of it. I was never allowed to go to school functions, or the movies, like my other brothers and sisters because I "couldn't be trusted." Every time the subject was brought up, she would say, "Do you want the same thing to happen again? Didn't you get enough the first time?" I would become physically ill and want to disappear, which is usually what I did.

My sister and I became friends again after about six months. It was hard, but I missed her and she missed me also, so I gave up leaving the house altogether, and opted for leaving the room he was in.

On June 21,1979, one week before my fourteenth birthday, my sister's best friend was getting married, and they wanted me to go. I was very excited because all three of us girls were very close. The time came to go, and I became very leery. I knew I would have to stay all night with them, and I hadn't done that in over a year. When my sister called, I said that I had decided to go to one of my older sister's houses and that they should take some pictures.

That night I had a dream that I was chasing my sister. She would stop long enough to let me catch up, then she would run again. I followed her into a large building where all my family was gathered. They were all sitting around crying, very unaware that I was even there. I looked up and my sister was standing in another room, looking down. I went in, and she looked up at me with the saddest eyes I'd ever seen. She looked away and I followed her gaze. There she was, lying in a powder blue coffin.

I jumped awake to the shrill ringing of the phone. There had been an accident and we had to get to the hospital. We pulled up to see all of my brother-in-law's family standing outside. I called his brother over to ask what had happened. He told me that they'd had a car accident, and that my sister hadn't survived. All I could do was stand there and scream. Her husband had been drinking and driving way too fast. He lost control of the vehicle on a straight stretch of road and hit a tree. My beautiful sister was dead at the age of twenty.

The only thing I can remember about the funeral services was looking at her and thinking, *She never wore red lipstick ... her nails are all broken ... if she could see her hair she would just die.* I guess I thought anything and everything to keep from knowing the reality of the situation. The one vivid memory I have of the visitation is when my mother looked at me and said, "I hope you're happy. You made your sister's last year on earth miserable." It was as if she'd hit me full force in the stomach. I looked at my brother-in-law, who just sat there with his mouth open. At that moment I felt such hatred of him that I was sure I would never survive it. At the funeral I couldn't even look at my sister. Every time I glanced at her, I heard my mother's words, so I watched a black spider building a web in the corner above her head. When it came time to say goodbye, I had an uncontrollable urge just to touch her hair, so I fought my way through the crowd and rubbed her hair and said my good-byes.

I was pretty much a loner from that point on. I never could bring myself to talk to my mother about what had happened, so I went through most of my life harboring a deep bitterness in my heart. The situation was made worse because I bore an incredible resemblance to my sister. I started high school the year after she died and had a teacher come up and strike up a conversation, thinking I was her. My entire sophomore year another teacher called me by her name. It became so upsetting to me that when I looked in the mirror for very long, I would actually see her staring back at me. By the time I was a senior, I had become used to it, and it didn't bother me as bad. I supposed it was people's way of keeping her alive, but in the process, I was once again disappearing.

Immediately after graduation, I cut my hair. I was very excited about the new look, but when I got home, my mother went into a rage. She said, "What have you done? You don't look like her anymore – you're ugly!" All I could do was stand there and whisper, "I'm not her. She is dead, and I'm sorry that you wish it was me instead of her." She just stared at me as I turned and left the room. From that moment there was a truce of sorts: she wouldn't say hurtful things to me, although she never did apologize.

There was a change in me at that point also. I was determined to make it. I applied for college and was accepted. Because I was seventeen, I needed my parent's signatures. They flat refused and wouldn't even discuss it. I was a girl, and there was no way I was living away from home and not be married. Education was not an option and definitely not a necessity. So I did the only thing that was acceptable: I got married.

By the time I was nineteen, I had my first child and my first dose of reality about my unfaithful husband. By twenty-one, I had our second child, whom I practically reared alone for the first year of his life. There were many bad times in our early years, but I wanted my marriage to work, so I overlooked the negatives – the drinking and late nights, the women, the phone calls in which he would sit and talk to other women right in front of me. When I wouldn't give him the phone, or tried to tell them to stop calling, they would call me a "bitch" and a "whore." He would get on the phone and say, "Oh, she's like that sometimes." He used the excuse that he didn't know who the caller was and, therefore, was trying to be nice so he could find out and make her stop calling.

In my mind, this was my life, forever, so I tried to dwell on the good aspects: he was a good provider, we had wonderful camping vacations with the kids, and we would sometimes stay up all night talking. I was determined to make my marriage work, so we decided to go to marriage counseling. After the first session, he decided I was the one with the problem, so I went to counseling alone for a year. I began to drink and party on the weekends, without him, because I was "somebody" when I was out. I could dance well. I was slim and somewhat attractive. The attention became addictive. I realized that it was becoming a problem when I ended up in the arms of another man. So, I stopped going out and returned to my counseling sessions.

I still felt a burning need to go to college and make something of myself. I had been lost my whole life, and I wanted to find my own way in life. I wanted people to recognize me for my talent and who I was, not because I was someone's wife or mother or look-alike. My husband never understood my need to better myself. When I would mention wanting to do something productive with my life, he would say, "I'm sorry you aren't happy being my wife or the mother of our children. I'm sorry we aren't enough for you." I tried to make him understand that it wasn't that I wasn't happy, it was that I wanted to do something for me and not everyone else. I had always taken care of everything for everyone else, and I wanted to take care of me for a change.

My father had started drinking again at this time. One night, around midnight, I awoke to the shrill, insistent ringing of the phone. My father's voice was on the other end saying, "I'm on my way to town and I'm going to kill every one of you damned kids."

Instantly I was wide-awake, my heart jumping through my chest.

"Dad, what is wrong with you?"

"Where's your mother? Every time I go out and am gone for very long one of you comes and takes her away."

"I don't know where she is, Dad."

"You're lying! I'm on my way to town and I'm making the rounds. I'm going to kill every one of you damned kids."

"Dad, you're drunk. You'd better stay home before you get thrown in jail."

"I ain't drunk and I ain't scared of no damned cop; I'll kill them too. You'd better be the one who's scared."

The phone clicked and went dead. I jumped out of bed and threw on my clothes. I ran through the house and grabbed my seven-year-old daughter and five-year-old son and headed to the car. I was in a panic. My dad's voice kept screaming in my head. The terrified little girl inside me kept crying, "We gotta go, Daddy's drunk and he's coming. We gotta get away."

I stopped long enough to call my brothers and sisters, who lived in town, and their reactions were pretty much the same. We all met at one of my sister's houses and pieced together what had happened; my father had left the house early that day and hadn't come back by dark. We recognized this as a sure sign that he was on a binge, so my brother had gone to take my mother to his house. As we all sat there, like scared children waiting for the demon to jump out of the closet, one of my sisters suggested that we leave town so Dad couldn't find us. So, off we went. My brothers returned to their homes because they felt they couldn't leave their homes unprotected, but we five girls, with Mom and our children, left town. We loaded everyone into two cars and went to a parking lot a couple towns away until we could figure out where Dad was. We sat there all night, huddled together, scared to death.

The breaking point for me was around 6:00 a.m., when I looked into the faces of my two children. They had no idea what was going on except that they had never seen me panic before, so they knew it had to be bad. I not only saw myself as a terrified little girl again, but I saw terror in their eyes as well. I knew what my children were feeling and, at that point, something broke inside me. I knew that I would never put my children through that horror and confusion again, I would not make them grow up with the hurt and fear that I had grown up with.

We returned to our homes to find that my father had been arrested and was in jail. He had been involved in a high-speed chase with police officers and had been caught with a loaded revolver in the car. His sentence was to seek alcoholic counseling and five year's probation. He would have done some hard time had any of us revealed what he had threatened to use that gun for, but we couldn't. Our mother had always reared us to protect our father, no matter what, because "he never meant what he said when he was drunk, and he was always sorry when he sobered up."

That night was the last time I would ever run. If I couldn't stand up for myself, then I would definitely stand up for my children. I never visited my dad while he spent his thirty days in jail. I got a major amount of trouble over it but I didn't care. When he got out I went to my parent's house and I looked my dad in the eye for the first time and stood up to him. I told him that I would never run again, and if he came to my house drunk, I would fight to the death, even if I had to kill him. I would never again be that scared child.

My husband's drinking became an every night thing. I loved him very much but I couldn't live this lost life anymore. My house was always a mess. Sometimes we had supper, and sometimes we didn't. I didn't care if I got out of bed in the morning, and sometimes I didn't bother. I stopped writing, I stopped painting, and I very rarely left the house. I was still going to counseling once a week and one day the counselor looked at me and said, "I have never said this before, but you are fighting a losing battle. One person can't win the war against the army and your husband isn't even trying." I knew that she was right and that I had to get myself together for my children. I talked to my husband about how I was feeling and what was going on inside me. We separated, but for a year still tried to make it work. It was hopeless. I was already too far gone. We divorced after eleven years of marriage.

I had a very good friend who encouraged me to go to school. I'd felt that I couldn't do that because I had bills to pay and kids to raise, so it was another year before I considered it. He was in a bad marriage also, and separated from his wife. We became confidants, then best friends, talking about everything and anything. He encouraged me to write, to paint, and to get myself back. The longer our friendship went on, the closer we became. Intimacy between us became so very natural, and it was a beautiful thing. I grew to love him very much, which I thought could never happen, and my life was beginning to feel good.

He called me one day to say that his wife was ill and he was moving back home. He said he loved me very much, but we couldn't be together. He loved his wife, too. They had talked about divorce, but they still had a friendship and they needed each other. He said they had been together for twenty years and wouldn't know how to go through life separately. He told me a lot of things that I didn't hear because my head was pounding and my heart was breaking. We had been seeing each other for two years, and I had allowed myself to fall in love with him, although I was determined to never love again and to never let myself be swayed from taking care of my kids and myself.

I was accepted at college and, at the age of thirty, was scared to death about it, but I was determined to go. Two weeks before I was to move away, I found out that I was pregnant. I couldn't believe it! We had always used protection and there was no way I could be pregnant. I thought about leaving town and not even telling him about the baby, but I knew he would find out because all our family lived in the same town and knew each other. We met and I told him I was carrying our child. He was shocked and very upset. He was just trying to get his life and marriage back together. We talked about what a child would do to our lives at this point. He asked me to think seriously about an abortion. I took a week to think about all the options and decided that, no matter what effect a child would have on my life, I couldn't abort. He wasn't at all happy about my decision.

I moved to Berea, Kentucky, and started college. I felt it would be better to wait and tell my family about the baby because they weren't going to be at all supportive in this matter. Not only was I having a child outside of my marriage, but I was having a bi-racial child, which was a big obstacle with my relatives. The hardest part was telling my kids. I knew they would have a hard time with another child, because we were already having a hard time adjusting to moving and to the divorce.

Basically, when I did tell everyone, they freaked like I knew they would, but after a few months everything mellowed out. The baby's father kept somewhat in touch. He would drive up and make sure we had what we needed. Things were very stressful between us; he still hadn't told his wife about the baby or me.

I started classes and met some really wonderful people. It was a very different life than what I was used to, but I was really enjoying it. When I was about six months pregnant, I began to have complications. I started having seizures and went into premature labor. I was ordered to spend the next three months on complete bed-rest, and had to take a leave of absence from college. I called my family and told them I needed help, and my mother came to stay with us. I was very nervous about her being there, because our relationship was strained and I was already under a tremendous amount of stress.

She came and immediately took over, which was wonderful. She got the kids up and ready for school every day. She made them breakfast every morning and made sure I ate right and took my vitamins when I was supposed to. What I thought would turn out to be another tragedy in my life was, instead, one of the greatest blessings I have ever received. My mom and I were together every day for two months, and we had a long time to talk to each other. We opened up for the first time in our lives, and I realized that my mother was proud of me and loved me very much. There was such a burden lifted from my heart in those months we were together. For the first time in my life, my mother and I were friends. We made comforters and curtains for the nursery and laughed at soap operas. She went to the doctor with me, and made sure they checked me out from head to toe. It was a wonderful time. We never brought up the past, but I was able to let it go and look to a better future between my mom and myself.

On the day of my son's birth, his father came to visit. He took us shopping for Easter and while we were out, I went into labor. I felt that God must have had a hand in all of this because, not only did I reconcile with my mother, but my child's father was there when he came into the world. He held him in his arms and kissed him, touched his fingers and toes, and held my hand while I nursed our son for the first time. Two days later, we left the hospital and he was waiting for us at my house. He said he was going to tell his wife about our son, because he couldn't have a child in the world that he didn't know anything about or take care of.

Things were really rocky for while. She accepted the situation, even though she didn't like it. Since that time, they have come to love our son very much, and he loves his father and stepmother also. It is very hard for me because I still love his father very much. I felt that he was my true soul mate, but we found each other too late. I am grateful that he is the person that he is, because he takes good care of our child, and all I have to do is make a phone call if there is anything he needs.

My son turned out to be a blessing in more ways than one. My family began to see how stupid racism really is. They have learned a great deal through the love they feel for him, and for the love he gives back in such great abundance. His brother and sister worship him, and he feels the same about them. My father has stopped drinking and says that he wants to be around when the kids grow up. My youngest son says that his papaw is his "bestest buddy," which makes my father stand like a peacock in full bloom.

Things were good, but just when I was beginning to settle back into college and adjust to a new child, my mother's health began to fail. She developed pneumonia and suffered kidney failure. She seemed to be going downhill fast, and I was terrified that we were going to loose her. She was a born fighter and seemed to bounce back after two years of dialysis treatments. She was weak often, but could still get around and do things for herself until she suffered a fall and broke her leg.

From that point on she was bed-ridden and in and out of the hospital often. Her body was so badly deteriorated that her bones wouldn't knit together and her leg would never heal. For the next year, I drove the two hundred and forty miles home every weekend to help take care of her. Two of my sisters alternated days of the week, and I took weekends. It was very difficult, but I loved my mother, and I wanted to spend as much time as I could with her. She was there when I was down, and I wasn't going to let her down when she was in need. My children became very close to their grandparents at this time because we spent so much time together. I was happy to see them together, and my parents seemed to have new life with them around. My parents would tell stories of when they were young, the things they would do and the mischief they got into. My children would sit in amazement and laugh at them, and then they would go home and retell the stories to their friends. It was wonderful.

I knew my mom was going down hill but she was always smiling and said, "I'll walk again as soon as I get my strength back. I'm not going to stay in this bed." In a year's time she went from being able to do some things on her own to not even being able to roll herself over. Her skin became thin as tissue paper, and if you took hold of her too hard, it would rip in your hands. She bruised at a touch, and developed huge blood tumors in her upper arms. Still she smiled and stayed strong. I had so much admiration for her. The strength she had was amazing to me.

July 31 was a great day for her. She felt good and wanted to go outside, so we took her onto the porch. She sat there and admired her many rose bushes and played with the kids. It was a wonderful day. At 5:00 a.m., August 1, Mom awoke with a fever and chills. I gave her medication and bathed her, but the fever wouldn't break. At eleven a.m., I called one of my sisters because Mom was having trouble breathing. We took her to the hospital and she was diagnosed with pneumonia. She refused to stay in the hospital so they gave her a shot and sent her home. All day she alternated between chills and heat flashes. We called my other brothers and sisters and they came to help us take care of her.

It was one of my brother's birthday, and when he came to the house, she looked at him and said that she would give him his spanking later. He began to cry and she said, "Don't worry, I'm not going to die today. Not on your birthday." She fought and fought. We had every fan in the house on her, but she still insisted that she was burning up. Family members came in all day and we took turns washing her off and fanning her. I watched her gasp for air and felt as if my heart would explode from trying to breathe for her. When her hands and feet began to turn purple from lack of oxygen, we begged her to go back to the hospital and called the paramedics. She asked for my dad and told him she was dying. They held each other's hand and said they loved each other.

The paramedics arrived and took her back to the hospital. At 2:30 a.m., August 2, 1999, my mother died, at the age of sixty-six, from congestive heart failure. Her hands were totally blue from lack of oxygen; she literally suffocated to death. That image will haunt me for the rest of my life. I was filled with incredible anger. I was so mad at God for taking her just when I had gotten to know her. There is such a void in my soul and a deep burning pain forever present in my heart.

Everything seemed to lose its meaning for me. I couldn't make myself do anything. I returned to college a month later, but had a very difficult time focusing on anything. I was angry at the world. I spent every spare moment creating flower arrangements for the graves of my mother and sister. It was my senior year in college. I was failing my classes and didn't even care. I had always been determined to make it through college to prove to my parents that I had made the right choice and that education was important. I had planned on getting a great job and helping my parents to have a better life. But now, my mother was dead and she would never know whether I succeeded or not. I could walk across that stage, but she would never know it and there was nothing I could do to help her now.

I found myself in a state of deep depression. Thank goodness, I had some real friends at college who helped me and wouldn't let me give up. I realized I had to pull myself out of it for the kids if I couldn't do it for myself. I put my grief on hold and refused to think about it. Instead, I focused on my classes and on creating a great senior sculpture show. I am now in my last semester and will graduate in May 2000.

This is where my story comes to a standstill. Where do I go from here? I will take some time to rest and to deal with my mother's death. I have a very hard time thinking about her and I know I need to let go and cry until I can't anymore. That will probably be my first goal after graduation. My long term goal is to get my master's degree in art therapy so I can help others overcome the hardships we face in life. I plan on moving back to my hometown so I can be close to my family for a while. From there, who knows?

– *Cheyenne Kade*

The Trip

I
want you to know
what it has taken
for me to get
this far –
much lost
to time,
lonely days
spent sitting
in a hard chair
trying to recall
why
I am
so numb.

– Trish Lindsey Jaggers

Sheila, February 2000 –

My name is Sheila Mitchell. I was born on May 1, 1955, in Kentucky. I began school in 1961 in a segregated school in Glasgow, Kentucky. I went to the third and fourth grade in a one-room, segregated school in Hiseville, Kentucky. Finally, in the fifth grade, I attended an integrated school in Hiseville. I went to high school at the Hart County High School in Mumfordville and graduated in 1973. Next, I went to a business college in Louisville for about a year.

I have always worked. My first job was working a motel when I was fifteen years old. I worked in a factory that made batteries, and operated a sewing machine for a company that made blue jeans. I've worked as a file clerk, a health records clerk, a secretary, a retail store cashier, a substitute teacher and a recreation specialist with the Job Corp. I even worked as a part-time secretary at a police department. Some of these jobs I held before 1975, and some I have worked at since 1995, but, from 1975 to 1995, I worked for one company, which is really where my story starts.

In September of 1975, when I was twenty years old, I took a job with a company in the agri-business field. I worked there for over 19 years, from September 1975 to January 1995. I began at $2.30 an hour and ended at $8.19 per hour regular wages, $12.29 per hour for overtime. I worked from forty to fifty-five hours per week. There were fifteen men in the plant, and three women in the office.

When I started there, I was the lowest paid person they employed, but I was thrilled to have an office job. In the late 1970s, it was rare in this part of the country for a black person to work in an office. I was young, from a small country town, and aware of my status as an African-American woman in that setting. I realized before long that I was stuck doing most of the work and that I was expected to work overtime. After working

there three weeks or so, I knew I was not accepted. My co-worker, who eventually became my supervisor, always tried to humiliate me. She often tried to make me look stupid, as though I was unable to comprehend anything. I remember how she introduced me to a customer on the telephone, "This is our new customer service clerk. She is black." I could have just died then because I knew I had a hard road ahead of me.

But I found out that as long as the customers who called in didn't know I was black, I would be all right. My job consisted of taking orders over the telephone. If my co-worker hadn't told every customer that I was black, they wouldn't have known for a long time. It was difficult for me, but I finally won over all the customers with a lot of hard work. I received more respect from my customers than I ever dreamed possible. But my relationship with the customers was going too good for my co-worker to accept, so she began to destroy it. She started answering the telephone, pretending to be me, and speaking to the callers in a cold, hateful way. She worked hard to undermine me and my relationship with the customers. From then on, it was like a race with the devil to get to the telephone before she did. I had come a long way, and I was not about to let her ruin it for me. Only the Lord and I know what she put me through.

Once, she even drugged me. She expected me to wait on her hand and foot, get her lunch every day, get her a cola drink at the break, get everything out of the filing cabinets she wanted. I was only allowed a thirty minute lunch break, after I had seen to it she had her lunch and drink. At some point, I refused to be her personal servant and it made her angry. She surprised me one day by asking if she could bring lunch back for me and, like a fool, I said, "yes." I won't ever forget, it was a pimento cheese sandwich and potato chips. The sandwich had a bitter taste. After I finished eating, I became very sleepy. It was all I could do to remain conscious. I held on to my chair with both hands to keep from falling to the floor. She kept watching me and telling me how the nerve pills she took made her the same way. She kept saying that, and I realized what she had done and why. She wanted me to know it. From then on, I never accepted anything from her, although she kept offering. One day she wanted to bring me a soft drink. There was no reason for her to do so, since we had a soft drink machine in the break room. I thought I would be safe with a cola drink, if I asked for it in a can, but, when she brought it, it was in a bottle and the cap had been opened. I was afraid to drink it. She was a cruel person who would go to any lengths to control me.

But my real ordeal was much more serious. I was only twenty years old when I went to work for the company – young, bashful, naive, and unable to recognize motives. I was a victim of sexual harassment and abuse for years, as well as racial harassment. As a young, black woman, I was a target for both. They seemed to think that since I was African-American, my morals were such that the sexual advances were welcome. And I didn't know what to do about it, except try to get through each day. Every morning for ten years I hated the thought of going to work, knowing I had to face harassment and intimidation. Although there were several men who sexually harassed and abused me, there were two who were most persistent.

It began as what I perceived to be an act of kindness. Two men at the company began sharing their lunch with me. Sometimes one would buy my lunch; the other would bring tomatoes and apples and share them with me. Occasionally, they would buy me a cola drink at lunch or break time. On Valentine's day, they gave me a box of candy. Then I realized they wanted payment: for their kindness – they wanted me to be their sexual play toy.

The sexual harassment took many forms. Often it was verbal. One of the men would ask, "Can I feel your pussy?"

He'd say he was going to pinch my breast, or ask, "How about us getting some?"

Every morning he told me I looked nice and that I smelled so good he could "eat me." The other one would tell me I looked nice, smelled nice, and had nice legs. Once at a company picnic, I had just gotten out of my car and walked to the picnic site when he came to meet me, rubbed my leg and said,"black legs." Everyone thought it was funny. He would often do that sort of thing, making insulting me or touching me seem like a joke.

One of the men told me he wanted to experience sex with a black woman. He was the one that asked to feel my "pussy," and seemed to think that because he was a white male, and I was a black female, I should have been flattered and willing to go along with his suggestion. A third man once asked me, "How much would you take for some sex? ... would you take $7,000?" He told me that he and another man were making bets on how big my nipples were.

But the physical harassment was worse. Several of the men constantly touched me. One was always trying to pat me on the behind, rub my legs, rub up against me, and grab at my breast. One man grabbed me between my legs and tried to pat me on the behind.

Another man would say, "You've got something on you," then rub at "it" and "it" would always be in my breast area.

Another would grab me, hug me, and pat me on the stomach and say, "After you have your first baby, you won't have that flat stomach any more."

Another dirty man, in his late fifties, would offer to buy me a soft drink, then try to grab my breast. A company salesman liked to rub and pat me; it got to the point I would pull out all the drawers on my desk to keep him away from me.

One morning one of the men came into the office when I was standing by the computer printer and rubbed his penis up against me. I stood there in shock; I really couldn't believe what was happening to me. If it had not been for another person yelling, "What's wrong with you?" I don't know what he would have done next. He just shrugged and walked away, as if what he'd done was all right.

One morning he asked me, "How about us getting a little?"

By then I was angry because I was getting no respect. I felt like I couldn't even demand respect because, being a black woman. I couldn't act the way I would have loved to act. All I could say was "No," and then he had the nerve to ask me, "Why?" I was really boiling by then, but I managed to tell him my boyfriend wouldn't like it.

He replied, "No more than what I'd get, your boyfriend wouldn't miss it."

One day, I got stuck doing inventory with one of the supervisors who closed the door because he said it would cut down on the noise. That was the day he decided to grab me between my legs. I was shocked, scared, and didn't know what to do. I was a black woman and who would listen to my complaint about a married, white man?

One of the men began trying to kiss me, putting his hand on my rear and trying to grab my breasts. When I objected, he said, "I'll twist your titties!"

This same man rubbed my legs in front of the plant manager who didn't object. I was told by another woman, my immediate supervisor, that when a woman goes complaining about sexual harassment, or a man doing such things to a woman, only the woman gets in trouble, so we should keep our mouths shut.

Then, there were the sexual innuendos, the gesturing and the stalking. One of the most disgusting acts was the man who was always making facial suggestions by wiggling his eyebrow up and down and licking his lips, telling me how good oral sex would be and that he bet the hair on "it" would be real kinky. Another man would say "Ooooh!" like he was so excited – like a sixteen-year-old just learning about sex. He was forever winking his eyes at me in a fresh way. One of his favorite things to do was grab his penis and raise his leg, kind of like a dog peeing on a tree. And I was stalked.

Being stalked was worse than the verbal or physical abuse because, unlike verbal abuse where you could leave to keep from hearing the vulgarities, or physical abuse where you could jump out of the way, stalking made me uneasy all of the time. I never knew where they were going to show up. Even outside, they would suddenly appear and make vulgar sexual gestures, grabbing themselves or asking me for sex.

I was going through so much at one time, and was so stressed, that I went to the doctor for my headaches. He put me on medication to reduce the anxiety. I went through a period where I drank a large glass of wine before I went to work. I was in and out of the hospital emergency room for asthma attacks that I knew were brought on by stress and anxiety. Every time I thought I couldn't go on, I'd get sick and end up in the hospital. I was a nervous wreck. But what kept me going was the determination that I wouldn't be run out of my job.

Even so, I was at the point that I couldn't talk without becoming confused and rattled, so I didn't make sense. I knew I had a problem, and I didn't know how to correct it, so I went around tight lipped. I would not talk to anyone. When I did, they would look at me strangely and avoid me, as if I were crazy. I started to think maybe I was. Everything had taken its toll. I remember telling one worker that if a particular man kept following me around, I'd take a straight razor to his neck. The worker said, "You don't mean that," but at the time, I was really thinking that way.

When I wouldn't allow them sexual favors, they found other ways to harass me, trying to make me give in. One man would abuse me with cigarette smoke. He knew I had asthma and was allergic to cigarette smoke. He always made a point of coming in and smoking when I was at lunch or on break. It would bring on an asthma attack. He tormented me with smoke.

Then, of course, there was my working environment as well. One of the things I faced was the intimidation my boss directed toward me. I was never sure why, but think it was because he was the plant manager, with a degree, and I was the accounting clerk, without a degree. When he fired the plant accountant, I filled in for two months, then he hired a man. He said a man would be better in the position than a woman. He started the new man in the position at $14.00 an hour. After the man had been with the company for fifteen months, he transferred to another plant, and I took over the accounting position, doing the job along with my regular work load. My boss gave me a sixty cent per hour wage increase, taking me from $5.95 an hour to $6.55. I had to learn the accounting and train two new employees.

After I held the position for three months, my boss requested an internal audit over the books because he was sure I didn't know what I was doing since I was a black female. It turned out to be one of the best internal audits done. I was really proud of the results, but my boss was not. He thought the auditor was going to find something wrong. One year later, he requested another audit. The company never had audits so close. It turned out he was hoping to put someone else into the job, a young, white female. Additionally, when I was training and supervising two white females, trouble erupted. It was all right for me to train them, but they didn't like the idea that I might be in charge.

From that day on, my life was made a living hell by my co-workers and my boss. He reprimanded me for working too much overtime, for not getting along with other employees. My boss was intimidated by my will and my ability to do my job and get things done. He tried to fire me. He denied me a raise for two years straight.

I was written up for working too much overtime in 1986. I was suspended in March of 1986 for one day because I refused to work over the weekend without pay, just prior to having fibroid tumor surgery. The suspension was meant to be three days, but sick leave intervened. I was written up by one person for not doing enough "checking," but later he apologized when he found out that I had been reprimanded previously for doing too much "checking."

In the early 1990s, when the sexual harassment was at a peak, I complained to the plant manager who acknowledged that he'd seen one of the men rub my legs, but he did nothing to stop it. When I tried to tell another boss, he said he didn't want to know. Because one individual's sexual harassment was so constant and extreme, I complained again, and the company made a gesture to keep him away from me. It only lasted for one week and he began to stalk me at the office.

Finally, in May 1992, the company asked me to resign after an investigation. I was offered $10,000 to quit my job. I was told the company did not want to spend more time monitoring the situation. I was told it was cheaper to get me to resign than to fire the man harassing me, and lose his wife who was also an employee. I refused the offer, and they increased it to $15,000 plus severance pay of around $10,000. I refused to sign, and I was told by the company not to make any more "frivolous" complaints. I received a letter stating that if I made any more complaints about sexual harassment, I would lose my job. I then took legal advice from the company's personnel manager and recorded the stalking incidents in writing. I was fired in December of 1994.

Six months before I was released from my job, I had a talk with a man about my getting a permit from a federal judge so I could bring a gun to work with me. He was worried about my mental state and suggested I go to Life Skills (mental health organization) for help. He told me it was obvious I was stressed out. I thought he was talking about help for the sexual harassment, but he really meant help for me; he thought I was going to snap. The next thing I knew, I was on the way to a "shrink."

On the day my job was terminated, I went to a doctor for chest pain. He checked my heart, and ordered an X-ray for stomach ulcers. For seven months I had the chest pain and only slept three hours a night. During that time, I experienced so many physical problems from the stress: asthma attacks, severe headaches, hives, abdominal pain, diarrhea. I even began losing my hair. I would wake up and find I had dug my nails into my arm, almost to the point of drawing blood; sometimes I would do the same to the palm of my hand. I found myself doing normal things to excess – overeating and even compulsive shopping. I just sought any diversion that would block out the pain and stress. Ultimately, the psychiatrist provided help. I was able to talk to him without getting embarrassed or tongue-tied. He put me on medication for depression, Zoloft, and gave me sleeping pills.

After losing my job, I went back to Western Kentucky University, where I began taking classes in paralegal studies, accounting, and all the general studies courses leading to a degree. Currently, I hold two associates of arts degrees, one in office technology and one in information systems. Now I am working toward a bachelor's degree in accounting and business education. I expect to gain that degree in May 2001. I substitute teach at Caverna High School and Elementary School. When my degree and teaching certificate are awarded, I plan to teach business education. I am slowly putting my life back together. I have also brought a lawsuit against the company for sexual and racial harassment.

– *Sheila Mitchell*

One Day Soon, There Will Be a Revolution,

and they will accept us
as we are,
when words no longer sweeten
the truth,
but fly like grey-white pigeons
dropping hints and feathers
from their tilting roosts –
abandoned straws,
matchsticks,
threads of cloth,
headliners, one-liners,
and want ads from week-old newspapers
padding newborn attitudes –
stretching wings
before feathers free our flight,
leaving behind the nesting urge,
until we reach the apex,
scaling words
of advice on how to climb,
how not to fall,
how to land,
feet first.

– Trish Lindsey Jaggers

Kim

My name is Kim Stacy. I grew up in Leslie County, Kentucky. I am the youngest daughter of seven children. I graduated from Leslie County High School and really didn't have much thought of going to college. Most of my brothers and sisters didn't go to college, and I really didn't have a plan for my life. Then the Title 9 sports program came into effect in 1974. Title 9 was a federal mandate stating that if the schools offered athletics for boys, they also had to offer athletics for girls. That was one of the big highlights of my teen-age life, and we started the basketball program. I only got to play my senior year. I thought I could possibly play college basketball, because it was a new program for all girls my age, and I knew our skill level was all about the same. I had high hopes. I went to Eastern Kentucky University and took my shot. To my horror, I was not as good as I thought. I didn't make the basketball team, but it did get me out of Leslie County and gave me some direction.

Going to school at Eastern was great because of the experiences. They were all new, fun, exciting things to do – experimenting with partying, that sort of thing. So, needless to say, my grades weren't too hot, and that eventually meant I was probably wasting a lot of time and money. I was eighteen. I knew of a program in Lexington that was offered through the Urban League. It was designed to teach women nontraditional jobs, so I had to make a choice. I was old enough to start making choices about what I was going to do, how I was going to make money to support myself. I decided to drop out of college and enroll in this program. Because of my experiences in growing up with my dad, I had a fair amount of background knowledge of tools and how to work with my hands. So, I kind of had a foot in the door already.

I knew when I made the decision to drop out of the college that it was going to be hard telling my parents, because I

was the first one of the kids to go to college. I knew it was going to disappoint them. That was very difficult. After I told them, my dad went outside and took a level out of his tool box, and a hammer, and gave me his tools. They were my grandfather's tools. He was okay with it. He is okay with it.

When I was four years old, my parents took a home movie of me successfully nailing two blocks together. That was my first carpentry project.

I started the program. It was a job site in Lexington. There were probably 16-20 women enrolled in the program. The building contractor paid half our salary, and the state, the Urban League, paid the other half. It was great deal for the contractor because it was cheap labor, and there were women that were in the carpentry business, concrete, electrical work, just every aspect of construction. Needless to say, it was not a very welcoming environment for the women. The guys – I don't know if they were threatened because of their jobs being taken away, or they were threatened because, if a woman could do it, then it must not be too hard. Therefore, it was a reflection of their ability. This was in 1977-78. We got a lot of the whistling, the boy talk, the drawings on the port-a-potty walls. Sexual acts drawn on the bathroom walls, some woman's name beside it, anything you can think of. It's amazing the gestures and the things that guys can do with a hammer! Or tape measure for that matter. And it was most of them who acted that way. I have to say, it was most of them. That first job site was where I met most of God's gifts to women. They were there, all of them.

There were a very few exceptions, but they just sort of kept to themselves. They were quiet about it. Occasionally, when no one was around, they would say, "Nice work," or something like that. The crew leader was an older man. He was kind of trying to be like a father. He would always want to know how things were going. I think older men have learned a lot along the way so they seem to be a little bit more accepting. I was doing really well. A lot of women couldn't tough it out; they quit early on. One woman sawed a 45 degree angle across her finger, and that was traumatic enough that she had to stop. For various reasons, they couldn't take the physical work or emotional pressure. Of the twenty women that started that apprenticeship program, only three of us remain in the trades today. The other seventeen dropped out of the program, or quit shortly after their first job. It was not due to lack of interest, but because of the constant struggle of working in a hostile environment.

It was on that job that the crew leader came to us one day and asked if we would talk to the other women and ask them to wear bras. Some of the women were smaller breasted and didn't wear bras, didn't need to wear bras, but he said that it was "distracting" for the men on the job. They weren't able to concentrate because they were looking at small breasted women, which is a switch. So I told him that maybe it would be a good idea if all the women would wear bras on the day that all the men wore belts because we had to look at the cracks of all those guys, but it didn't distract us from working.

It was tough physical work. I was in the trim carpentry so it really wasn't too hard. If I had been in the framing end of it, I think it would have been more so. In this business, as in most businesses, women tend to use their brains and men use their backs, more often than not. I can carry just about anything that your average man can carry because I balance it. If I can find that counter balance point of any piece of wood, or anything, I can move it. Some doors were heavy, some kitchen cabinets were heavy, but I could always figure out a way to do it.

My crew leader came to me one day and told me I was doing a really good job and he was going to ask his boss about giving me more money, so I was thrilled. That meant that the building contractor would have actually been paying another 25 cents an hour for me and the Urban League would have picked up the other 25 cents: a raise of fifty cents an hour. He came back to me in a couple of days and told me his boss denied my pay raise because, if he gave me a raise, he would have to give all the women a raise.

I responded, "Every time you give a man a raise, do you give all the men a raise?"

Then I asked the building contractor that same question and he said, "No, I don't. Can't you understand the difference?"

I said, "No."

It wasn't the first time I had a door slammed in my face. In 1973, the superintendent of the Leslie County School systems, when I was still in high school, wouldn't allow me to take a carpentry class. I was told, "The vocational school is here to teach you students a trade. Girls cannot take carpentry classes." That was the beginning of my struggle with discrimination and working in the "man's world" of construction. Now, it had happened again.

A woman from the Urban League stayed in very close contact with all of us to make sure that we were all doing okay. She wanted the program to succeed. It may have been her, it may have been someone else at the Urban League, but someone decided that the Human Rights Commission should get involved and investigate. If this program was going to go forward, then this guy shouldn't be able to refuse me the raise if the supervisor recommended it. It was investigated, and there I was, back on the job site and all the men knowing there was a little investigation going on. And yes, I was a troublemaker, just like they knew I was going to be a troublemaker.

"Once you bring women on, it's going to be a mess. Why should we do it?"

We all got those kinds of remarks. It wasn't just me; there was a backlash for all of the women.

Finally, I said, "It is too difficult and I am getting more trouble than 50 cents an hour is worth, so I quit."

I guess I'm a quitter in that regard. I quit the job, and I quit the investigation also. One of the guys that was nice to me had also quit earlier and gone to another job, so I knew that they were hiring. I knew that he was there, and I wouldn't have to start out brand new. At least he could say, "Yeah, I worked with her at the other place."

So I did. I followed him. I was 21-22 years old then. I was hired and this was my first experience at framing. They tested me, and I became the cut "man" for two crews building apartment complexes. I was basically cutting the whole building package for two crews. They would yell at me to bring them a piece of 2 x 4 that had a zillion measurements on it, and I was supposed to cut all these 2 x 4s, all the lengths, to keep all these guys going, to keep them busy. Otherwise, they would all be standing around going, "Hey, Baby, come on, hurry up. Let's go."

That was a really difficult time. I was exhausted, but it was on a Friday so I had the weekend to recuperate and rest my right arm. I was back on Monday, and they were better. They were easier so I guess I had proven myself. I don't know if they thought one day on the job would get rid of me, but it didn't. If it had been a Monday, they would have. Actually, I got fairly close to that group of guys, and then I moved on to several other smaller jobs.

During that time, my dad, who is a plumber, had a job going that he needed some help with, so I went home. It was in the middle of the winter, and he was putting the plumbing in a restaurant. It was cold and I was all wrapped up in coveralls and a toboggan coat.

We worked there for a couple of days, and the owner of the restaurant said to my father, "That boy of yours really works well. He is one of the best workers I have ever seen."

My dad said, "That's not my son, that's my youngest daughter."

The guy really didn't say anything then, but that evening he called my dad's house and said "I can't work the girl any more."

My dad said, "If you can't work the girl, you can't work me."

It was so wonderful that he stood up for me like that. He had the plumbing permits and everything in his name, so he just pulled out. It was a lot of trouble. This guy had to hire another plumber and get all the new permits because of whatever strange beliefs he had going on in his head.

Dad was progressive. He had four other daughters before me that I am sure taught him a lot, and we certainly learned a lot from him. He's 82 years old now and still working. He and my mom are both impressed with my building career. They are two of my greatest fans.

I had a series of jobs and was in my middle twenties when I moved down to Lake Cumberland, Monticello, Kentucky. I worked down there for about seven years. I worked for two guys that were timber primers, that is using large timbers, like 8 x 8s or 6 x 8s. The best way I can relate it is, it was like the old barn raisings. All the large timbers are mortised and tenoned together to create a skeleton of the building. We built houses around the lake, and I learned a great deal from those guys. They were "hippy" kind of guys so they were pretty accepting, although they could be difficult. But they were nice guys, and I learned a lot about cabinet making. When I lived there, I also built a house. After I left Lake Cumberland and Monticello, I came back to the Lexington area, but I really missed the lake. I loved the lake. Anne, whom I will mention later in the story, and I built a house there, over the last seven years. We go down on weekends.

I got fed up with working for someone else when I was with my Monticello buddies. As nice as those guys were, they had an edge: some of their ideas were hard. A discussion on the way home from work one evening was the turning point. We were talking about men and women dating, and one of the guys went into great detail about how, if a young woman says "no" when they are making out, she doesn't really mean "no," it's just that she is trying to come across as a nice girl. He should just go ahead and continue his pursuit because, no matter what she says, she doesn't really mean "no." I objected and it led to a big blowup.

That was my last straw. At that point, I decided that never again would a man sign my paycheck. I left Monticello and moved back to Lexington and decided to go into business for myself. It wasn't just that; there were a lot of other factors. I wasn't making very much money down there. House building was slow, and my family was in Lexington – my sisters, my mom and dad. I had a lot of things pulling me back in this direction.

I had good connections in Lexington, so I started building decks and room additions in the city. I did that for two years. Then I met Anne Harrison and we decided to buy property out in Willisburg, which is about an hour west of Lexington. We started building the house in 1989. We moved in six months after we started. It's still not a completed house, but it is mostly completed.

I've had my own business for a little over ten years. It's called Custom Designed Woodworking. The name sort of evolved, and it seems to fit. I build homes. I've built five in the Willisburg area. I build about one a year or one every two years. It takes me about six months to do one. I sub out a lot of it. I sub out all the concrete, the electric, and so forth. I used to do the shingles, but I don't do those anymore. They're too heavy. But, I do a lot of it myself, and it's slow. It's pretty much a one-woman thing, especially near the end.

Once, when we were on the job site at Lake Cumberland we had this guy working. He was talking about his strength, and my lack of strength. It was after work. Somebody had brought some beer in, and we were sitting there drinking it. It's a dry county so those guys were crazy to do anything for a beer. He kept talking about his strength, and my lack, so I bet him a tall Budweiser that he couldn't carry three bundles of shingles up on the roof at one time. He did. He was a fool. He got his beer, but I always think that it was a great example of lack of knowledge. To think he would try to prove himself by actually hurting himself, and for a beer. I won't even carry one bundle. I break them apart.

Down in Monticello, we were framing a house, and we were on the roof. I can't remember if we were putting on the shingles or the plywood. A man was working right beside me, and he stood up, and peed off the side of the house.

I said, "Do you have to do that?"

His reply was, "If you don't like it, or you can't take it, get down off the roof."

I ran into lots of things like that along the way. You know, you make a choice about whether you want to stick with it. You go home at the end of the day, and you think about it.

You think, *Why am I doing this? Are they just all idiots, or did I just happen to fall into a whole bundle of them?*

But, being in the business this long, I know that they're not all idiots. There are idiots everywhere, but I've met some really nice guys along the way who have been very helpful. I think, also, being in the business as long as I have, I now can pick the contractors, the sub-contractors, that I want to be involved with. If I don't like them, I don't hire them again. Now I am at the point where I no longer have to deal with that sort of thing. The sub-contractors that I hire now are very considerate and very nice guys.

I had some low points when I considered giving it up, but I didn't know what else I would do. I really love the profession. I love working with wood, the beauty and art of it. I love taking a truck load of lumber and arranging it so that it makes a beautiful house. Another thing that I love about it is the variety. It's not a profession where I spend twenty or thirty years doing the same thing. Every day I start a job, and work for these wonderful people that bring me into their homes. I get to know people when I start a job. But then it ends, and I go somewhere else, so it keeps my interest. Every job is a whole new experience.

When I began my business, I didn't start with loans. I started with a hammer and a skill saw. I wasn't afraid when I built the first house, because I had already built one for myself so I had one under my belt. Still, building the first one, with someone else's money, was significant. I started with room additions so it wasn't like hundreds of thousands of dollars at stake, only thousands of dollars. When I started, I would make the material list, they would buy the material, and then they would pay me by the hour. I did that for a while until I felt comfortable being able to put it all into a neat little package. That was scary, and it still is. After all these years it is still hard for me to do that. Material prices fluctuate. I can give a bid today and tomorrow material prices change, and I can lose half my personal profit.

I would like to move away from building entire houses, into cabinet making and furniture, but that's difficult. I feel like my career has been a great success, but I'm by no means wealthy. I live comfortably, but I just can't quit building homes and doing larger construction and devote time and energy to furniture making. Financially, I just can't afford to do that.

Being a self-employed person is kind of scary, as I'm sure it is for all self-employed people. You never get over being worried about the next job coming in, and it's hard to turn jobs down. But, in the last several years, I have always had more requests for my work than I can get to, and now I can be more choosy.

I have just completed building my woodworking shop, next to my home, and purchased some major woodworking tools. My shop has a working floor space of 900 square feet, with a second floor wood storage space of 600 square feet. I hope to further my understanding and knowledge of woodworking so I can do more cabinet making and furniture design.

The art of woodworking has traditionally been reserved for the other gender. While growing up in Eastern Kentucky, I saw the lack of job opportunities for women. Women worked hard to build their homes, barns, fences. They worked to dig water lines, dig coal and grow a garden to feed a large family. I did not see these women as the weaker sex! They were, and still are, my role models just for being themselves. I believe we have a responsibility to be role models for the young women yet to come, just as the women who came before me were for me. I would not be who I am today without those women. When I am working in someone's home, with my tool belt on and my circular saw in hand, the greatest compliment that I can be given is to be recognized for my skill and not my gender.

The percentage of women in the building trade is very small. I knew a woman in Lexington years ago who was in the building business. She was a contractor. Her father and brothers were in the business also, but she is no longer involved. I do get a couple of calls a year from women who are interested in working for me or training with me. We have a state plumbing inspector who's a woman, and I know a woman that got her journeyman's license as an electrician: she was the first one in the state. There's not very many of us out there. There certainly needs to be more.

According to the US Census Bureau, women in construction should be at 6.9 percent, but at this writing, we are only at 2.3 percent. That is national census. I am sure it is even less in Kentucky, because nationally you have cities like San Francisco, New York, Chicago, where the unions have to hire women. In Kentucky, the unions don't stress hiring women. I believe there must be women out there, and young girls, who would love this trade because it has been so wonderful for me. It's had the highs and the lows, but it is a wonderful career. It's a great love. It's independence. I think the times are easier now. Women are more accepted in some of the non-traditional roles, and I think the road has been paved by a lot of women, who have paid a lot of dues.

To those who want to try a different role, I say, "Take it. Try it."

I am at the point in my career where I can pretty much pick and choose the kind of job I want. Earlier on, picking was not an option. I kind of took what came along. It was dirty work, remodeling. Lots of jobs that some people might love to do, but I didn't. But, I would take the jobs. Now, I'm glad to say, I can turn down jobs if I want.

Yesterday, the house I am working on was being inspected by the electrical inspector. He walked all through the house, came back, and said "This is a beautiful house, a wonderful house. Would you consider coming to Lincoln County to build a house for me?"

That kind of conversation would have been unheard of ten years ago.

I was glad to say, "No. No, I don't want to come to Lincoln County, but thanks for asking.

– Kim Stacy

Just Like Blood

They say life's experiences
make you stronger – like vitamins.
I wish some of my experiences
belonged to another
where I could just read about them,
cry with them,
sympathize with their plights,
easily, because I haven't been there
and can't possibly know
what their pain hurts like,
or their darkness blinds like,
or their hunger twists like,
or their coldness hardens like,
so my "case" could never be
"that bad,"
or sunken that low
so as to have to talk to strangers
and have them say, "Oh, that happened to me,
once."
Just leave it all lying
on the counter by the sink –
because I never really like vitamins.
They tasted too much like blood.

– Trish Lindsey Jaggers

Jessie

I'm forty-one years old, a senior in college, and a mother of four, two gone and two left at home. I'm majoring in horticulture with a minor in women's studies. I'm doing my first big landscaping project right now, which is the yard of the new women's studies building. It was offered to me because I am the only women's studies minor in agriculture, so it was a natural. It's probably going to be the hardest job that I will ever do because there are major problems with slopes, erosion, too many trees, and crumbling masonry. I hope it will be the jewel of my portfolio. I love to design. I'm discovering that, more and more, as I take my landscape design class. I got my first project back and it had a big, red "Excellent" across it. I knew I was on the right track, and I really love to do it, so that just thrills me to death, to be validated in that area.

I've done a lot of thinking about my life. I know that the difficulties in my life began with my mother and her childhood. She was taken from her mother, after her father died, and reared by her paternal grandparents. Her father's family was all German and first generation Americans. They disapproved of my grandmother because she was more modern and wilder than they were used to. When my grandfather, their son, died, they took my mother, separated her from her own mother, and reared her. Knowing this, my mother spent her entire childhood, in fact most of her life, fighting for freedom and self-esteem, and trying to prove to her grandparents that she was as good as them.

My mom is an extremely talented person. She was a "jack of all trades" and, instead of "master of none," she was master of everything. She's been an architect, a waitress and a go-go dancer; she can drive an 18 wheeler and work on cars. She built the house she is living in herself, with her own two hands. She didn't just go out and buy the lumber, she went out and cut the trees down, milled the lumber, and built the house. She felt very stifled living with her grandparents and hated being made to feel inferior. Being young, she decided marriage was her way out. She married and had seven children. She then discovered that marriage and seven children was not a way to find freedom.

I grew up watching my mother struggling to be free. The best way I can describe her is that she was always like the butterfly trapped in a cocoon – always wanting to get out. The entire time I lived at home she never did get out of that cocoon, and she never proved to her father's family that she was as good as them. I saw that struggle but, as I was growing up, it seemed that she was just a terrible mother. She was a talented person who was a terrible mother, to the point where there was almost no contact at all. She was not there for advice; she was not there at all, emotionally. For example, she didn't teach me how to be a girl or a woman.

My mother and father divorced when I was nine years old. He was a very simple minded kind of person you could twist around your fingers, but he also turned out to be an alcoholic.

Their relationship became very abusive, so, she left him, packed up all seven of us kids and moved to Louisville, on her own. I'm the second oldest of seven. My oldest sister has emotional problems and that meant the responsibility for my five younger brothers and sisters rested squarely on my shoulders. From the time my parents divorced, I had to be the mother, the guardian and the shepherd who kept everybody gathered together. I had to be the one to cook, clean, sew, and attend to all the other household duties. My mother just left it all on my shoulders; somebody had to do it. That was the beginning of my feeling that I was responsible for everybody.

She worked and I took care of the kids, but we were also often on welfare when she was between jobs. We were poor most all the time, extremely poor. I can remember powdered eggs. I'd think, *Yea! Give me those powdered eggs.* Or a can of green beans, I'd think, *Oh my, we got a can of green beans. Everybody stand in line ... don't fight ... we'll share.* I remember many times we'd have just one outfit of school clothes, and we'd have to wear them until they were literally falling apart. We wore them until the seams were coming apart. Then she would make us another set, find the money to get us a replacement or find somebody to give us some. She kept us in clothes, barely, and food, barely.

When I was nine years old, right after my parents divorced and we moved to Louisville, one of the most tragic things that could happen to me occurred. My mother was working at International Harvester, building tractors at a factory. She had gone through this long series of baby sitters, trying to find someone to watch seven wild, unruly kids that had never had any kind of parenting. Mom had a boyfriend, and they were together for about a month after we moved to Louisville. He and Mom had gone out and she'd gotten drunk. When they came home, she went to bed. All seven of us kids were sleeping in two beds, in one bedroom, in the front of the house. Her boyfriend came and got in bed with us. He started on my sister. She got up, ran off to the bathroom, and locked herself in. Then he started on me. I got up and ran to the bathroom. My sister let me in and we locked the door. He started beating on the door and telling us if we didn't come out, he was going to go in and get our little brothers and sisters. My sister stayed in the bathroom, but I came out because I just couldn't let him hurt them. Even though I was only nine years old, I knew I could deal with him a lot better than they could. The youngest one wasn't even a year old at the time. So I came back out and I was raped – at nine years old. I don't know what I thought was happening. I guess I knew it was sex, but I didn't know what to expect.

The next day I painted an ugly picture of him, on the wall of the house next door, and got into all kinds of trouble. My mother's only words on the subject were that she couldn't keep a boyfriend because of me. I was traumatized because of the experience itself, but also because that was exactly the moment that I realized I was responsible for my brothers and sisters. Not her! She wasn't even passed out. She knew the whole time what was going on, as it was going on, and never even got out of the bed to come and help me. He never came back again.

I, my older sister, and my younger sister (the one next to me), all three of us, were molested several times – not full-blown intercourse, but to some degree. Our baby sitter's boyfriend, whoever, it just went on and on and on. The males always found ways of putting us in a position where we had no choice if we wanted to be safe, or get back home safe. They found ways to control us so they could have their way.

Another traumatic thing happened to me when I was twelve. I was diagnosed with juvenile degeneration. It's not common and it usually happens to boys, but it happened to me. I got it in my hips so I was in and out of the Shriner Hospital for three years. They would put me in traction and pull one hip out and go in and scrape cartilage away. Then they would operate and put pins in my legs to hold my legs together until the cartilage could grow back. Once one side was done, they would have to do the other side. Once I got both sides done, I would have to go back in to have all the pins taken back out. I gained weight during that period and didn't get to go to school. I was supposed to have home tutors, but they only showed up about once a month. The medical procedures took place from the time I was twelve until I was fifteen, from sixth grade through all of middle school. My brothers and sisters would be on their own while I was in the hospital, usually for about a month at a time.

The weight gain happened at a very bad time in my life. I was beginning to be interested in boys at that stage and here I was, crippled and in pain, getting fatter and fatter and fatter. I reached a point once where I weighted 300 pounds. The one thing I discovered, after I started putting on all that weight, was that mom's boyfriends, the baby sitter's boyfriends and all the boys in school didn't want me anymore. I was shielded. However, I wasn't shielded from name calling, and I wasn't shielded from pain, because I was taunted and called "the great white whale."

I turned inward and spent a lot of time thinking about my life. I learned a lot, about a lot of things, but I didn't mature in the area of relationships. I remember waking up at one point in my life, when I was about eighteen, and realizing I was immature. I was so wise about so many things, the really bad things, yet so immature about the rest of life. I was like an innocent little child in some areas. Having that time to think was good, and being protected from all the molestation was good, but to have gone eighteen years of my life and not had a normal life at all was not good. I had no foundation. I was not grounded. My mother was just so absent. Even when she was there, she was absent. It would be hard for me to say that she was loving.

I always got the blame for anything that went bad: the loss of a babysitter, her boyfriend problems, a dirty house, not enough to eat, somebody's illness causing her to miss work. The only thing my mother and I shared – the only good thing – was when she shared some of her talents with me. We'd move into a house, and it would be an awful house because we couldn't afford a good house. We'd proceed to tear down walls, hang wallpaper, put up paneling, take the bathroom out and put it somewhere else, pull the back porch off or build stairs. She and I shared that. I was always her helper.

School was hard. It was hard being raggedy all the time and poor, and not having a mother. She wasn't teaching me how to grow up to be a young lady, so I was this wild, raggedy child with no sense of what I should or shouldn't do in a situation. I had no guidance; I just evolved. We grew up in Louisville, seven of us, and it was a miracle that we all reached adulthood. We not only grew up with no direction at all, but no protection! I can remember us climbing up on two-story buildings and jumping off into trees, running the streets, going down alleys where there were bars and not very nice people and just scooting on through.

The first time I saw the look of murder in someone's eyes, I was sixteen and my mom had remarried (to her second husband). They were both working. He was an alcoholic. One day, my youngest sister, who was the wildest and most unruly of us all, was talking on the phone when he came in from work in a fury. He told her to hang it up, and she was trying to say goodbye, but it wasn't fast enough. He slammed the phone away from her, pulled it off the wall, stormed back into the bedroom and she followed him, screamed something at him. I was coming downstairs from my bedroom at the precise moment she got through screaming at him. She was standing in front of his bedroom door with the bathroom on her left side and the stairs that I was coming down on her right side. I heard him charge, and I just knew he was coming after her. She was only about ten. I ran the rest of the way down the steps, pushed her into the bathroom, and turned to face him. He was bent over like a bull: face totally red, eyes bloodshot, charging like a bull! He had gone insane, and there was nothing but murder on his face. He couldn't even see me. I was just a body to him. There was no familiarity at all. He came charging at me and I froze. He slammed up against me and smashed me into the wall, nearly dislocating my shoulder. I remember being totally frozen and helpless, knowing I had to do something or I was going to die. I remember urging my mind, begging my body to do something. All I could manage to do was start screaming, "He's going to kill me! He's going to kill me!" Everybody in the house came running at this point and everybody jumped on him and pulled him away.

He'd done it before. The previous two attacks were aimed at my mom, and he hurt her the first time. The second time it happened in the kitchen. I'd taught my brothers and sisters to defend themselves or each other with anything they could pick up – skillet, pan, rolling pin, big spatula, whatever, and beat the crap out of him if necessary. The second time he went after our mom, they beat him down to the ground and he had to crawl out of the house, on his hands and knees, with them beating him the whole time. That was when I discovered I couldn't lay a hand on anyone. I could tell them how to defend themselves, but I couldn't lift a hand and actually hit anyone. Years later, the second time my husband beat me, I again saw the look of murder on a person's face.

I didn't finish high school but I got a GED. When I was a junior, and going into my senior year in high school, the integration issue was a battleground in Louisville. I experienced rocks being thrown through the window of our car, best friends dying, blacks and whites beating each other up with chains, cops in the hallways. It was not a very conducive environment for learning. It didn't effect the younger kids in grade school as much as it did the three of us who were in high school. We all quit high school. At that time, I was also the only one working, even if it was just baby sitting. I had started working when I was nine. I baby sat, delivered newspapers, was a page at the library, did anything I could get my hands on, mostly so I could buy food because we were hungry – a lot. Also, since I was eighteen, my mother decided she had put all the effort she could into me. I had a job. She was tired.

While I was working on weekends, she was supposedly taking vacations with the rest of the kids at Rough River Lake, but, instead, she was setting up a whole new life for herself at Rough River. I came home from work one day and the house was empty. The doors were locked and I couldn't get in. Mama was gone. My brothers and sisters were gone. Everybody was gone. So there I stood in front of an empty house. She knew I was smart, and independent, and strong, so she just decided to leave me. That hurt, but by that point that I was so totally convinced that I didn't matter, that my whole purpose in life was to take care of everybody else that, rather than be upset about my own situation, I was completely destroyed by the fact that I wasn't there to stand between mama and my little brothers and sisters. What was going to happen to them when I wasn't there to be their safety net, their shield?

I broke into the house so I'd have a place to sleep that night. I stayed in a totally empty house. I called my mother's sister, in western Kentucky, and told her what Mama had done. We made arrangements for me to go and stay with her, so I only lived in the empty house about a week, just long enough to get a paycheck and buy a bus ticket. I went there because she could get me on at a factory which had a steel worker's union, so the pay was good.

We made car seats in the factory, and there was a lot of heavy work in the press department where I worked. I was eighteen, the baby of the whole place, working in a department with only men on third shift. I got picked on a lot, but I also grew up a lot. In one way they babied me, yet in another way I was their target, an easy target, and some of the men were not so nice. I worked there for about two years, and that was where I met my husband. During that two years, my relationship with my husband developed, and I got pregnant. At first, I didn't realize I was pregnant. I didn't know the symptoms. I just knew I could no longer stand the smell of the place and couldn't handle the work anymore. I quit and, about two months later, found out I was pregnant.

My husband is five years older than I, and black. My aunt couldn't handle the racial aspect, particularly twenty some years ago. She couldn't handle the gossip over my choice in men, so she booted me out. I got an apartment and started taking care of myself. He moved in with me, but we didn't get married then – we waited sixteen years – but I referred to him as my husband until we actually did get married.

I didn't know a thing about being pregnant or having babies. I had no money and no insurance since I'd quit my job. But, I saw a doctor whom we were supposed to pay after he delivered the baby. (That's poor people's way out. You just pretend you're going to pay, and then you don't pay.)

One of my major difficulties, when I began to have children, was I had nothing to look back on. I couldn't say, "Well, Mama did this or that in this situation." No modeling whatsoever. I was going to have a baby and we were scared. Neither one of us knew what to expect. I was twenty, my husband was twenty-five, and he had already started drinking.

My first child was a boy. About two weeks before I gave birth, my husband moved me in with his mother. Up to that point, I'd always had black and white friends, but I'd never been totally submerged into black society. His mother and I never got along. She's dead now, but she was the kind that refused to see the things she didn't want to deal with. Her husband, my husband's dad, was a really outgoing kind of person, a volunteer fireman, the best volunteer they had at church. He was always ready to go, ready to hunt squirrels if somebody wanted a squirrel, ready to fish if somebody wanted fish, always stopped if somebody needed help. He was that kind of person, but he had no influence on his family at all. My husband's mother stood between the kids and him. My husband grew up with no self-esteem, no sense of balance, no modeling either. Even worse, he was taught that, as a black person, he should never look anybody in the face, never speak out. He was brought up like that and, to this day, it's hard for him to look people in the face. He looks at the floor.

So there we were, these two young people, neither reared with a sense of security. He was still working at the factory, and we were living with his mom when I had my baby. Every time the baby made a little squeak, she poked her head in the door to see if I was killing it. It wasn't long before we moved out. I began to learn about budgeting and money. And my poor child? I just experimented on him, trying to figure out what worked in different situations. My relationship with my oldest son is good now, but we had a hard one then. He got really stubborn on me. I can't blame him because, although I wanted to do what was best for him, and truly loved him, I honestly didn't have a clue as to what I should be doing with him – not a clue. By the time the second one came around, three years later, it went a lot smoother.

But, my husband and I were in love. Our relationship would go back and forth. Sometimes I would love him more; sometimes he would love me more. Then, he decided to start modeling his life after his friends who were in similar situations, and their main goal in life became drinking and smoking marijuana. There was quite a crowd of them, about twenty, who bolstered and supported each other.

My husband had left the factory and was a sawyer at a saw mill. He always worked; if he lost a job he would go right back out and get another. He's a big, muscled, physical kind of guy and there was always manual labor to be done, but it didn't provide the best pay in the world, so we were always poor. A lot of times I was at the welfare office, begging for food stamps or going to a church and begging for this or that, or standing in the cheese line. I took my kids to doctors knowing I couldn't pay. I managed to clothe and feed them. My number one priority was to raise them right. I wanted to be everything that my mother wasn't. Sometimes, I had to be a mother and a father, because their father was drinking or smoking marijuana.

I had some talents. I could sew and crochet. I'd go to Goodwill, buy shawls, take them apart for the yarn and make things because I had to feed my artistic side. If you have an artistic side, you have to feed it or you'll go crazy. I began gardening and, when I couldn't stand to be home anymore, my father-in-law, who was always willing to help, decided he would go in with me and we would raise tobacco together. The kids were still too young for me to get a job without paying people to baby sit, so I decided I'd raise tobacco and take them to the field with me. I did that until I got the first two in school. When I got them in Head Start, I volunteered there. Again, it was to get out of house because being at home absolutely drives me crazy. I'm not a homebody. I prefer to be creative, and I like to help people. I started volunteering there. I was actually Parent of the Year in Kentucky twice, and Parent of the Year in the county four times. I also worked at the Senior's Assistance kitchen and gave out the cheese products, when they had the cheese lines, so I got volunteer awards from there too. I began teaching Sunday school and I did that for a couple of years.

When I got my younger son into first grade, I got a job at a sewing factory. I'd tried for six years to have another baby, because we didn't have a daughter, and I wanted a little girl. Well, two days after I got my job at the factory, I found out I was pregnant again. Typical! My third child was also a boy, but six months later, I got pregnant again! My fourth child was finally the daughter we wanted. I had my first child when I was twenty, and my last when I was thirty.

I went back to tobacco farming again. By then, my husband had worked at the sawmill for twelve years, but the man who owned the mill retired and moved out of state. My husband found another job building public housing projects. That job, at a small town in western Kentucky, only lasted a year. It was a pretty decent job, but the employer was from Tennessee and, when they finished that job, he went back to Tennessee. My husband was left to look for another job. He got a job at an aluminum siding and insulation place, but that employer turned out to be an alcoholic and lost his business about six months later. My husband likes being stable; he doesn't handle change well. He was beginning to get really frustrated and was having a hard time taking care of his family – and a hard time buying his alcohol and marijuana. As his worry increased, his use of alcohol and marijuana increased. His drinking and smoking became very heavy and he started on his final, downhill slide. I was involved in the church then, and he felt threatened by that, as well as the fact I was working and becoming more independent and knowledgeable. I had gained a little power and he was losing his.

One night, I got mad at him and slept with my daughter, who was about a year old. We'd never slept apart in all the fifteen years we'd been together. I woke up to him grabbing me by both breasts and yanking me out of bed, throwing me down on the floor, and kicking me all the way back to the bedroom, screaming and hollering at me the whole time. This from a man who'd never laid a hand on me in fifteen years. I was in absolute shock!

Somehow I managed to get past that by praying, crying, talking to people, believing it would never happen again, thinking it was a one time thing. And, it didn't happen again for a solid year. I don't know what set it off then, but it was the second time I saw the look of murder on a man's face – this time on my husband's face. Again, he attacked my female parts. Literally, I believe it would be possible to pull a person's breast off with just one's hands. It felt like he almost pulled mine off. I was bruised, scratched. Once more, I was in shock. I took the kids to the spouse abuse center in another county, one county over, and got an injunction to stop the violence.

Against all proper procedure, the judge in my husband's home county gave my husband the number to the spouse abuse center. I was scared. I didn't really have a good job. I didn't know how I could take care of the kids, and I had no place to live. I didn't have a decent car or decent clothes to find a job. I had no education, so I could only do manual labor. I was afraid of struggling on welfare, so I went back to him. Six months later, he beat me again. That was the third time in a year and a half. Looking back, it seems that my refusing to have sex with him would start it off. That's not what he was about, but that would set it off. I also think my becoming independent, and him viewing me as more powerful than him, was very threatening to him.

112

I started making plans in my head as to what I was going to do. I went back to work at Head Start. I decided I would save my money, and pawn everything I had ever bought to raise more money. Instead of trying to find another job or move out of town, I'd go back to school. That was my goal. I knew if I got a college degree, I could take care of the kids. It took me about six months to get myself together – getting the courage, pawning things, saving every penny, lying to him about the money I had, preparing the kids mentally to make the move. I tried to figure out where I was going and how it was going to work when I got there.

In the meantime, the violence continued, twice during the six months, then once more the day before I left. We had gone from fifteen years of no abuse, to one year, to six months, to two months, and finally one month. He was always drunk. The last time it happened, I had planned on leaving the day before. I had a friend and her truck lined up and had called BRASS (Barren River Area Safe Space: a shelter for battered women) in Bowling Green and made arrangements to stay there. I had a sister in Bowling Green at the time. I'd decided Western Kentucky University was the school I wanted to attend. I had a thousand dollars saved. I knew if we were going to survive and have any kind of decent lifestyle, I had to go to school.

He came home from work with plans to rape me that day. He'd bought a gold necklace. It was all premeditated. So he raped me. I tried fighting, but my legs weren't strong enough to hold him off. He just came into the bedroom and attacked me. It was violent. He was needing to vent and I was his target. Violence, not sex, motivated him. He did what he wanted to do, then threw the gold necklace at me and left. I called a friend, and she said I needed to go to the police. I went to the county sheriff's office. I cried and gave the necklace to the sheriff, and told him what happened. He said he would have my husband arrested. He did, and put him in jail.

I loaded up the trunk of my car and a truck with everything I could get in it. I cleaned the house. Every one of his immediate family came over to tell me what a horrible person I was. They all knew he was beating me. They knew he was drinking and taking drugs. They knew we were poor and had nothing, but they all came over to tell me how awful I was because I had him put in jail. His mom, especially, called me on the phone and asked why I did that to her baby. They had me in tears all day long, but I kept packing, and I kept cleaning because I was going.

We left sometime that afternoon. It was dark by the time we got to Bowling Green. My kids were 15, 12, 6 and 5. I had a thousand dollars, clothes, photo albums, toys, bicycles, dishes, pots and pans – stuff like that. We didn't have any furniture. I took my possessions to my sister's house and she let me unload them in her shed. I only kept out the clothes we were taking to the spouse abuse center. At the center, we had to go through the entry process. They told me we would all take turns cooking and cleaning. They gave us three sets of bunk beds in a room shared with another woman and her kids. We were all piled in this one big room. That was pretty stressful and I had my first panic attack that night, in the middle of the night. It was horrible. I realized I only had a thousand dollars, four kids, some junk and no place to live. As I look back on it, I know it was the bravest thing I ever did in my entire life. That was six years ago.

When I had him arrested for rape and abuse, I didn't know anything about the court system. I discovered they never had any intention of prosecuting my husband. The judge actually called around and told everybody involved with the case that I'd lied, made the whole thing up and that I'd done it because I wanted to go back to school. They never did a rape kit on me, never sent me to the hospital, never took pictures of the bruises, none of the usual procedures. After I was at the abuse center for about a week, I had one of the workers call and ask about the trial date and ask what they were doing with my husband. We learned that, the day after his arrest, they released my husband on his own recognizance – from a federal offense – which they weren't supposed to do. But they did.

The county authorities were very hateful every time the people from BRASS called them. Eventually, I found out when the hearing date was and one of the women at the center agreed to go with me. I hadn't been notified; I had to go pick up my own subpoena. I went to the courtroom with the worker from BRASS. My husband and his family, his friends, his whole gang, were there waiting for me. They were there to support him and intimidate me. The district attorney was there, but I'd never met or talked to this man who was supposed to defend me.

The worker from BRASS and I were sitting in the hallway downstairs, waiting to be told what we were supposed to be doing, when the sheriff came over and started yelling at me, "Your husband gave me a letter you wrote him saying you loved him, and when this was all over with you all are going back together. . . ." I had not; our daughter had written him a letter. The sheriff continued his verbal attack until the court worker from BRASS broke it up, because the sheriff was making me mad and I was starting to yell back.

He said a bunch of stuff that wasn't true, yet he was the one who was supposed to defend me, who was supposed to testify on my behalf. The court designated worker from BRASS got really scared because of the atmosphere there and called in the court designated worker from the spouse abuse center in the adjoining county. That woman knew my case, because that's the shelter I went to the first time. She told me the case was going to be dropped because they said I'd lied, that I'd made the whole thing up. She said I didn't have a chance; it was going nowhere. We sat there another ten minutes, then I was called upstairs to go into the grand jury room. I still had not met the district attorney, still had not been interviewed. He had no clue about my case – he knew nothing.

I opened the door and looked in. One of my husband's friends was sitting on the grand jury. This man had once asked me for my cigarette lighter and got mad when I asked for it back. He'd thrown the lighter back across the room at me, hitting me and giving me a black eye. There he was on the grand jury! I walked in and saw him and all these other people that I knew in this little bitty town, and I started shaking all over. I looked at the district attorney and asked him if he would step outside. I told him there was a man on the panel that was my husband's best friend. They'd gone to school together. I said, "You have extra people on the panel; can't you have him removed?" He refused to have him taken off.

At a grand jury, they usually don't have the defendant there, because they don't want the person testifying to be intimidated. However, my husband, his friends and his family were all there. I was so nervous. I went in, sat down in a chair by the district attorney, and he told me to tell my story. There was no coaching from him, no questions from him, no questions from anybody. I proceeded to tell this horrible story, but I couldn't get it out because at that point I was in awful shape. I barely knew my name. I could hardly walk because I was shaking so bad. I was just so scared, so nervous, that I couldn't do it. I could not do justice to my testimony. I couldn't do a good job of telling my story. So, I mumbled all this stuff about him hitting me and that he was an alcoholic, but that was about all I could get out.

I walked out of there, trembling, found the court designated worker and sat down with her. The sheriff went in and spent two minutes testifying. My husband got to testify. They came out and told us to leave. I asked how I would know how it turned out, and they told me, "Buy a newspaper." They weren't even going to notify me of the ruling. I found out a couple of weeks later that my husband's father had been a sharecropper for the judge and that my husband and the judge's son had grown up together. When I went back to BRASS, they couldn't offer me much encouragement, but they said I could file a complaint if I wanted to. I called the attorney general's office in Frankfort. They said they would write down my complaint, but it boiled down to my word against their's, and all they could do was add my complaint to everybody else's. That was the end of that; the whole case was dismissed.

While I was still at BRASS, I found out my oldest sister had told my husband where I was. I was in a panic. I had put him through the arrest and trial and now he knew where I was. He was going to come and get me. He was going to kill me. I just knew he was, so I asked that I be transferred to another shelter, in another town, in Kentucky. I went there, and it was horrible. It was headed by a nun whom I never saw. The place is on the city map so it's not hidden. I didn't need an escort to get there. I could walk in, but I couldn't walk out. The door was unlocked from the outside so anybody off the street could walk in, but the people who needed the protection, women who have run away from their abusive partners, cannot get out. Not only that, but they separate the entire family, the kids by age groups, so the parents are not allowed to be with the children.

My children and I were in four different places inside the shelter. The workers were all in offices with locked doors. I had to make an appointment and couldn't see them until they had a free spot on their appointment calendar. They checked our heads for lice. They went through all our baggage, wrote down everything that we had, every piece of clothing to make sure we didn't steal. In that place I felt as if I were a criminal. Rather than protect you and help get you out in thirty days, you're in jail and they don't care if you stay there for six months, a year, or five years. You're a deviate and they want to keep deviates locked away. That's how I felt there. Needless to say, the very next morning, I called BRASS and begged them to please let me come back.

I said, "I'm coming out of this place if I have to break the windows out. They're not keeping me and my kids apart; we need each other right now. I'm coming out a window if I have to."

She said I could come back. She said, "I thought you were afraid your husband is going to kill you."

I said, "I will get a baseball bat and keep it by the door. I'd rather face my husband, than live in this kind of a situation."

So I came back. A week or so after that they helped me find a place to live.

The people at the center took me to the welfare office and told me about Section 8 housing. At first, I didn't understand about Section 8. I looked at the resources I was going to have and thought I couldn't make it. I sat down and cried. I thought, "I've gone through all this and now I can't survive on welfare and Section 8." I thought it couldn't be done. But I didn't have a choice so I figured out a way to do it. I got lucky because one of the women had a fellow church member who was the landlord at a good apartment complex. He agreed to let me use my Section 8, so we got an apartment. It was unfurnished, but it was huge, and there was a swimming pool in the complex. Also, it was in a good neighborhood. We were lucky.

In February of 1993, I moved into the apartment, got the kids in school and settled down. Section 8 pays a part or all of the rent. In my case, the landlord agreed to accept the amount they would pay so I didn't have to pay more. I had a welfare check of around $360.00, and out of that I paid my own utilities. I got food stamps and a medical card. And, I still had my old raggedy car, a Buick. Part of the thousand dollars I saved paid a year's car insurance.

Six months after I moved into the apartment, my husband found out where I was, once again through my sister. He started calling me and his dad started calling; people from the church started calling; a lot of people started calling. They were putting the pressure on me, saying "Your husband is miserable without you. He's stopped drinking. He's cleaned up the yard. He's gone back to church. He's a changed man." I didn't believe it, but after a few months of the calls, I decided to take him back – on my terms. There was to be no drinking, no hitting. He was going to get a decent job. Everything was going to be on my terms. We would have sex when I was ready to have sex. Right down the line, things would be the way I said they would be. After about eight months, we moved back in together. For about a year after that, we struggled trying to rebuild our relationship and get the kids settled down. They were traumatized by all the violence they had witnessed. They'd felt just as helpless as I had. I think they even felt guilt over the whole thing because they couldn't do anything about it. They weren't responsible for doing anything about it, but they didn't really know that. Also, they had to deal with the change from the country living to the city living.

It was rough. I was seeing a counselor at the time to talk about my grief and pain, all the trauma. I was trying to figure out how to make it with him and deal with my anger. It was an extremely gradual process because he hadn't ever, one time, said "I'm sorry." He'd never acknowledged to me that he did anything to hurt me. His attitude was, "It's in the past; leave it in the past and we'll just start over." We struggled for about a year and a half, then the apartment building caught on fire and we wound up moving. We lost almost everything in the fire. We had to start from scratch once again. All we'd saved were our pictures, a few clothes and the cast iron skillet.

I'd started school in August of 1993, so, when the fire happened, a lot of our loss was replaced by people on campus, by a campus women's organization, and by the Women's Studies group. We wound up moving to another neighborhood, which was a horrible mistake, but school had already started – it was fall of 1995 – and we didn't have a lot of options. We wanted to keep the kids in the same school district. Six of us were trying to live in a two-bedroom townhouse, and my husband was once again looking for work. We were dependent on his wages because I'd had to give up Section 8, all welfare, everything, when he moved back in with me.

The pressure started building for him again, although he didn't hit me. The guy next door was an alcoholic, and my husband had already drunk with him, nothing serious, but he had slipped a couple of times. Then one night, when I picked up the downstairs phone, I heard him on the phone upstairs making a drug deal. I quietly set the phone back down. That night, I had my second anxiety attack. At the time, everybody in the house was asleep, so I drove myself to the hospital. I was terrified I was having a heart attack, but it was just an anxiety attack.

I made plans to leave again, because I couldn't have my kids in a house with a man that was planning to sell drugs. I could live without him; I couldn't live without my kids. A guy was buying from him, so that meant he was selling. That was pretty scary and shocking to me. I could just see the cops knocking on my door and both of us going to jail. Since I was an adult, I would have gone to jail also and the kids would have been sent no telling where. I couldn't handle that. So, in less than a week, I was out of the house again. I packed up one day when he wasn't there. I had another domestic violence order served on him because he had become verbally abusive. The fear was still there.

Within a week, my wonderful friends at the campus women's organization, and all the other people at Western that knew me, pitched in once again, paying my security deposit so I could move into a trailer park. My husband found me the day I was signing my lease. He saw my car when he was driving down the road. He came in and we had this confrontation right in front of the landlady. She was in another room, and I was trying to keep it quiet. It was very embarrassing.

We were apart about two months this time. He swore up and down that he wanted his family more than he wanted the alcohol. I wasn't convinced, but then my son's leg shattered. His muscles got so strong that they literally ripped apart the bones in his leg; his muscle strength had advanced ahead of his bone strength. My husband wanted to be able to see his son, so I had to rescind the domestic violence order so he could get into the hospital room. That put us together, and I let him talk me into going back again.

It has been about three years now, and he has stayed sober and is improving himself. He is working hard and steadily getting better. He's driving trucks in the city now, getting a good reputation, and shifting up to a better and better place of employment. There have been no drugs and alcohol. He's been going to Alcoholics Anonymous for over three years now and has gotten his three-year pin. He's been chairman there and, as they give him all these positions, his self-esteem increases. He listens to me now, and he's trying to learn. I think he's serious; I don't think he's going back this time. When we've had troubles, when times have been rough, instead of him turning to drugs or alcohol, we've actually worked things out. Our relationship has improved, too, although that is still hard because I carry a lot of anger at him and a lot of pain.

That anger probably goes right back to when I was nine years old. That's probably why I chose a black man, because he didn't represent those white men who hurt me. Black men are not part of the big old boy's network, they're not part of the court system and they're not that big, scary, white sheriff standing there.

So now, in our relationship, there's some promise. He doesn't feel threatened by my going to school anymore. He's actually proud of me now. He's a very earthy type person, very physical, hands-on, common sense kind of person. He's not a book person, but he is taking plumbing classes now.

I've begun to realize that my decision not to work, to go to school and concentrate on my kids, is beginning to pay off now. I'm beginning to get the dividends back. I'm rather proud, outside of all my accomplishments right now, that my kids are doing so well. My oldest son is married and in the army now. He is a communication's specialist, which is great, because he has a $100,000 job waiting in his future.

At a recent high school ball game, my eighteen year old son, who'd been injured in the game, was giving the pep talk at half time. He's always been outgoing and re-spected. He's been head of Christians Taking A Stand, head of Just Say No to Drugs, that kind of stuff. I was amazed to find out that it was my son who always gives the pep talk during half time – not the coach, but my son. He's got all this athletic ability, all this common sense, makes good grades and gets along with everybody. He is a week-end manager at a Hardy's, and he's in line for a football scholarship at one of the top ten colleges. He became a father in August 1999, and takes his responsiblity seriously. He is a great father.

My two youngest are both in the sixth grade. The boy got held back a year from illness, asthma. He's in the leadership program, he's a peer mediator at school and he's been head of his level of Just Say No to Drugs. Although I've gained a lot of power since being in school and I've never hesitated to pass it on to my kids, my daughter scares me to death. At eleven, she's an extremely powerful, self-confident young lady. She is strong, and head-strong, and it will be a challenge to keep her in hand until she actually reaches the age where she develops a moral sense and can handle so much power and independence. Some-how, I actually was successful as a mother. I have some really awesome kids who are going to do a lot in this world.

We're still living in the trailer. My husband and I are at the point where he totally respects me and we make joint decisions; he asks me what I think. He has learned patience. He is willing to wash clothes, wash dishes, cook supper. He is trying to have a good rela-tionship with, and be a daddy to, the kids. Our relationship is balanced now; we are more equal. I work weekends, and that gives me money and independence until I get out of college and keeps me in shape physically.

Good things have happened to me. I was president of a campus women's organization for two years, the same organization on campus that helped me when I first started. Then I served in two advisory positions with that organization. The best thing for me was meeting a lot of women on campus, professors and administrators, who have been role models for me, have given me hope and helped me to see just how far I could go. That and going to school itself was a big ego booster for me. I remember I was terrified my first year. I'd thought there was no way I could jump into college. There was going to be too big a gap and I couldn't handle it. But, after that first semester, I figured out really quickly that I could handle it, and do it well. I started at the community college and took beginning classes like study skills, career planning, typing, developmental English (the starter classes), then eventually transferred to Western.

Other things have added to my self-esteem, have made me feel good about myself. I was asked to moderate a session of the National Women's Studies conference. That was a thrill! I got to be on television and radio. I got to lobby on behalf of women on welfare who were attending college. That was quite thrilling because my efforts resulted in a policy change, not only here in Bowling Green, but statewide.*

My motto is that people look for big organizations to change the world, but if you've got one million people, helping one million people, one-on-one, that's the greatest power there is.

When I think ahead, my husband will be a partner with me in the landscaping business. We are going to start our own business. He has the strength and muscle power and knows how to use every kind of tool and drive every kind of equipment. That is a bonus. I have the knowledge. It may turn out to be a family thing because my two oldest boys talk about moving back to the country. They love the country. They like raising things and they both feel the need to put their hands in the dirt and pick it up and hold it and smell it. It's part of them. My oldest has his computer knowledge and his communication skills now, and that could all be worked into one big family unit. My second son can do carpentry and engine work because he's going to college for that. It may or may not work out that way, but I would be very happy if we owned a large farm that had several little houses on it. It would be wonderful. Plus, I want to travel. Ignorance is not bliss and I want to understand the whole world. I want more knowledge. I want to learn for the rest of my life, and travel is one way to do that.

– Jessie (pseudonym)

---

* The problem was that legislatures had put a two-year limit on the time that women could receive benefits. But, getting a college degree takes about five years because if a woman has kids, she can't push it and do it in four years like the younger students can. So they need to go to college for five years, but with the two-year time limit on welfare, the amount of time they could draw benefits stops them half way through. After two years of being on welfare, if they wanted to stay in school, they'd have to work. The minimum amount of time was twenty hours of work plus school which meant seventy hours a week, and that didn't even include time with their kids or time for homework. It was just going to be just a straight seventy hours of work, going to school and transportation. And it was only going to get worse, because each year they were going to make them work more hours until they got up to full time.

The reason I lobbied was on behalf of the women in school. I thought they deserved a break on that twenty hours because they were trying to make themselves into people who would be good for society; they weren't trying to avoid working. They weren't "welfare queens," and they weren't "welfare moms." They were moms that got laid off from a job, or their husband got sick, or their husband had left them, or somebody died, or a parent had moved in, they knew they needed more money and they knew that the best option was to go back to school. Even if it meant, and it did, sacrificing while they were on welfare, sacrificing while they were in school. They made that decision and it's the right decision. The government decision of forced work after two years was making it impossible for anyone except the strongest women out there, and that wasn't right. In Kentucky, everyone knows we definitely need educated people.

I am happy to say the legislature has now changed the rules. They are now going to let women that are in college go to school without having to do the twenty hours. Hallelujah! I know that my activities helped change that. I was the first to bring it to the forefront at our university and to the heads of the cabinet (Kentucky legislature).

Woman's Creed

The extent to which a woman will go
doesn't depend on what
she can accomplish,
but on what she's willing
to risk –
for everyone's price is
another's loss.
A woman trades the paper
for the art upon it,
and in drawing her mark
beyond the limit,
she frees herself to color
outside the lines.

– Trish Lindsey Jaggers

Debbra

My name is Debbra Smith and I am twenty-four years old. I have two sisters: Lisa, who is fifteen years older than me, and Kelley, who is eleven years older than me. My sister Kelley took over raising me when I was an infant. Nicely put, my mom was lazy. She was older than most when she gave birth to me and I gather I wasn't quite wanted. I wasn't going to be sent away or anything, but I wasn't quite wanted. They let Kelley take care of me and, when I was almost seven, my mom got very jealous of the fact that I listened to Kelley instead of her. A conflict developed over how I should be reared, and Kelley realized she was the big sister, not the mother. So she relinquished control to my mother.

She was seventeen then and going to high school, but left school and went into the Air Force. She ended up in the Philippines. She wrote to me, kept in contact until she came back in 1991. The next year, 1992, was just the year of years. In 1992 my mom found out she had cancer, and I had a baby and got married.

I got pregnant on my sixteenth birthday, on October 26, 1991. I wasn't married then, and my boyfriend, Shawn, wanted a baby. We'd discussed it, but I didn't want a baby until I got out of school. At that time we weren't able to get married because of our age. I was 16 and he was 15 and we couldn't get married without parental consent, not in Maryland where we were living. We had been seeing each other, first as friends, then as boyfriend-girlfriend, since we were eleven and twelve years old, in junior high.

Even though I was on birth control, and he was using his nice condom, I ended up getting pregnant anyway. I think it was meant to be. I was meant to have my child. I didn't find out I was pregnant until March of 1992. I went to several doctors but, at my age, none of them listened to me. They didn't test me to find out if I was pregnant. I went to a doctor the first time because I was bleeding – bad – really, really bleeding. I thought that as bad as I was bleeding, I was probably hav-

ing a miscarriage, so I went to the school nurse. Before we even talked, I asked her, "If I tell you something, you won't tell my parents?"

Of course she promised, and being naive, I thought she would keep the promise. She set an appointment for me with a doctor, then called my mom, who met us on the way to the doctor's office. My mother was furious. We talked to the doctor and he never checked me out at all. He just told me it was a uterine infection and gave me some medicine and sent me on my way. I went to another doctor and he never checked me either. He said it was a urinary track infection, and gave me more penicillin. Another doctor told me it was a yeast infection and gave me medication for that.

This was in the November-December time period. I got pregnant October 26 and started having trouble the second week in November. I went to yet another doctor because, throughout December, I still hadn't stopped bleeding. By that time I was taking three different medications. This doctor told me, "You're fine, sweetheart, your body is just trying to get back where it should be because of everything that has been wrong with you, and it is just going to take couple of weeks to get back to normal..."

I finally stopped bleeding in January. February and March went by without a drop of blood, so my mom finally said, "You're going to get a pregnancy test." She was not angry. She was more in denial than anything. I don't think she thought it would ever turn up positive. I took a pregnancy test, and it couldn't have come up more positive, even with the many protections I had taken to make sure I wouldn't get pregnant. My heart hit the floor. Shawn was ecstatic. He was bouncing off the walls; he couldn't have been any happier.

My due date was July 15. You couldn't tell I was pregnant. The most aggravating part was that when I got pregnant, I was the smallest I had ever been. I was wearing the smallest clothes I have ever worn in my life. Mom talked to one of her friends, and they suggested I go to another obstetrician. We went to him, but I should have stayed with the first one. This second one told me my due date was from July until November – he couldn't pinpoint it. Couldn't pinpoint it within five months! I had ultrasounds, one internal and one external. He should have been able to tell, but there was not a thing I could do. He was an older, old-fashioned doctor and my parents liked him.

I was still living at home and still going to school. My parents convinced me not to get married to Shawn until after I gave birth to my daughter, Shawntay, because their insurance would cover it as long as I was not married.

Around my seventh or eighth month, I started gaining weight, and I gained it quick. I mean really, really quick. July came and went. I asked the doctor, "Don't you think we should look into this?" He said to wait a couple of weeks. August 1 came and went, and I asked the same question again. He said we could wait a couple of more weeks. August 14 came and went, and I said something again. I guess I got on his nerves because he told me to come up with a day I would like to have labor induced.

Mom had found out she had cancer before I found out I was pregnant and the doctors only gave her six months to live. Actually she didn't die until April of 1994. But, my mom's cancer was being treated with chemotherapy, and she would only have about one good week out of the month, a week when she felt the best, so I arranged to give birth the first day of that week. They finally induced labor. I was sixteen when I gave birth to Shawntay, on August 21, 1992. I had it in my mind that I had no business being a parent, that I couldn't love her like I should, that I was too young to love anybody. I'd heard it all the time, a baby giving birth to a baby, and that was obviously on my mind. I didn't know how to love; I didn't have a clue how to love. I believed that I had to earn love, and that nobody loved me unless I gave them a reason to love me. That's why I went through as much as I did, because I tried as hard as I could to do what everyone wanted. I was afraid I wouldn't know what my daughter wanted, so I figured she wouldn't love me and I was afraid I couldn't love her.

When I gave birth to Shawntay, there were complications. They gave me two epidurals and they didn't work. I felt everything. I was fully awake, completely, mentally there. I'm just plain stubborn and I insisted they let Shawn be there although they weren't going to allow it because of our age. I told them if they wouldn't let him in the hospital delivery room when I gave birth, I would give birth to my child at home, and there wasn't anything they could do about it. It made the doctor extremely angry that I wouldn't sign the permission papers, but as soon as Shawn was there, I signed them. I was very adamant that no one was going to touch me unless my man was there. Shawn doesn't like blood, yet he stood there the whole time, and he was only fifteen. He held my hand and said, "I love you, Baby." My labor lasted four hours and thirteen minutes. I gave birth to my daughter and Shawn held her. Oh, it was just amazing watching him hold her, seeing the love go through them! He asked me if I wanted to hold her and I had no interest. He handed her to the doctor and they took her into ICU. This was about 11 o'clock in the morning. At 6 o'clock in the evening, I still didn't have my baby, although I had indicated (signed a form) that she was to be breast fed, to have no bottles in her mouth. I knew she couldn't go that long without a bottle. Something was wrong. Every time I asked, they wouldn't answer, so, of course, I was imagining the total worst.

Finally, at about 7 o'clock, they brought Shawntay to me and her right arm was completely paralyzed. I realized I should have been cut, had a caesarean, because she was too big to come out, and her right arm got caught on my hip. I held onto her. She was supposed to be in the nursery, especially with her arm, but I wouldn't let her go. She was already focusing her eyes. She had nails so long I'd felt them scratch me as she came out through the birth canal. She was even holding her head up and eating a lot more than she should have. Clearly, she was a lot more mature than she ever should have been, so I know she'd been very overdue.

The doctor told me there was nothing I could do about her arm. I asked about physical therapy and he told me it was hopeless. Her nerves had all been severed and there'd be nothing we could do about it. Well, I'm stubborn, so I worked with her. I started balling her hand up with my hand and, two or three days after she was born, she started moving her finger. So we worked with her. I got her a good pediatric doctor, and he was the first doctor I had gone to that had any sense at all. (By two years old, she had 90 percent use of her arm; at six years old she had 99.7 percent.)

I named her Shawntay Amanda. I gave her her father's name. Even though we weren't married, I knew we would be. I got home from the hospital the next day after I gave birth, although I had been hemorrhaging. My mom was laying in the recliner, ill with cancer. Dad was sitting in the other recliner. I proceeded to make dinner and put my clothes away because I knew if I didn't, it wouldn't get done. I had Shawntay with me. Shawn was there because he lived with us; he was living with us when I got pregnant. I was standing at the stove and just like a man would do, a good man, he came up and put his arms around me. I went into the bathroom. I was still hemorrhaging, and it was bad, but I came back in the kitchen and finished cooking dinner. Shawn was scared to death because I was so pale. I had no color in me. He asked me what was wrong and I told him. He finally put his foot down and told me to go sit down and said he would finish dinner himself.

I stayed home and took care of Shawntay for a while, then got a full-time job, a darn good job, as a secretary-receptionist, getting paid $8.00 an hour. We were both going to high school. There was a half day program, so we would go to school for a half day. I was a sophomore then. When I was at work, Shawn stayed home and took care of Shawntay. We figured it was more beneficial to her for one of us to stay home, and he loved being with her – she was his pride and joy. He took care of her better than he's taken care of anybody in his life. We got married November 14, 1992. We had a wedding in church. The wedding party numbered 15, and we invited over 200 people to the wedding. It was an awesome wedding. The ceremony itself was as quick as could be, but the reception was one heck of a party.

I did the best I could on my job. I was supposed to be a backup secretary/receptionist. I ended up getting fired because I took on other jobs. I could do them all, so I became a threat. It was apparent that if I could do all the work by myself, the other workers must not be doing much. After I was fired, Shawn got a job, but we started to have trouble. My mom would put things in his mind, telling him I was cheating on him, that I wasn't being faithful. She said it was me that ought to be out working, that I would be paid more. As often as he heard things about me from my mom, I can understand why he started to believe it.

Shawn had begun living with us in 1990, and Mom and Dad treated him like a son they never had. Everything Shawn wanted, he got. If I requested something through Shawn, I would get it, but if I requested it myself, I wasn't really heard. It had been like that the whole time Shawn lived there. Before I got pregnant, dad caught us upstairs doing what we shouldn't have been doing, and he about blew a gasket. I was afraid to go downstairs and face my dad's temper, but he called me downstairs and Shawn went with me. My parents called me every nasty name in the book, and told me to get out of their house, so I walked out the front door and Shawn started to follow me.

My mom looked at him and said, "Honey, you don't have to leave. You're our son and you always will be."

He told her if she was kicking me out, he was leaving also. So they discussed it really quick and she said, "I guess that whore can stay too."

We stayed but things were really going down hill.

Then I got pregnant and gave birth to Shawntay. Even after I gave birth, in their eyes I was still a bad person. I didn't fit. I'm not high class. I'm not prim and proper, and I never have been. A couple of months after Shawntay was born, Shawn went to another town, about an hour away. While he was there, he cheated on me. I think the love he'd felt for me diminished because of everything Mom put into his head.

That's about the time my sister, Kelley, came up from Kentucky and took me back to Kentucky with her. She saw how bad things were for me, and realized I had no clue which way was up. She saw that I didn't know how to love my baby or how to love myself. She said I was one of the worst cases of depression she had seen. So, we loaded three kids, a crib, bags, and ourselves into a 1979 Nova and made the trip.

My daughter and Kelley's children are about the same age; her daughter Chyenne was born in April 1991, Shawntay was born August 1992 and her daughter Skyler was born in September of 1992.

Kelley worked extremely hard teaching me how to think for myself and how to tell right from wrong. It sounds really silly that I was seventeen years old then, and just learning right from wrong, but I had always just done what I was told, and didn't have to know right from wrong. Kelley taught me how to feel emotion, and she taught me how to, basically, be a person. Kelley was living in a trailer in Bowling Green with her husband at the time, and he didn't much like me, but I loved keeping her trailer spotless and raising the three babies together. She sold Avon and while she was selling, I took care of the three babies. Shawntay was eight months old, Skyler was seven months, and Chyenne about a year and half. So it was a handful, doing baby food and diapers. Lord, have mercy!

While she worked selling Avon and I worked at home, her husband at the time worked as a mechanic. I planned to stay there until I graduated. I started my senior year of high school in Bowling Green. She watched the girls while I was in school; then when I got out of school, I watched them.

I was still having emotional struggles. There were evenings when I'd lock myself in the bathroom just to get away from people, because Kelley loved me and the three girls loved me, and I wasn't sure how to handle it. Locking myself away from everybody was a way to figure out my emotions. Eventually, in February, we moved from there to a log cabin out in the country on twenty acres. It was a really old cabin that needed a lot of work, but it was gorgeous. Things were going pretty good. I changed high schools because I could bring Shawntay to school with me at the new one.

In February 1994, Dad called Kelley and requested she come back home because Mamma was fixing to die. I was very angry because I saw no sense in making Kelley go through it when I could have done it for her. There was a high school there and I could have transferred. I'd taken care of my mother while she went through the suffering and the pain before. Later, I found out it was Kelley who said I couldn't go up there. She was the one who put her foot down trying to protect me. We were both trying to protect each other.

She went up there, and I was stuck down in Kentucky, out in the country, with her husband. I kept going to school. When spring break came, Dad sent me a bus ticket to go home, with Shawntay, to spend some time with Mom before she passed away. I had no interest in seeing Mom, but Kelley needed the break. Mom was an evil lady, especially then. I know a lot had to do with the medicine, but she was evil. I went up there and tried to help Kelley. The first day I was there, we explained to Mom that I would take care of her the next morning and let Kelley sleep – she needed rest – but, when Mom woke up, she started screaming for Kelley. I told her Kelley needed a break; I would take care of her. She refused my help with breakfast, with taking her to the bathroom. She threw a fit, just like a child. She refused all help unless Kelley did it. She tried to make me feel bad, and the whole week went like that, but I won. Kelley got a break and that's what she needed.

We could tell my mom's chair was her death bed. We could tell she was fixing to die. She said, "I've got some last requests." I said, "All right." As far as she was concerned, I wasn't even her daughter then, but anybody that's got a heart says "yes" when someone makes a last request. She said, "I want to make sure that you play a couple of songs at my funeral."

I said, "Okay, what songs?"

She looked at me and said, "I want 'One' by Metallica played, and I want 'We're Not Going to Take It' by Twisted Sister played."

They were Shawn's songs. He listened to that type of music. Metallica meant something to her because it was Shawn's favorite band. Her second request was to let Shawn know immediately when she died. Her last request was that Shawn would be at the funeral. I told her I couldn't promise that. If he didn't want to be there, I couldn't make him be there.

She said it didn't matter, she wanted him at her funeral. I told her I would do the best I could. He either would want to come or he wouldn't. She looked at me, then grabbed me by the scruff of my neck, pulled me down to her face, and said, "You don't seem to understand. I don't care if you're there or not. I want Shawn at my funeral."

I pushed away, looked at her, and said "I'll do the best I can. As far as I'm concerned, you can burn in hell."

And I walked away. She'd broken the final straw. There was a lot of things she did, but that was it. Still, I kept my promises. I went back to school after spring break, and she died about a week later. I tried my best to play those songs at the funeral, but that was not about to happen. However, I did play them the day of the funeral, and Shawn was at the funeral. I was there because Shawn wouldn't have gone if I didn't go. I went for him, and for Dad, and for Kelley – for moral support. I did the right thing.

We all came back, and I graduated from high school in May. Then one day, when Kelley wasn't around, her husband looked at me and said, "I really don't want you here."

I had a 1986 Pontiac Sunbird. It is an itty-bitty little car, but I packed it with all my stuff and left because, as far as I was concerned, if I wasn't welcome, I didn't need to be there. Kelley didn't know anything about it, and I left before she came back. This was in late spring.

I drove around for quite a few nights. I had a lot of friends then, but they were my age so none of them had a place of their own. I slept in the car that first night. I slept in that car for quite a few nights.

When I started sleeping in the car, I'd take the car down to Boat Landing Dock, on Boat Landing Road off Barren River in Bowling Green. I'd let Tay sleep and I would meditate. I wasn't about to go to sleep with her in the car. I didn't know the area that well, and I didn't know who went down there, so I was afraid to lose consciousness and let her get hurt. We lived in the car from May until late August of 1994. We lived in the car, and I wrote bad checks to get food and diapers for Tay and cigarettes, gas, and soft drinks for me. Nothing else. I knew at that time that, if I wrote bad checks, eventually I would have to pay them back. I was thrifty.

I tried to get jobs, but I couldn't get a job without a baby sitter, and I couldn't get a baby sitter without a job. It was a circle. I had no income and I couldn't get one. I called Social Services to get a baby sitter or help with baby sitting, but there was a couple of months wait. I tried to get someplace to live, a Section 8 place, something like that, but it was six months to a year wait unless it was an emergency.

I said, "Well, it's an emergency; I'm living in my car."

They asked me if I had proof of residence. Did I have proof I had been kicked out? I said I could get the proof I had been kicked out.

The social worker said, "Well, then it's only about a three-month wait."

I did have an opportunity to stay in a shelter, but I would rather be in my car with my baby than with a bunch of folks I didn't know. My car door locked and I knew we were safe; if someone tried to break in my car, I could guarantee I'd wake up. I kept my keys in the ignition in case something happened.

A typical day was going to the park early in the morning, before everybody woke up. It was summer, and I'd sit there and let Shawntay play at the park. Living and sleeping in the car was an adventure to her. Often we slept in the park. They're supposed to run people off, and if they caught me there they ran me off. They'd ask me what I was doing there, and I'd come up with some excuse because, if I'd told them I was sleeping in the car, they'd take me to a shelter or they'd try to take my baby away.

We'd sleep in the park, at the dock, wherever nobody else was. We used truck stop showers. Shawntay would get a bath every day. She was easy to bathe because I would take her to a bathroom, any filling station bathroom or restaurant bathroom, put her in a sink and bathe her. I would take a shower once or twice a week, depending if I was lucky or not. I wouldn't let myself get to the point that I smelled though. If I started stinking, it was about time to find something. I'd go into the same bathroom where I gave her a bath, shave under my arms, brush my teeth, brush my hair, grab a roll of toilet paper, and be on my way. We also used creeks for bathing. They did it a hundred years ago, and it's still good enough.

I had a couple of friends that I would go see, but I didn't like using my friends. Whenever I went to see them, they would try to get me to go to sleep for an hour, or they would try to get me to eat. I felt guilty because they were trying to help me, and I had nothing for them in return. I felt like I was using them, so I didn't go see them unless I needed sleep so bad I didn't have a choice. I did have one real good friend whose mamma didn't know I didn't have a home. When she wasn't home, he'd let me take a shower there. He made food for me and made me take three or four hour naps. He'd watch Shawntay for me.

By that time, I lived mostly on crackers because I could go into a restaurant and crackers were free. Shawntay was easy to feed. Before I lived in the car, I had bounced around, working at a number of fast food places like Hardys and McDonald's. I had friends there who gave me food for Shawntay. They would have given me food for myself if I told them I needed it, but my concern was for Shawntay. I didn't want to waste an opportunity. I wanted to be able to go back there two or three times and get food for her, instead of just food for both her and me just one time.

If worse came to worst, I would go to Minit Mart, write a check, and get her food. It took an awful long time for anybody to stop accepting my checks. It took four or five months for them to figure out I was writing bad checks. At that point in time, I had written about a thousand dollars in bad checks.

When Kelley found out what happened, she made me promise to let her know I was okay, although there wasn't much she could do. She knew I was bouncing checks and didn't have a home, but she didn't know I was living in the car. I wasn't about to tell her because I knew she would want me to move back in with her, and I didn't want to put her in that position. She was doing the best she could at that time.

Toward the end of the summer, I moved in with one of my older friends who had a shack, literally a shack, off Russellville Road. Shawntay and I ended up staying with him and his roommates for a little while because it was a guaranteed roof over our head, a guaranteed shower, and a guaranteed bathroom. It turned out it wasn't the best place to be because it was a house full of guys who were full of hormones, and they expected me to be available. For a roof over my baby's head, I gave in.

I also wrote checks for them to have alcohol and wrote checks for them to eat. I was now paying for a place to stay by writing bad checks, and paying in other ways, but I had a place for my baby and that was all that mattered to me.

One day I called Kelley and she told me Shawn was trying reach me and was extremely upset I wasn't living with Kelley. She let him know I didn't really have a place to stay, so he told Kelley to have me call him, to give him a chance to help because it was his baby too. By that time, I had divorced Shawn. I finally called him, and he wanted to come for Shawntay. When I said, "No," he said he would come for both of us. I figured I had no choice.

He came and took us both back to Maryland that weekend. I gave him permission to provide for Shawntay until I got my feet on the ground. He invited me to stay with him, but I knew not only was he was involved with another woman, but he was staying with John, a friend of his, at the house that belonged to the mother of John's girlfriend. It was only a two-bedroom house, and there were already too many people staying there. I had a friend, Amy, pick me up and I moved in with her, where I stayed until October. Amy and I had been real close since high school, and she was the best person I could have come across. She worked with me to teach me how to eat again, teach my stomach how to eat again, because I couldn't eat. She tried to get me to eat a full-fledged meal the first night I was there, which would be the first full-fledged meal I had since May, and of course my stomach couldn't handle it. She weaned me from crackers, to soup, to harder food. I had taught my body not to be hungry. I stayed with her and her brother for a while, then I went out and got a job.

Amy's brother really couldn't afford for me to stay there, so I called Dad to see if I could stay with him for about a week. I told him I had a job and asked if could stay there until I could save up enough money to get my own place.

He said, "No."

I said, "Okay, fine."

Amy's brother Steve never said for me to leave, but I didn't feel welcome so I left and walked down Highway 355 to Rockville, Maryland, where my old friends still hung out. The woods there were safe, so I'd have a place to sleep, and I'd be okay. But Steve was feeling guilty, so he came and took me back to their apartment.

My baby was with Shawn. I made sure she had a roof over her head and good food. I stayed with Amy and Steve for a while. I got another checking account, and I started writing more bad checks. It was the same thing: I didn't want to use my friends so I said, "I will give you food for a week if you give me a place to live for a week." That's what we did. By that time I had written two or three thousand dollars' worth of bad checks, combined. That's a lot of money, and I knew it.

I had weekend visitation with Shawntay. Shawn kept her during the week so I could keep a good job. I knew I was already in a hole and that I couldn't get out.

I thought, "Who cares anymore, really?" Tay had a good place to live and nobody cared where I was.

When Shawntay's second birthday came around, I spent close to a thousand dollars on her birthday party. I bounced checks, and I didn't care. I was so far in debt that a thousand dollars more wasn't going to hurt. I had a helium tank for her balloons, and we invited friends and we had food. We ended up having an adult party for a child. She made out like a bandit. If she'd been a couple years older, she would have loved it, but, to a two-year-old, it didn't mean a thing. Somehow, my dad found out about my bad checks in September, and he "went off." I had a job at an ice cream parlor then, and I basically told him to mind his own business.

Kelley and I were writing back and forth at that time. She was happy I had a place to stay, but nobody was happy that Shawntay was with Shawn. Everybody thought Shawn would run with Shawntay, but I knew Shawn. I knew Shawn would never run with her. For a while, everything was peachy-keen. It was a party. It was the teen-ager's life that I had been looking for and couldn't have as a child. I was actually enjoying it, but it couldn't last forever.

I eventually stopped writing bad checks when they stopped accepting them. At the beginning of October, Kelley called me and told me she had kicked her husband out, and she wanted me to come back home to Kentucky. Once again, she came up to Maryland for Shawntay and me. She grabbed all my stuff, and moved us back to Kentucky. We lived together and it was the best thing in the world. It was just Kelley and me and the babies, and it was my family as far as I was concerned. We were all under one roof with nobody else involved. I would take care of the kids; she would go to work. It couldn't have been any better. It really couldn't have been. We were happy. It was the best time in my life because it was where I wanted to be: I had a home. I had love.

But, things change. I began dating a guy, a little older than I was, who seemed to be a perfect gentlemen. He had a job and was staying with us. He was helping us financially. But, he went out one night and got drunk, and he beat me. I resisted. Kelley came home and we threw him out.

Then, Kelley started dating a guy who moved in and everything was hunky-dory for a while, but it ended up being too much to have two families under one roof. He didn't want me there, so I called my oldest sister, Lisa, and asked if she would watch Shawntay for a week at her home in Memphis. My intention was for her to watch Shawntay for just one week. I knew I'd find a place to live by Friday. I didn't want to make Shawntay live on the streets again.

Lisa said "Okay."

I dropped Shawntay off. It was Easter of 1995.

That following Monday she went to the court, and said I had abandoned Shawntay. She was granted temporary custody on grounds of abandonment. She was going for full custody. Today, I know she was trying to help me, trying to help Shawntay and trying to do the best she could for both of us. But at that time I could have killed her. I learned Lisa was going to take it to the courts and make it final and Dad was paying for the court and the lawyers.

Then, out of nowhere, my ex-husband, Shawn, showed up and said, "You're not getting my child."

It turned into a custody battle, which Lisa wasn't expecting because she never expected Shawn to stand up for his rights, but he did. Shawn didn't care if I had Shawntay, but he'd be damned if Lisa would have her. Eventually it got worked out, and everybody gave me permission to have my daughter back in October. I'd gone six months without her. Within that time period, I learned that I loved my daughter. And I learned how to love her, how much she meant to me, how much I missed her. I learned an awful lot about love. I got Shawntay back two weeks before my twentieth birthday that year.

With my fathers's help I bought a trailer. It was an old trailer, a 1958, 8 foot x 20 foot trailer, but it was big enough. I started working at McDonald's but it wasn't cutting the bills, so I tried a second job, working at the Shell station. When that didn't help enough, I quit the Shell station and worked at McDonald's during the day, 40 hours a week, and the Waffle House at night, 40 hours a week. Even then, after paying the baby sitter and paying my bills, the money wasn't stretching far enough, so I got a third job. I'd work at Waffle House from nine o'clock at night until seven o'clock in the morning, then go straight from Waffle House to McDonald's and work from seven o'clock to anywhere between three and five o'clock. Waffle House was only four nights a week, and so the other nights I worked at the Shell station again. I was working, on average, 20 hours a day, every day but Saturday and Sunday. I was forking out money to the sitter, who wasn't charging me nearly as much as she could have, but I still wasn't earning enough.

I'd take Shawntay to the sitter, then pick her up when I got off work at McDonald's. I'd spend an hour or two, playing with her, watching movies with her, and then take her back to the baby sitter and go back to work. I'd sleep on Saturday, and I'd spend Sunday with Shawntay, then start the week again. But it still wasn't covering the bills.

I had to decide which were the most important bills to pay. We were out in the country, in a trailer park in the middle of nowhere, so I couldn't lose my phone in case of an emergency. I had to pay for gas for the stove, and I had to buy food. That left the electricity bill. I knew how to survive without electricity, so we did. We'd lost the electricity at the time of the blizzard in February 1996, and I never did get it turned back on. We had the gas stove and blankets galore, and we used candles for light. I heated water on the stove for dishes and baths. We also had a friend at the top of the trailer park that would let Shawntay take a bath there. We always had food, and I didn't worry about the refrigerator because it was winter, and I could put food outside to keep it cool.

I enjoyed that time of life because it was my place. It was my rules. The trailer was mine and nobody could tell me what to do. It wasn't that bad living without electricity. I worked twenty hours a day for quite some time, but I ended up having trouble with my stomach again. I realized something was really wrong when Shawntay offered me three or four M'n'Ms and I got very, very sick!

I went to the doctor and I was told it was nerves and was put on several different medications for nerves and to help me keep my food down. The doctor told me to take time off and go away for a week, away from Bowling Green. That seems like a good idea. So I did it. Shawntay and I went down to Linden, Tennessee, for a week, and we had a blast. Once again we slept in our car, but we had fun. We really did. We slept right on the side of the creek, and there was a swimming hole. During the day we would swim, eat, and have fun. Shawntay just loved it to death. We did that for a week and I came back, refreshed. When I got home, there was a note on my front door from my father. He wanted me to call immediately. By then, he'd bought a house in Bowling Green. When I called, he said he wanted to have a family meeting with my sisters and me.

We all got together and he said, "Well, I want to help you. I'd like you to move into the house with me, and I'll pay you $50 a week to live here. All I want you to do is go to school and raise your child and help out around the house."

That sounded great. Even living with him sounded great. I was fixing to say "okay" to it, when he looked at me and said, "If you choose not to, we're taking Shawntay away from you."

I was furious. I said, "You know what, I was ready to go for that. I was more than willing to move in here and do the right thing, but you're never going to hold my daughter over my head because, I guarantee you, if you ever do it again, you'll never see her."

I just went off. Too many times people had held her over my head, one way or another, even calling social services on me. When I was living in the trailer without electricity, everybody was threatening to call social services. I called them myself and told social services to investigate my trailer. They did and told me I was doing nothing wrong and that my daughter had the necessities.

We worked it out finally, and I agreed to move in with my father in June 1996. I moved in with him, went to school, and took care of my daughter. I'm in college, going after my two-year degree in paralegal studies. Then I want to earn a four-year degree in accounting, with a minor in criminology, and, eventually, a law degree. I'd like to be in criminal law and work as a defense attorney. I really enjoy debating and argumentation, and am interested in helping people. Last fall was a tough semester because I had emergency gall bladder surgery. I had to miss a lot of school. I have taken the spring 2000 semester off school, but will resume this summer, stronger and healthier.

As we have gotten older and watched our children grow – Shawntay, Chyenne, Skyler and Jeremy – Lisa, Kelley, and I have realized the importance of family. Now, my sisters and I are not just sisters, we're friends.

Shawntay and I are now living with Kelley and her girls again. She bought a good sized house that has five bedrooms and three bathrooms. It has been good for all of us. Shawntay is now eight years old and turning into a young lady. I've gotten an awful lot of compliments on how intelligent, responsible and mature she is. I love the three girls, Kelley's and mine, and I love Kelley with all my heart. We are a family.

Today I know myself: I know I'm stubborn, but I'm also straight-up, honest and blunt. Now, I like who I am.

– *Debbra Smith*

In My Attic

In my attic
there is a book
of poems
I have been meaning to
write
if only I could find the nerve.
There is a page
from a chapter
I have been meaning to
finish
if only I could find the strength.
There is a story
I have been meaning to
tell
if only I could find the will.
There is a person
I have been meaning to be
behind my attic door
if only I could find the
key.

— Trish Lindsey Jaggers

Anonymous

The author has chosen to remain anonymous because she believes the message is more important than the messenger – that the good she aspires to do is through His Grace. I'm forty-five years old. I've never been married, and I have no children. I was born and reared in northern Kentucky. My mother is in her late seventies. My father passed away fourteen years ago. I grew up in a typical suburban family in a small town in northern Kentucky. My father worked for a railroad and my mother stayed at home. My father developed rheumatoid arthritis when I was seven or eight years old. By the time he died, he had diabetes and emphysema. My entire childhood was dominated by my father's chronic illness. My mother doted on him, and our life was governed by his needs. It was a difficult adjustment for me as a child. For example, I couldn't have friends come over to the house to play because we might be too noisy and interrupt Dad.

I refer to my father's illness as the "alcoholism" in our family because I never knew what to expect when I got home from school. I didn't know if he would be feeling good and be in a good mood, or if he'd be feeling bad and be in a bad mood. Either way, our behavior had to correspond with his moods. He took an early retirement from the railroad because he couldn't physically perform the work any longer. He was an engineer, but he couldn't make it up and down the steps into the engine anymore. The arthritis progressed to the point that, when he came home at night, he'd have to literally crawl up the basement steps because his knees and his ankles would be causing him so much pain.

My mother and father both came from a very rural background, in a place where education was not valued. In a way, I was kind of the "black sheep" of the family because I absorbed books as a child. I was like a sponge. The year that I turned ten, while my friends were out in the yard playing all kinds of games, doing the kinds of things children do, I was in the house reading the *Rise and Fall of the Third Reich.*

When I was thirteen years old, I spent the summer working as a candy striper at a hospital in northern Kentucky. I wanted to work with folks that needed my care. I ended up working in the psychiatric ward, which was the first time they'd ever allowed a candy striper in that ward. I really enjoyed that experience because the folks were sick, but not the kind of sick you think about. I learned a lot about human behavior then, and about the need people have to connect to other people. Since this was not a regional or state hospital, the cases that they got were mostly people with depression, nothing that was too severe. A lot of it was brought on by loneliness and neglect from their families. I remember, we had one young man who was admitted to our hospital psyche ward every time his parents decided to take a trip around the world. They would check him in, and that's where he would stay. I'm sure that he was depressed, but mostly he just really needed to be connected to somebody.

When my dad died, folks at his funeral said that the reason he had been sick for so many years, the reason he had been virtually an invalid for the last couple of years of his life, was because God was trying to teach me compassion. I remember, even at that time, not really believing in God that much. I thought, *If that's the kind of God they worship, that isn't the kind of God I want any part of, not One Who would make someone suffer to teach them a lesson.* That was not the kind of God that I was looking for. However, my father's illness did teach me compassion. Four months after he died, my mother had a heart attack. I think, more than anything, it was brought on by stress and the fact that, as she puts it, the morning after the funeral she woke up and realized she didn't have anything to do with her life anymore. He had been her entire life; she'd lost her identity along with her husband. My mother was always a good worker in the church, and she was always the kind of person who would be there to help somebody in need. I learned a lot from her and expressed it through volunteer work.

When I graduated from high school, I worked in retail, mainly office work. To use a cliche, I was making a living, but I wasn't making a life. I still expressed my compassionate side by continuing in my volunteer work. I worked as a buddy, a friend of folks with AIDS who lived in a home in a neighboring state. I was a personal reader for a woman who was blind. I worked with different community centers, that sort of thing. I really enjoyed that. It made me feel better about myself if I was helping someone else.

I went to church with my family until I was eighteen years old. When I was eighteen, I looked at my mother one morning and said, "I don't have to go anymore, and I'm not going." I decided church and God was not for me. Although I still believed there was a God, I couldn't see that He had anything, personally, to do with my life. With the exception of going to church on Mother's Day or Christmas, I didn't go for the next eighteen years. My mother never stopped praying for me. She always wanted me to come back, nagged me like crazy to come back. I always had an excuse. Part of it was working in retail – I usually had to work on weekends – but, in truth, I didn't want anything to do with church.

I'd been involved in a couple of relationships that were not good ones. When I was twenty-four years old, I was involved with a man who was forty-eight years old. (We worked together.) He was your typical "bad boy." He'd been married a couple of times, had several illegitimate children, had a fourth grade education and worked as a truck driver. It was the kind of stupid thing you do when you're a kid, and even at twenty-four I was still a kid. I liked him because he was dangerous. But he wasn't any good and prided himself on not being any good. We were together for six years and, although it was not a really an abusive situation, he did damage to my self-esteem – more damage to my self-esteem than my physical body. I finally got out of that relationship, then was in a series of other really uncommitted, but intimate relationships. I dated a lot of guys who were musicians in bars, and I drank and spent a lot of time in bars. I drove home nights when there was no way in the world I should have been driving. It really got to the point where I was getting disgusted with myself, and felt my life was going in a direction I knew it shouldn't be going. I don't know how much I actually articulated that in my own mind. There was just that sense that things were not going well.

I was dating a guy that I'd met at work. One night he came over to my house with a friend of his. He wanted me to have sex with his friend. I said, "No." He tried to force me. There was no rape involved, but it was very frightening, and it was a turning point for me. It made me see just how low I had dropped. I asked myself how I could even associate with someone who would suggest such a thing. That night, after they left, I was sitting in my bathtub, feeling absolutely at the end of my rope. The adrenalin was still pumping through me from the fear I'd felt, and I was overcome with an incredible amount of self-loathing. I was thinking I didn't have anyplace else to go in my life. I was backed into a corner and really and truly at bottom.

I sat there and said to God, "You know, I don't even know if You're there, but I am in so much pain that I really need for You to either become real to me or just kill me, because I can't go any farther." At that very moment it all changed. I have never felt so loved and so clean in my whole life as I did then – never in my whole lifetime. When I first sat in that bathtub and prayed to God to either reach me or kill me, I was completely desperate. I had nowhere to go. My dad was dead and my mother had no idea what kind of life I was living. But, when I finished that prayer, I felt clean and so incredibly loved. I've never lost that feeling. There are times when I think back, and I can really experience it again. When I climbed into that tub, there was no amount of water that was going to wash away the dirt. Then, I felt reborn, newborn. The slate was wiped clean. At that instant, my whole life turned around. I really and truly found Christ that day in the bathtub. I was thirty-four years old.

Of course, the guy tried to come back several times, but I just flat out told him, "No." I'd had ten years of bad boys. I'd wasted my best years on men who wouldn't commit, but I really hadn't looked for men who would commit because I hadn't wanted to either. I used to say I didn't want anybody that would be there for breakfast. But, my life had turned around, and I began going to church. I knew next to nothing. I would go into the Sunday school classes and sit and the lady would be talking about things that I had no idea about. I grew up with the little, typical Bible stories, but I didn't know anything about Scripture.

Two months later I lost my job. Previously, I'd bought a house and lived in it for a couple of years, but when I got laid off, I lost my house. I really believe that part of it was timing. I don't believe God treats us like puppets and pulls our strings, but I do believe that, even though the job I had was a really good paying job, one I loved and was sorry to lose, there was a timing, an order involved. I know that God knew I would never choose to give up that good paying job. I would never choose to give up owning my own house.

After losing the job, I knew I was going to have to go back to school and get an undergraduate degree. I'd never been to college, except for taking one class in psychology when I was twenty-two years old. As painful as it was for me to lose the job and the house, it had to happen for me to make the change, to continue to grow, to continue in the direction God wanted me to go.

I moved back in with my mom which was hard for both of us, because, although she's never liked living alone, she was accustomed to it. Then, all of a sudden, there I was, back at home. I had to sell all my furniture because there was no room for it. I felt like a little twelve year old, packing my bags and going back to Mommy.

I started my college education then, going to school part time and working part time. I was able to finish in three years because I took a lot of CLEP tests (testing out of a course) and did a lot of portfolio work.

The idea to become a minister was kind of percolating around in my head. In the meantime, I'd found a full-time job and played around with that for awhile. Then, through my involvement at church, and talking with some friends who told me I could be a minister, I began to think about it. I thought, "Well, I don't have a voice like James Earl Jones. I don't look like a minister. I certainly haven't had the background that I'd think a minister would have." Of course, I've found since then that, as Henri Nouwen, a Catholic theologian, says, "The best healers are the wounded healers." The ones who have been through all that, and know where people are, don't have to guess about where people's pain is, because they've had their own pain. Nouwen was very instrumental in my spiritual life. So many people kept telling me they thought the ministry was something I could do that I started to take them seriously.

The United Methodist Church has a candidacy program. What you do is declare your intentions to want to explore the idea of being in the ministry, then they match you with a mentor who helps you to really look at your faith development, and look at whether or not you have the gifts to be a minister. I started into that program. One of the parts of the program is that you're supposed to pick a couple of people who are pastors, talk to them and find out what their experiences have been, that sort of thing. There was a woman pastor here in the area and I decided I would contact her because women in ministry are pretty rare in this conference. I went to see her and, while we were talking, I told her one of the big issues for me was finances. I'd always been a really extravagant person with my money, never saving it, blowing it the minute I got it. I didn't know how I was going to continue financially. I'd had scholarships for my undergraduate degree, but I had no idea how I was going to go to seminary, which costs about $12,000 a year. We were sitting there talking, and she was talking about a theological seminary in the state. She said, "Well, you know, they have full scholarships for Methodist students." I would have never known that if I hadn't talked to her.

I applied and I was accepted. I went to the theological seminary for three years with no tuition. In fact, the first year I was there they gave me a $100 a month stipend in addition to the tuition. I still had living expenses, but the tuition was taken care of. It was just another confirmation from God that it was the way I was supposed to go. It seemed like every time I'd run up against a brick wall, somebody would come and give me a piece of information that I needed so I could continue. When I was in seminary, I used to walk up and down the seminary halls and think to myself, "I am so lucky to be here." Now, I wake up and go about my day and just think to myself, "I love my life. I *really* love my life!"

I graduated from the seminary in 1997. I've pastored three churches so far. I am in my second year at my current church which is also located in northern Kentucky. I have found that with congregations, the fear of having a woman pastor is a whole lot worse than the reality of it. People are very tentative when they first find out that they're going to have a woman pastor, but a woman brings qualities to ministry that men don't necessarily provide. I don't like to stereotype, but while I may give up a few inches on the authority issue, I'm a lot more collaborative in my ministry style. I'm not as autocratic as a lot of men tend to be. I've had training in hospital chaplaincy, and I'm accustomed to sitting by people and listening to their problems, their stories, and being with people in the middle of their pain. I think that is another thing my father's illness prepared me for.

I still think about the people at my dad's funeral who made the comment that God made my dad suffer to teach me how to be compassionate. I think they had the spirit of it right, but the explanation of it wrong. I believe that God allowed that to be a lesson to me if I wanted to learn it, and I took the opportunity to learn from it. My theology of suffering is that God allows things to happen in our lives that God wants to bring good out of, but we have to want the good too.

It's very seldom that anybody comes to me and tells me anything that surprises me, because I've already done it. If I haven't done it, I thought about doing it. While a lot of folks who have strayed away from church, have strayed away from God in the past or may feel reluctant to talk to the traditional pastor, my door is open, and they know it is. In my preaching, I'm very candid about my failures and my shortcomings, about my own troubles with sin, and I think that makes me approachable.

There's a story that I tell, when I serve as a spiritual director on a retreat called The Walk to Emmaus. In the Bible there is a story about Jesus walking on the road to Emmaus, and this is after his crucifixion and resurrection. He meets two people on their way to Emmaus, and they're walking along very sad and very downcast because the person they thought was going to be the Messiah has been killed, and they wondered what was going to happen to them now. Jesus meets them on the road and tells them all the things the prophets have said over the years, about who the Messiah will be. He really gives them encouragement and educates them in their own faith. As they get ready to part company, the two ask Jesus to stay and have dinner with them, because it's dark and dangerous for him to go on alone. They have no idea who He is. Jesus blesses the meal and breaks the bread. The way the scripture reads, "And their eyes were opened with the breaking of the bread," and they saw who He was. Well, this Walk to Emmaus retreat is a way of taking people through kind of a mini-course in their faith history, and allowing them to be with Jesus for those seventy-two hours. Then, hopefully, in all these different encounters, they come to see Jesus face to face, and they know Him.

I act as a spiritual advisor and director on these Walks. I talk about the grace of God and how God's grace can work in our lives and change us, transform us. I use the metaphor of the caterpillar going to the butterfly. How do you take something as ordinary as ugly as a caterpillar and turn it into this remarkably glorious creature, a butterfly? I don't understand the scientific theory; I can't tell you what kind of process that is. I also don't know how God can take somebody whose life was as meaningless and corrupt as mine was and turn me into the kind of person who speaks for Him now.

I tell about a time when I was at the job that I got laid off from. There was a woman that was working with me. I was the office manager, and she was a thorn in my side. She was lazy and hard to deal with, and she made fun of one of the younger girls who worked there. So I found out I was going to have to fire her. I'd talked to her and talked to her and nothing happened, so I was told to get rid of her. Purposely, knowing the animosity I felt, I waited until the day before Thanksgiving to fire her because I knew it would ruin her holiday. That's the kind of person I was. I hurt people. That's not anything I'm proud of, but that tells people that I've done some really rotten things in my life, too. God can turn that all around. You can look at me and tell it's not theory; it's true.

When I started considering the idea of going in the ministry, my mother said to me, "I know you too well. What do you think you're doing? How in the world are you going to do that?" For a long time, that was in the back of my mind, that she was right and I was not worthy. Well, the more you get to know Christ, the more you know it doesn't have anything to do with being worthy – not a thing to do with being worthy.

When I look at the different things I had to overcome in my life, I see an isolated and painful childhood lacking normal experiences because of my father's illness. I often think I was kind of like a ghost, around the edges of the family. I can remember coming home and wanting to do the kind of things kids do, sit at the table and talk to my mom and dad, that kind of stuff, and my mother just didn't have time for me. It wasn't deliberate neglect; it was just the idea that she only had so much time. Now, she's my biggest supporter.

In the United Methodist Church, in Wesleyan tradition, we talk about God's grace being a prevenient grace, which is a preventing grace. It's the grace that God surrounds us with before we ever acknowledge that God is there, and it's not necessarily protecting grace, but a grace that really and truly kind of stalks us until we finally stop and turn around and accept it. That's called justified grace, when God justifies your life. I believe it was that prevenient grace of God that kept me as unencumbered as I was. It would have been very difficult to go back to school and seminary if I'd had a child. So there are so many ways that guardian angels were watching out for me, and I was giving them a run for their money because I was doing everything I could to thwart their protection.

Now that I'm a pastor, I have a church and a parsonage that's part of my salary package. I have a house two blocks away from the church. I even have a pension and health insurance. I went for eight years with no health insurance because I couldn't afford to pay for it myself when I was in school. Now, the idea of having health insurance is a luxury for me, especially since I've been sick and undergone eye surgery. The main thing I struggle with now is being diabetic.

I hold a Bible study class on Thursdays, at noon, and again Thursday evening. I teach a Sunday school class and a youth group. My week is filled with hospital visits and meetings with other pastors to discuss what is going on in our church. We read over the week's Scripture together and talk about sermon ideas. There are always weddings, funerals and baptisms. Sometimes I do all three of them in one day. It takes me about 20-25 hours a week to write the sermon for Sunday because of all the preparation, but my favorite thing is delivering the sermon because there are times, when I am in the pulpit, that whatever I have written on the paper gets ignored and, somehow, God seems to tell me, "Here is what you need to say." Then I just do it. It's a Zen moment.

When I was growing up in the 1960s, the church (the church in general with a big "C") was going through a time where the emphasis was on being a good person, and doing things right: obeying your parents, doing all those moral things. So, I never really learned anything about God, or about the Bible, or about Jesus. I learned how to be a good person, and that's why I think that when I got to be an adult, and began doing all kinds of volunteer work, I was trying to fuel that good person side of me. I did it because it made me feel good. Now when I do something for someone, I do it because that's what God commands me to do. What I do now is not to earn God's love, but to show God how much I love him. I don't believe there is any big, cosmic scale where you have to weigh your good points against your sins and hope the good points win out. The only thing that any of us need to do is profess our faith in Jesus Christ, then everything is taken care of. But, in any relationship, when you really love someone, you do as much as you can for them, because you want to, not because you think it's going to make them love you more. Now when I do something for someone, it's not because I hope God will notice and put a little star next to my name, it's because I'm doing it to show God how much I love what He's done for me.

People ask about my being a woman in the ministry. I've been very fortunate in having some really supportive mentors in my life. I've been lucky that there have been some women who have gone before me,who have greased the skids for me. In the United Methodist Church, each of the churches sets their own salary scale, according to their budget. The typical career track is to continue to go from church to church, making more money in a bigger church with a bigger budget each time. If I were following the career track, if that was my aim, I would be looking toward growing into another church with a higher salary. Maybe it's because I'm a woman, maybe it's because I'm in my forties, and I'm already past the mid-life stuff, but I'm more interested in God using me where my gifts can best be used. If that means putting me in a bigger church, that's fine; if it means putting me in a smaller church, that's okay too. In the end, the idea of me being obedient to God's call is the gauge for success.

I hope to have a long and successful career in the United Methodist Church.There's Scripture that says when you're faithful in small things, God will give you greater things. That may not necessarily mean number-wise, it may just mean the next church I'm in has people who have the desire to be spiritually deeper. Maybe that's bigger for me. I think that one of the reasons people have been supportive of me is they can see that my call is genuine and sincere.

A lot of people enter the ministry bringing so much personal baggage and so much woundedness that they have not resolved, that they try to work it out in the church. They end up being ministered to instead of being the minister. A friend of mine once said that the ministry is a great place to go and hide, especially if you have intimacy problems, because as a minister you're looked up to. As a minister, people treat you with a certain degree of respect you might not get in a different line of work. You can be falsely intimate in the ministry; you can act as if you care about people's problems, and you can have people really trust you and share things with you without you ever having to share with them. So the ministry can be a hiding place, if that's what you're looking for.

But the ministry can also be a place that is this strange mixture of joy and sorrow, where you can interact with people in ways that you know are on a deeper level than you ever had in any other sphere of life. When you're sitting next to somebody that's dying, it is not a time for small talk. When you're sitting next to someone who has gotten themselves into a lot of problems, because they've made bad decisions, it's not pleasant to sit there and tell them they are messing up their lives, to tell them they have to stop blaming other people and take responsibility.

The criteria for authentic ministry is being able to not only say the hard thing to people when they need to hear it for their own growth and own good, but also to be there to hear the hard things from people. That's tough. I can remember when I was working as a chaplain over at a hospital, doing volunteer work. I was sitting at the bedside of a man who was all crippled up from arthritis. He was in his sixties, in failing health, with a family which wasn't very involved. I remember walking into that room and immediately thinking about my father, and having to put that aside so that my own feeling about my father didn't get in the way of what I was doing with this person.

There are people, every single day, who remind us of somebody, whether it is someone who has loved us, or someone who has been an enemy of ours or betrayed us in the past. We run into these people, and we have to interact with them on the basis of who they are, not on some kind of preconceived notion. That's what makes ministry authentic, when you can put away all the baggage you carry around so you can be available to somebody else. A lot of ministers can't do that. I think that's the reason our culture makes fun of the stereotypes of ministers who seem overblown, egotistical and power hungry. The ministry tends to attract people like that, because they can get away with it.

Some people are comfortable talking to me about their darker side because they know I have one, too. It's not because I've done some magical self-improvement regimen to change myself; it's been strictly God Who has changed me. I think the only time we actually throw ourself on the junk pile of life is when we've not only lost faith in ourselves, but when we have come to the point that we don't have faith that anybody cares enough to pull us off the junk pile. I just don't believe that anybody has the right to be hopeless because you never know what tomorrow will bring, and you never know what resources God has for you.

I believe that everything that led up to the night in the bathtub happened for a reason. Every job that I held, no matter how much I disliked it, prepared me for this job. Every person that I met, and everything that I learned from them, prepared me for the people I know now. All my habits of loving to read and study serve me well now. None of that, no matter how mundane or distasteful, none of that was wasted. It was all to bring me to the point where I am right now. Even the things that happen now, the conflicts that I have in my church, the conflicts that I have with people in general, the disappointments that come in my life, with people I think are my supporters who end up not being that, those are all teaching me lessons. My big question in every situation, good and bad, is "Where is God in this? What is God trying to teach me in this? Is He teaching me that I need to be more humble? That I need to be more obedient? Is He teaching me that I need to remember to trust in Him? Is He trying to teach me that I'm not the hotshot that I think I am? I really believe that is necessary to be spiritually attuned to what looks like everyday life. We're not human beings who have isolated spiritual experiences. We're spiritual beings who happen to be living a human life. We don't disappear; we just die.

All the time that I was growing up, up until the time I went on my own Walk to Emmaus, my favorite Bible verse was, "For God so loved the world, that He gave His only begotten Son, that whosoever believeth in Him, should not perish but have everlasting life," which is John 3:16. But that wasn't the way I heard it. The way I heard it was, "For God so loved the world (except for you), that He gave His only begotten Son, that whosoever believeth in Him (except for you) shall have everlasting life." And I never, ever, ever heard John 3:17, which says, "For Christ did not come into the world to condemn the world, but that through Him the world might be saved." That speaks to self-esteem. Now when I hear it, I know that I'm included in it.

For years my names were "Unlovable," and "In the Way." Of course, these names weren't intentionally given to me, but they were my names just the same. Each time I was ignored or rejected, each time I was ridiculed or disregarded, I accepted that as evidence that I, indeed, was unlovable and in the way. Until I was willing to change my name, I had little to offer anyone. I was trying to hide who I was from people so that they wouldn't see me as the truly imperfect person I was. Now, instead of being "In the Way," I am "Sought Out by God." Instead of being "Unlovable," I am "God's Beloved." We are all "God's Beloved."

– *Name withheld*

A Penny, on Heads

One copper sparkle
in the dirt of poverty
catches my eye,
where dank boxes shelter lives
with lengths of wrinkled
corrugation
on the foundations
of past houses.
Clippings of forgotten years
sit warming by a barrel
of rags, paper, books –
all burning.
Standing across
the stench of trash,
where charred scraps of half-words
slow-float,
a woman watches me, her fragmented clothes safety-pinned –
chain-link fences staggering
across her breasts –
her hands withdrawn
inside a raveling, ashen wool sweater,
long past scratching,
or warmth.
Threads of unfinished sentences
hang like wet, black fibers clinging to a pen.
Hunger,
or some other form of deprivation,
weeps from the corners
of her eyes
as they ricochet
between me
and the ochre head in the dust.
I stoop to retrieve the small, cold
silhouette that places souls
in this hell to freeze,
fingering the edge
of inclination –
knowing she needs the money,
but I need the luck
more.

– Trish Lindsey Jaggers

Valerie

My name is Valerie Yonko. I was born in 1975, in Detroit, Michigan. I have nine brothers and sisters. I'm in the middle: number five. I'm Puerto Rican and East Indian, I think. I'm not sure exactly what my father was; he was really dark, almost a red color. My mother is Puerto Rican. I had two birth certificates, and didn't know which one was valid. It finally got straightened out, and I discovered I was a year older than I thought I was.

I don't know much about my father's history. He used to be in trouble with the law all the time. His family was involved with the mob. He was a gypsy. My brothers and sisters and I think his name is Yonko, but he moved everywhere, and I'm not even sure my last name is Yonko, because he often changed it. My mother doesn't talk about it. My oldest sister, Sue, had a different father and so did my older brother, Sam. Sam's father was my mother's brother-in-law. But the rest of us belonged to my father, all eight of us. Sue and Sam were his step-kids. I don't have much memory of Sue because she was about fifteen years older than I, and because she was always running away –

we never knew where she was. Sue ran away because my dad used to sell her and my oldest brother, Sam. He used to prostitute them for money, when they were little. We hardly ever saw her. She would come back every once in a while, but they would always hit her. I remember Dad always hitting her. That all happened before my father got sick. He died when I was almost seven. He died of cancer. He wouldn't go to the doctor.

Before he died, we lived in Detroit for a little while, but my dad moved us around a lot. We'd lived everywhere: in Michigan, in California, Ohio, New York. We were referred to as "the gypsies." People called us that because he schemed – scammed – for money. I remember my parents told people they could tell fortunes. My mother would tell older men their fortune. My dad would say he was

her brother, so that the men she was doing things for would think it was all right with him, and would give her money. He used to fix cars a lot. He'd go up to people and ask them if he could fix their car. My dad also used to steal cars, and I remember him stealing a Cadillac one time. He wrote hot checks. I don't know where he got any of the IDs.

He and my mom always used to fight, and once they separated. They were both alcoholics, and my father was into a lot of drugs. I remember going with him on drug deals when I was four or five. I didn't know what he was doing then; I had no idea. I was his favorite; my brothers and sisters would pick on me and he would take up for me. He did hit us, but in our household, he was the kindest person I was around. He was always good to me. Many times I was in the bed, though, when he was molesting my older sister, Sue. I'd wake up and think, *That's okay. That's what he does. That's normal.*

When he got really sick, we lived in Knoxville, Tennessee. He had cancer of the liver. He used to drink – a lot! He used to drink so much that when he didn't have money to get alcohol, he'd drink rubbing alcohol. I mean, he was in bad shape. We moved from Knoxville when he knew he had cancer, and we landed in the projects in Nashville. We moved into the projects when I was six years old because my dad couldn't work anymore. I think my mother is in her sixties now. (I'm not sure how old she is.) She was maybe forty or forty-five at that time.

My parents told us, "Don't ever let anyone know we're gypsies, and never talk to black people."

That was a big deal in our family, not to ever speak to black people. Then, when my father died, my mother started dating men in the projects, black men. Not even a week or two after my father died, my mother had a boyfriend, a black man. That's why it was significant, because all our lives they had told us, "They're bad."

She didn't like me because I saw her cheating on my father while he was sick with cancer, lying in his hospital bed She used to call me a "little reporter," because I always told everything. I hated what she was doing, and I was mad, so I told him. I was scared to death, but I told, because he treated me better than he did her. She almost killed me over that, almost strangled me.

She took me in a room with a bunch of black people and said, "Now did you see that happen?"

I said, "Yes, I did. I saw him touch your breast."

She grabbed me by my throat and carried me upstairs and tried to suffocate me. My brothers had to get her off of me.

She was on crack really bad. She got involved with crack and drugs, and would leave us alone for months. When she left us, we'd hardly ever get to eat. We didn't go to school. We didn't have clothing. We weren't trained in hygiene, manners, anything. We were all little. I've heard a lot of stories about what she used to do. She was pretty much a prostitute. I don't know if she did it for money, or because she was on drugs.

People used to break into our house. We had to learn to fight. There was a lot of sexual abuse. My older brother Sam would abuse all of us! He would make us watch pornography, and then he would make us act it out, or he would make us fight naked until we were bleeding. I mean, he was really controlling. He was about fifteen then. Maybe he behaved that way because he was the one that got sold to men or women – whoever my dad wanted to prostitute him out to, whoever wanted him – ever since he was little. Sam abused us, physically, mentally, in every way. We used to have to stand in a corner for hours, on our tip-toes. If we didn't, we would get beat up. Or he would have my brothers and sisters, all of them, line up to punch me in the stomach.

So, there was this older stepbrother and eight of us. Melissa, still at home, helped Sam. She was really physical with us. She used to hit us a lot. But that's all we knew. That's what our parents did to us. I understand it now, but then it was just abuse every day.

Sam would show us the Kool Aid packages and ask, "Which one do you want? Tropical Punch?" I knew what was going to happen.

I'd say, "I don't want either one."

He'd say, "Pick one."

I would pick one, and then he would punch me in the stomach. I already knew what was going to happen, because he would tell us to line up even if there was no reason to hit us.

He'd say, "Everybody line up and get punched in the stomach," and we would just have to do it.

I don't know why he did it. He also used to use a plastic bat. On one occasion – this is really hard for me to deal with – my brother told my little sisters to hit me with a plastic bat, until they were both hitting me as much as they could. I was bruised from head to toe, and I was so mad. Then he gave me a bat and said, "Now we've got to do it to Tony."

So we did it to Tony, another one of my brothers, and I just remember the pain in his face. I thought, *I know what you're going through, but I can't stop it. I can't help it. This is what we have to do.*

We always had to fight like that, or do whatever it was he wanted us to do. Sam was the king of the house, and he would keep us in a room. He'd separate us, take the ones he didn't really like, and put them in the back room. He would make us sit on a bed, in the summer time or after we got out of school, all day long. We couldn't get out of the bed. We didn't eat. We didn't do anything. In order for him to control us, he kept us in a bed. We weren't allowed to get up. We were too scared to get out. We could crawl across the bed, but we could not step out of the bed. If we did, it was whatever he'd decide to do – burn us or hit us with metal. Whatever he decided was what he did.

My mother came home one time, after she'd been away about a month. She came to get the welfare check and the social security from my father.

She said, "Get out of the bed." She knew what he was doing, because she wouldn't have asked me otherwise.

She said, "Go get that cup off the dresser."

I said, "I can't. I can't get out of the bed." I was crying.

She said, "Listen to me. Go over there."

I wouldn't. I didn't get up and I didn't go get the cup.

"They don't even listen to me; they listen to you," she said to Sam. "You guys make me nervous. You make me sick." Then she left. We knew we wouldn't see her again for another month or so.

The house was filthy. The rooms were just, you know, cat feces and just ... then another room with absolutely nothing, windows broken out, from where people, neighbors, threw rocks at us, or broke in. We always had to fight off everything.

We were never allowed to say we loved each other. We always had to say, "I hate you." We always had to act mad, angry. One time Sam made us hold up our arms for thirty minutes, just because he wanted to have control.

He said, "You're going to hold your arms up. If you don't, I'm going to have all the rest of them beat the shit out of you."

And if he did that, then we were in trouble. We knew we weren't going to eat. We weren't going to be able to eat. He didn't let us go to the rest room. He'd only let us go two or three times a day. If we were good we got to go three times. We couldn't take baths or showers because he said he didn't want our dirt in the tub.

Sam made us cook for him, but we had to ask permission to eat. I don't remember food being around that often. When my mother got food for us, Sam had all the good stuff, and we would get whatever was left. On Friday night, he would steal my mother's food stamps when she came home drunk with whatever man she brought home that night. She would only come when she didn't have anywhere else to get laid. He used to steal the food stamps, and then send me, with John or Tony, to the store. We'd have to go in the middle of the night, on Friday night, where all the drug dealers hung out. We were chased. People stole from us. All we did was buy candy, cakes, cookies and ice cream and bring it home. Then he would let us watch videos. That was another thing he made us do: stay up all night. We had to stay up until six in the morning, or whenever he wanted to go to bed.

Sam was bisexual. It was very confusing. He was a really sick individual. He molested us when we were younger. He molested both my brothers and my sisters. He stopped after my father died, but he expected us to do each other. He made us touch each other for his pleasure. He made me do things like that with my older brother, but I don't like to talk about that. He did it just because he wanted to watch. He wore makeup and tried to look like Boy George. He used to send us to the neighbors with letters saying his name was Nikki, and he was a girl, and he was attracted to them. This man named June Bug wrote Sam letters, telling him what he wanted to do to him, like he was a female. My brother acted like a girl.

He'd send us out to do vandalism. If he argued with the neighbor, he'd send us out that night to mess up her yard, or bust out her windows. You know, we did all his dirty work. My mother didn't do anything about it. Nothing. I think she was so messed up that she didn't even care.

I'm not sure if she was always on crack, but I know her boyfriend was, and I know from other people telling me, who used to party with my mother, that she used to buy his crack with her food stamps. She used to get a couple of thousand dollars worth of food stamps, for ten kids, and she'd trade them off and get crack.

People would say, "I didn't know she had all these kids."

That was because she was never with us. She kept us out of school, and it started becoming a problem. The truant officer came to see my mother.

He said, "You've got a big fine. You have to go to court. Your kids aren't going to school. You have to pay these fines."

She said "I can't handle them anymore. They make me nervous. They're bad."

She said that with us standing there. So, they offered Potter Children's Home, an orphanage in Bowling Green, Kentucky, to us. We all got sent there, and I was so happy. It was the first time I ever had clothing that fit. I had my own clothes, a room I shared with my sister, a shower. I loved it. I loved the freedom from my brother. Freedom from having to hide. I got attention.

The day I stepped out of the car, I thought, *This is great! I don't have to be hit anymore; I don't have to be told how awful I am anymore.*

I went there when I was nine years old, in 1984. Seven of us went: Melissa, Tony, Mary, Johanna, John, Tiffany and me. David wasn't old enough to go. Sam stayed home. My oldest sister, Sue, was long gone. So there were only my oldest brother and the baby at home, but my mother soon threw my oldest brother out. I don't know really what happened, but she threw him out, kept the baby and then took Tiffany, the next youngest, out of Potter. She kept David and Tiffany for the welfare money. That left six of us in the children's home.

Melissa was bad, but we all had bad tempers. We fought the very first day we were there. The first hour we were there, we were in two fights, with boys. We were killers! I remember those days, We were really bad. We would pick on anybody. We would say whatever we wanted to, because we didn't know any better. We thought that was how you had to live.

Potter is a Church of Christ orphanage school and home. I grew up there and it was difficult. We went to school there, learned manners, and we took "Women: How To Be a Lady" classes. It surprised me, the how-to-be-a-lady stuff I was learning there. It was hard, at first, to do as we were told. I was expelled from school for fighting, running away, doing whatever. I even hit the house parent out there, for spanking my sisters. We'd always had to protect each other, and I was not about to let the people at Potter hit my little sisters. If anyone stepped in our way, all of us would take care of whoever was in the way. That's just how we were.

They did behavioral level systems there. They'd grade us on level one to four. Four was the highest. We'd get privileges on four; on one, we didn't. I was always on one. I was always in trouble. I didn't care. I did what I wanted to do.

Then they brought in Chuck Miller as administrator, and Pam Butler as counselor, and that's when it all changed. That's when they started to talk to us.

The first day I went in Pam's office, I thought, *Who is this lady and why is she trying to tell me I can't hit anyone, telling me I can't do this or that?*

I told her right then that I didn't want to talk to her. That's how we were, just mean. We talked to people like they were dirt. But that's how we knew everything to be. That's all we knew.

When Chuck came, everybody had to go by guidelines. Previously, it was pretty much no rules. We ran away at night and went to Kroger and stole things, went to the mall, whatever. We'd wait until the house parent went to bed, then we'd get away. At that time, they had single mothers, or fathers, there as house parents. They didn't have couples. It wasn't a family. It was whoever they could get. So we all sneaked out. I think there were about fifty-five kids who lived there. It was a school as well, and sometimes we'd go upstairs and tip over the desks or mess up the classroom. It didn't matter to us what we did. We were all dysfunctional, and we were just doing what we did best.

The stealing was just fun. In the past, my brother used to make us steal things. He would take us out once in a while, and we would go downtown. He would have us steal makeup and things like that for him. Then we'd come home, give the items to him and we would get rewarded. I mean, he would like us! He'd put makeup on us or fix our hair. That was our reward, the attention. Good attention.

A lot of people came and went at Potter. They would stay and get really close to us for about six months. We would try to be good for them, but then they'd leave. It was always a temporary show. They were good people, but they didn't last very long. When Chuck came, it was a different story. I'd been in a lot of trouble at Potter by then.

He said, "You have to make a choice. You have to change or you have to go."

I left. We all did. We said, "We'll just go."

I was ten years old when I went home for six months. I was living at home with Sam, my baby sister, my youngest brother, and my mother. Then Melissa, Tony, and Mary followed a couple of days after. So we were all there again. Back at home, I got the same treatment, the same abuse, and I couldn't take it anymore. Everyone was still hitting each other. I knew I had to go back to Potter.

I thought, *I don't want to live like this.*

I realized that at Potter I had clothing and food and love, and I wanted to go back. I wanted to live a better life. Since I was little, I'd always wanted to get out of the other life. I called and asked if I could come back. Another counselor, Debbie, came and got me. Slowly all of us returned to Potter.

When we went back, Chuck Miller was still there. After Chuck, it was Roger Wood. Roger came to Potter when I was fourteen, and he and his wife Brenda created a family atmosphere. They started celebrating Christmas. Before that, holidays, like Thanksgiving and Christmas, were a chore because people who didn't even know us were sending us things. We were supposed to smile, and enjoy it and pose for a picture. I pretty much just put on a show. The holidays were celebrated in the cafeteria with whatever church came that year. We had to smile and put on big hair bows. I hated those big bows.

But, when Roger and Brenda came, it changed. They treated us like a family. Before, we used to eat in a big cafeteria where everyone had to go, but they changed that. Roger organized a family structure. There were cottages for big girls, older boys, younger boys, younger girls, but everyone had to come to the kitchen to eat or for meetings.

Roger and Brenda were wonderful. They taught us about Christmas. They stayed with us for four years, from when I was fourteen until I was eighteen. They made us want to do good because they loved us. They were good examples, wonderful examples. Roger enforced manners and taught us things. They ate with us, made us dinner, treated us like their own children. They had one child of their own, and adopted three others. So when we saw they loved children who didn't belong to them, we could believe they loved us, too. They were super!

I turned eighteen. I went to prom. I was getting to do things. I went to Warren Central, but every summer we had to go to church camp. We were still bad, but we were getting better.

Once, another dysfunctional girl who lived in Potter hit my sister, Mary, at church camp, so I hit her. They broke us up, but they didn't punish me. That was the first time I didn't get punished and told that I was bad. Russ King, our youth minister at the time, grabbed me and took me behind the canteen where we ate.

He said, "What's wrong with you?"

He didn't say, "You're going home." He didn't yell at me or ground me or tell me I was bad. He talked to me, and when he did, it changed me. I got up, and, although I'd never been able to do it before, I apologized. We had a devotional down by the creek, and I apologized to everyone about what happened. It was the first time I'd ever done anything like that and I felt good. Right then was when I thought, *I don't have to be angry. I don't have to fight. I don't have to always be on the defensive.*

I started going to Church of Christ and started living their way. Russ King was wonderful. He was super to me. When I turned eighteen, I had to move out, but they came up with a transitional living program at Potter.

Roger and Brenda said, "We don't think you're going to graduate from high school. We don't think with your temper and the way you are, you're going to make it through high school so we suggest you get your GED this summer."

I didn't go my junior year. I got my GED that summer and then, in August of 1993, I started school at Western Kentucky University. I didn't know what I was doing. No one in my family had ever been to college. My parents didn't finish high school, I know that much. I know my dad only went through sixth grade. My mother finished her junior year, and then she didn't go back. No one in my family ever went to college. I was eighteen when they put me in college. I didn't know what I had to do to get my degree; I just went with the flow. That's how it had always been.

Roger and Brenda were telling me, "You can get through. You're smart enough, and we just want the best for you."

But, they pushed me in a little too soon because, when I left high school, I lost all my school friends. I didn't know what I was getting into, and I wasn't prepared. I went for two years, but I didn't do well in school.

Also, I got into drugs when I was nineteen years old. I'd just moved out of Potter. I decided to do so on my own, to try it. I had a lot of money in the bank. I'd worked as a waitress at a local restaurant for four years. I saved every bit of my money. I used to make pretty good money, and I didn't have to buy anything at Potter. They provided everything, so I just put it in the bank. I decided to move out and ran into a lot of trouble, because I moved in with this guy, a friend of mine, and he did drugs.

I'd never really been out on my own, even though I'd drunk my first beer and smoked my first joint when I was about six years old, because it was around the house all the time. But that was when I was living at home.

Before long, I met a guy that I fell in love with, and he smoked marijuana. I got more into drugs. I wouldn't drink, but I did everything else. I thought if I didn't become an alcoholic like my mom and dad, then I wasn't an addict. But I became a drug addict. I was just doing everything to numb myself, because I started getting memories about what happened to us. It started when one of my friends got raped. She was telling me about it, and I was surprised that I understood how she felt. Then I started remembering what my brother did. I had blocked it. I tried to commit suicide; I cut my wrists.

During that time, I took in my brothers and sisters. Mary, Tony, and John, all of them. Tony got kicked out of Potter because he started using drugs. Mary left because she wanted to be out on her own. The relief house parents took Johanna home and adopted her, so she was okay. I never had to worry about her. But Mary and Tony were the ones that were having as hard a time as I was. When I was nineteen, Mary was almost eighteen, and John was five years younger than me. Sam had messed them up, too.

During this whole time, even when I was on drugs, I was working forty hours a week, waitressing. I worked, went to school full time and tried to take care of my brothers and sisters. I moved around a lot. We would get evicted from an apartment because I didn't have enough money to pay the rent, so we would get another apartment. I just wanted my brothers and sisters to never go without.

I also lived with a lot of my friends. I was in apartment after apartment. I estimate I lived in about fifteen places, sometimes with people, but mostly I rented the places. I was living in a trailer at the end. I was broke. My sister and brother were living with me; I couldn't afford to take care of them because my bills were getting bad. I had a habit to take care of and I spent all my money on drugs. I couldn't do it. I couldn't do it anymore. I didn't have anywhere to go. I didn't have money saved up. I was having a hard time. I had already failed out of school. I weighed eighty-seven pounds.

I lost everything I owned. By then, my boyfriend was sleeping with my best friend. I didn't really have anything left. I was so bad on drugs that I didn't even care enough to get out of it. I didn't care what happened. I did marijuana, cocaine, LSD. I smoked danks, that's a joint with cocaine in it or crack sprinkled in it. Then, when I couldn't afford those drugs – crank, opium, hash – I started drinking.

No one ever taught me anything about relationships. I was in relationship after relationship. One boyfriend, Michael, who smoked marijuana, and I got along really well. He as just as bad as I was. But he was also running around on me, always had other little girlfriends. During this time there were other ordeals that are too painful to even talk about. I finally left him, but it took me a year. I kept going back no matter how bad he talked to me, how much he told me he didn't want me. I didn't care. I just kept going back. I think I just needed somebody. I thought that was love, thought that was how it went.

Finally, I went to Fuller Center in Mayfield, Kentucky. It's a drug rehabilitation center. That's when I stopped drugs. I stopped for eight months. But, I got mixed up with a guy in there that was an ex-con and an alcoholic. I moved to Eddyville, Kentucky with him. He didn't want anything at first.

Butch had just gotten out of prison at Eddyville. He was older, twenty-eight or twenty-nine. He raped me and he beat me up all the time. I wasn't doing drugs or any drinking, but he was doing both. He controlled me. He used to pour sodas on me. Like when I was driving, he would pour one all over me. He wouldn't let me drive unless he needed me to take him to the bar and wait for him to drink. If I didn't, he would beat me up pretty bad.

I'd wait for him at the bar and I'd think, *Maybe I should run.*

But, I stayed. He'd leave me in the house, all day long. He'd take my car and tell me to stay home. There was no telephone. I just sat in a chair all day long with nothing to do – I mean nothing. No television, no way to get out of there. If I walked, he would see me leaving, because the driveway was about five miles long. It was way out in the country, near Eddyville. I couldn't get away. He wouldn't let me do anything, and I was scared to death. He'd told me that if I ever left, he was going to bury me under cement. He said he would kill me and kill my family. I didn't know how to get out of it because when I moved out of rehab, I left everybody. I thought I couldn't go back because I'd messed up all those relationships.

Then, one day, I had to sit at a bar waiting for him, his brother and his friend and I wondered, *What am I doing? Why this?*

I was pregnant by then, and I was so miserable. That day, he kicked me out of my car, and I didn't even know where I was, just at a bar. I walked down to a lady's house to call his sister. I didn't call the police. I called his sister and she came and got me. For two days I stayed at her house, and then I went home.

I was starting to get really sick, so I went back and told him, "I have to have my car. I have to have my car to go to the hospital because something is wrong."

He wanted the baby, so he said, "All right. Okay. I'll give you the car. You better not go anywhere else."

I said, "I'm not going anywhere else. I'm not going anywhere. I promise. I love you."

I dropped him off at work, and then I hit the road. There was a lady who had known me since I was really little. She's a Catholic lady, and she's been a good influence, too. She'd helped us when we were little, helped us get to Potter. So, when I left Butch, I went to her and she helped me get to an abuse center, a safe house, in Franklin, Tennessee. But it was too late, and I lost my baby. I lived there for a couple of months, and he was looking everywhere for me.

After I went to the shelter, I became a nursing assistant in Tennessee and did in-home care for a year or so. First I got a job by myself. Then I called a woman who ran an in-home care business because I saw her ad in the paper. She showed me training videos and sent me to different houses every week. I liked it because I was helping somebody. I was taking care of elderly people, living with them and staying with them, every day, all day. I made a thousand dollars a month doing it. I got food, phone, television – everything was provided

I left that job and came back to Bowling Green because I missed my family, and I wanted to be back home. When I first got back, I went to the Holiday Inn for a week, stayed with my brother for a couple of weeks. Then I met P. and took a job with her. I met P. in 1997. She was seventy years old or so, and she had an ad in the paper saying she would furnish board for helping her. She'd been through surgery for cancer, and was paralyzed from her waist down. She read the Bible every day, and reminded me of how I used to live. She had a good attitude.

I wanted to get back in school. I was desperate to get back in school because that was the only way I was ever going to make anything of myself. So I called Pam Butler, who was the counselor when I first went to Potter. She was living in Virginia, and I asked if I could come out there and stay.

She called Chuck Miller, who was in Chicago, and talked to him and said, "Let's pay for her to go back to school." So they paid tuition for six credit hours. I came back through the community college.

At one point during that time, I went back to Potter to live in the transitional living program again because I knew I was about to start school, and I knew, if I was taking care of P., it would be too hard to do because I was up with her all night.

I told her, "I've got to do school. I can still come on weekends, but I really want to do well in school."

When I went back to Potter that summer, I did really well, except I began doing drugs again. Amy, a girl I knew, had quit because she was pregnant again. I'd gotten really close to Amy, but she left. Again, someone left. So, I thought, *All right, I'll do drugs.*

That's what I always did when something bad happened, someone left me or I was abandoned. I know I have abandonment issues. For a couple of months no one cared what was going on with us. For a couple of months there we were just doing whatever we wanted, and no one cared. Nobody checked on us. They were pretty much just taking care of the young kids. We were adults, but we were dysfunctional and shouldn't have been left alone. But, they left us alone for a while. Then Candy came. Candy was really sexual. She drank, partied, and always said things like, "Go get me a joint."

She was supposed to be the supervisor of the transitional living program, but she was doing the same things I was doing, so I thought, *I don't need you. This is a joke.*

Then they tried to throw my brother, John, out. John had just gotten into the transitional program. He was eighteen, and he just wanted to have fun. He was going out, drinking once in a while, but he didn't do anything really wrong. He passed a drug test. I was the only one there who couldn't pass one. But, it was assumed that, since I had drug problems, automatically John had them. I was so mad.

I said, "Why are you doing this to my brother? He didn't do anything wrong."

I felt like I had to leave because the whole reason any of that drug stuff started was because I was talking to him.

They thought, *Oh! Oh! She must be getting him on drugs. He must be on drugs too.*

They threw him out, so I told on Candy. I told them about her getting on the Internet, and having sex on the Internet. I told them about how dirty she talked, that I didn't even want to go around her because of her vulgar language. I told about her smoking, taking us out to smoke cigarettes. We were adults, but to take a bunch of dysfunctional people and act like them? She was supposed to be an example, especially in Church of Christ. She was coming to God's place to work with God's children.

Well, I told them, and none of them believed me. I left. I moved out, and went back to P. I went to school full time, cared for her full time and worked thirty hours a week at Kroger. I was dead tired, but I made a 3.5 grade point average anyway. Eventually, Candy bought some alcohol for one of the girls out at Potter and the girl got a DUI. She was underage, so it finally came out, and they got proof of everything. Candy got thrown out, and everyone believed me then.

But during that time, I was smoking marijuana just to cope with taking care of P., going to school and working thirty hours a week. When they found out, they sent me to psychotherapist, a psychologist, a neurologist. They didn't want to deal with it. They didn't want to talk to me. They wanted somebody else to do it. They sent me off to all of these doctors who were putting me on lithium, Prozac, Serzone, all kinds of anti-depressants, and I was going to sleep. I slept most of the time for a month. I remember when I was leaving class one day, I couldn't even walk across the street. I was falling asleep walking across the street. I messed up in school since I wasn't going, because I was sleeping all the time. I could not get up!

So I decided to take all of the pills. I knew they weren't helping, so I was getting ready to take them all. I poured half of them in my mouth and started drinking some water and Roger walked in.

I said, "Roger, I'm getting ready to take all these pills. I can't handle it. I can't deal with it anymore."

He said, "You have to go back to Rivendale. We've got to evaluate you. Even the psychologist says you have to go back there so they can evaluate you, so they can figure out what kind of medicine you need to be on."

They were still saying that.

I said, "No, you've tried everything. Just leave me alone."

But, they put me in Rivendale. I had a hard time. I was in there for two weeks. They did EEGs, sleep deprivation EEGs. They did tests, the little "touch your nose" kind of things.

I was familiar with the routine. I have been studied. I have been in hospitals, with psychiatrists and psychologists, all my life. I was sent to Louisville once because I had anxiety attacks so bad that I would pass out, but I felt so much better after I passed out. If I got too stretched out, then I'd pass out. No one was able to tell me why I was passing out, but they figured out it was anxiety.

Anyway, after Rivendale, I switched again. I stopped doing drugs. An English teacher at the community college made a difference. When I passed his class with a "B," I knew that I could make it, that I could get through. I'd worked so hard for that grade. At one point, I thought I was just going to give up, like I had on everything else in my life, but I thought, *No, I've got to get through this.*

I used to just give up and think it wasn't going to work out for me, and I wasn't worth it, so I'd was just do drugs and fail. But, when I took his class, it really helped because he made me earn my grade, and I needed that, because I thought, *You know, I can do this.*

Now, when I think I can't do something, when I get frustrated, I think, *You can pass. You can do it. You did it before.*

That class changed my mind about everything. Now I am patient enough to wait until the end. Before I couldn't do that. Before I thought, *I already know how it's going to end up: terrible ... I'm awful ... okay, let's go do drugs.*

I continued helping P. until I strained my back and I couldn't lift her anymore. She was getting so weak. I wanted to lift her, and help her into bed, so I did a lot more than I should have. I didn't want her to hurt, so I did too much, and it finally caught up with me. I had been caring for her for two years, but I left her at the end of July 1999, because I strained my back all the way down to my leg. I couldn't walk for a week. I couldn't lift anything or bend over. She gave me three days to get out. I had no money. I'd used all my money to fix my car and for school. She gave me three days and I understood. She was in a wheel chair and didn't want to go to a nursing home. I had to leave so she could get someone else.

I didn't know what to do. I called George Peterson, an elder at our church. He had helped me through all the drug stuff. When I absolutely needed help, he would be there. When I called, he told me I could move into his house with his family. He has three children.

Now, I live in his basement and it's nice. I have a room, a bathroom, a desk, a computer, and a television. They provide. I'm part of the family and in a way that's hard to deal with because I've never had that. I just live day by day now. I'm back in church and I have been back in school for almost two years now. I'm a junior in college and have a 3.0-3.4 grade point average. I really want to do well.

Every now and then emotional problems hit me. *What am I going to remember? What's going to happen today?* But then, when I get discouraged, I remember I made it through that English class. I can do it. I realize that all I needed were parents. All I needed was somebody to love me no matter what.

I'll be twenty-five on my next birthday. For my future, I want to help any kid that I can. That's my goal, to make a difference in kid's lives, to change them when they're at the point I was. I'm going to be a social worker. I'm going to get my degree, get a job and get my master's degree. Then I'm going to get my Ph.D. I want to open a children's home, and I want to write a book. I want it so bad. I have ideas about what a children's home should be, and I think my version is pretty good. I think it would make a difference. I want to take care of our future.

– *Valerie Yonko*

Valerie has changed family members' names to protect their privacy. She has changed the names of individuals who were harmful in her life, to protect herself. She has used her own name and the true names of those individuals whose support, love, and faith have helped her through her transition.

My Turn

Wipe my tears from your eyes;
sympathy is not what I want.
What I want
is understanding,
a little compassion,
and silence
when I speak.
Words escape me, and I stammer
over you, and her, and them.
Give me room,
give me freedom to move
my will.
That's all
I ask.
Just stay,
but don't hold me.
This time I need to shake;
I need to sob;
I need to swear
and make enemies above,
friends below.
Until the anger is over,
don't hold me; let me be
full of everything
I've always been told is bad.
It's my turn
to judge
what size shoes fit my feet,
or whether I'm tough enough to run
barefoot through snow.

– Trish Lindsey Jaggers

Marti

My name is Marti Knipp. I was born in July 1945 and named Martha Rebecca after my great-aunt Martha and my grandmothers who were both named Rebecca. Years later, when I lost a baby girl, in my heart I had already named her Rebecca also. I was the fourth child of six, the first daughter of two. When I was four years old, my baby sister was born, and my mother was confined to bed for several months with a bad back. At the age of five, I was changing my baby sister's diapers. Those were the days of cloth diapers and diaper pins, so the family must have been very desperate to allow a five-year-old to do the job.

We lived in a rural neighborhood. We had a garden and all of us were required to hoe corn, pick beans, and do other chores, such as milking the cow and feeding the pony and pigs. We were rewarded with good food and the experience of learning to live off the earth when necessary, in addition to the joy of riding a pony across the field when chores were through.

At six, I experienced separation anxiety when I entered first grade at Summit Elementary School. I was so shy and insecure I cried almost every day for the entire year. Ultimately, I learned to enjoy school and became less fearful of being alone. My teacher, Mrs. Meade, a sweet and sensitive woman, seated my best friend, Regina, close to me, knowing I wouldn't cry so much if she were near. During my sixth grade year, there was a scarlet fever epidemic, and I caught it during Christmas vacation. My skin broke out in a thick rash, and my temperature shot up to 107. When I recovered and returned to school, I was a skeleton of a girl. In the seventh grade, a new school was built and my friend, Regina, was transferred there. I was lost without her, but I grew up and began dealing with life without tears. I graduated from eighth grade in 1959 and went to Boyd County High School. Regina got married when she was

a sophomore, and moved to Germany with her husband who was a soldier. I really missed her, and my life seemed very empty when she'd gone.

My father was a Baptist minister and also owned a service station. My parents were strict with us. In their church, women and girls were not allowed to cut their hair, wear makeup or wear pants. We didn't go to movies or participate in many of the school's extracurricular functions. That was difficult in the early sixties, but we survived. I learned how to style my long hair, and I would put on a little makeup when I got on the school bus in the mornings, then take it off before I got home. Dad and Mom caught me a few times before I had a chance to wash my face, and I was chastised, but that didn't stop my trying to fit in with the other girls at school.

In spite of how strict they were, and how different we felt from the crowd, we knew our parents loved us. They taught us values and taught us to respect them and each other.

My first boyfriend was Andy* whose parents held the same religious beliefs as mine. He was a very handsome boy. We were great friends, but he lived in northern Ohio, so we saw each other only when our parents would travel to visit each other's churches, maybe once a month. I was only fourteen years old when we met, and a couple of years later, when a boy in my school asked me to the prom, I wrote a long apologetic letter breaking up with Andy. He and his folks were supposed to visit the next weekend, and I just assumed he would stay at home and grieve over his loss. But that Saturday Andy's family's car rolled into the driveway, and the first one out was Andy. He said "hello" to everyone and then ignored me as if I were invisible. In a way it was a relief not to "have it out" with him in person, but, in another way, it hurt that he really didn't seem to care. I was sixteen and believed someone who was in love with me, as Andy said he was, would fight for his rights, but that just showed me I wasn't that special to him. That took some of the wind out of my sails.

After that, I became engaged to Carl. Although I was only sixteen, my parents seemed willing to let me get married. Mom had married Dad two weeks before she was fifteen. I believed they were worried I might get into trouble and cause a scandal, and it would be safer to marry me off as soon as possible. Carl went into the Air Force because he couldn't find a decent job, and we wrote to each other for a year or so before we grew apart. He stopped writing suddenly, and later his sister told me he was dating someone else. I returned his engagement ring though I was heartbroken. I was much too young to be engaged, but rejection was hard to take at that age. I wondered if that was how Andy felt when I rejected him.

The summer before I was a junior in high school, I found a lump in my breast. Mom took me to the doctor and there were two marble-sized lumps which the doctor surgically removed in his office. He sent them to the lab and found they were benign. That was a traumatic and physically painful experience for the insecure young girl I was then. The surgery was in August, and I was too ill to start back to school, so I dropped out for a year. My parents agreed with my decision, and I spent the next year keeping house for them. In the fall, I went back to school, but missed another three weeks when I had an emergency appendectomy.

In 1964, I finally graduated tenth in my class of 250. I wanted to go to college then, but my parents did not have the money. I had sent my application to Morehead State University and been accepted, but I put it away and went job hunting instead. I went to work at Ashland Oil and worked there for four years as secretary to the personnel administrator. The first thing I did when I got my first paycheck was buy some great looking work clothes. I went to several expensive stores I'd never shopped in before, and opened charge accounts which seemed to grow all by themselves. It was years before I finally paid it all off, and I have been terrified of debt ever since.

I met Danny when I was 19. He had just graduated from Rowan County High School in Morehead, Kentucky, and had come to Ashland to stay with his cousins and work at

McDonald's. We became friends and a year or so later became engaged. We broke up a couple of times, and Danny moved on to Mansfield, Ohio where he worked at a steel mill. He was soon drafted into the Army, and we wrote to each other while he was in basic training at Fort Knox. We were married after he completed his basic training, six days before I turned 21. Danny and I took a short honeymoon trip to Michigan.

The Vietnam War was going on and Danny agreed to stay in the Army for an extra year because the Army promised him he would not have to go to Vietnam if he signed up for a third year. We spent only a few days together before he was sent to Aberdeen, Maryland for training. My first train trip and my first airline flight were to Washington, DC to visit Danny on the weekends. Three months after our wedding, he was sent to Korea for 13 months. I continued working at Ashland Oil and moved in with my brother and his wife in Russell, Kentucky, just a few miles from my parents' home. I wrote letters to my husband every night, and prayed for the longest year of my life to pass.

While Danny was in Korea, I became interested in finding a religion I could identify with. My sister-in-law, with whom I lived then, was from California and was a member of the Church of Jesus Christ of Latter Day Saints. I didn't know much about the church, but soon learned it was the church I'd been searching for. I joined the Ashland Branch of the LDS Church in February 1967. My parents and most of my family and friends were disappointed with my decision. Danny was not happy about it either, but I had to follow my own feelings. I was, and still am, happy with the church, though many of my family and friends disagree with my beliefs.

John Stuart Mill taught that "individuality is one of the basic elements of well-being," and that "unless a person is free to follow his own interests, to develop his own lifestyle, and to act spontaneously when and however he chooses – insofar as his actions do not harm others or restrict their individuality – a person is not genuinely free." Though it bothered me that my family and friends were unhappy with my choice of religion, once I became a member, I found that I just couldn't live with myself if I abandoned my faith. It's been difficult at times these past 33 years, but I've never regretted that I found the church.

The bishop advised me years ago that the church did not believe in breaking up marriages, and that I should not alienate my husband to become active in the church. I was grateful for that advice, because it would be hard to leave Danny for any reason. I sometimes worried that not being able to attend meetings would cause me to possibly stray from the teachings of the gospel, but sometimes it's easier to just try to make everyone else happy, and wait for your own happiness to come later. I've never liked arguing about anything, and to argue about my religion would tarnish the beauty of it. My husband attends church with his father every Sunday. Sometimes I take my mother to her church, but most Sundays I stay at home. Life is too short to spend it fighting about how to live it. I defined my feelings in a journal:

> When a person reaches a milestone, she begins working toward another. The mile between the two stones sometimes seems long and sometimes it seems you're there before you know it! What makes the difference is your attitude as you travel down the path of your life.Those you associate with can make the journey more pleasant or more difficult. Sometimes you carry them with you, sometimes you leave them behind. Sometimes they drift away into a different path – one you aren't comfortable following and so you sadly wave goodbye and continue. Sometimes you love them so much you attempt to go with them only to find you've been led away into a way you'd rather not travel, and by then you're so attached by obligations and loyalties you begin to lose sight of where you were headed and why. What then?

When Danny came back to the states from Korea, I left Ashland Oil, and we moved to Colorado where he was stationed for the next 18 months. In Colorado Springs, we lived in a small upstairs apartment, and I worked for an interior decorator as a bookkeeper. The beauty of the Rockies was endlessly fascinating, but it seemed a long 18 months until Danny was discharged and we were free to go wherever we wished. When that time came, we invested in our first new car, a 1969 Chevrolet, and headed east toward home.

In May 1969, my parents moved to Chicago. Danny and I decided to see what the big city was like. He worked for my dad, and I found a job as a bookkeeper at a poultry factory. We lasted the entire summer there before we decided Chicago was not our kind of town. We had a small apartment in a suburb of Chicago, and one evening as I was driving to the fiberglass plant to pick up Danny, I was followed by two members of a motorcycle gang. They were dressed in the traditional sleeveless leather vests with skulls and crossbones, had long shaggy hair and beards and smiled menacingly. On a country road, they caught up with me and rode very close to my car, one on either side of me, following me for several miles. I was so frightened that by the time I turned into the driveway of the plant, I was shaking life a leaf. I was afraid to get out of the car because I didn't know the two gang members had gone on by when I turned off. I sat and blew the horn until Danny and my dad came running out to see what the problem was. The remainder of the summer I spent looking over my shoulder, afraid I would see those guys again. By the end of the summer we had decided to move back to Kentucky where we belonged.

We moved to Morehead, where his folks lived, and Danny started college at Morehead State University in September 1969. I got a job as a clerk at Commercial Credit, and worked there for a year, and then was hired by the university to work for the dean of students. I stayed with the dean's office until Danny graduated and accepted a teaching job in Fremont, Ohio, just south of Toledo. We moved north again, and I found my first legal secretarial job with an attorney. He took me to court with him and showed me firsthand how the legal system works. I was fascinated by the machinations of a simple trial, and determined one day to find out more about why the American judicial system is so complicated. But first I wanted to start our family. We'd never tried to prevent pregnancy, but somehow I'd never been able to get pregnant. The Army doctors said maybe we were just trying too hard and should settle down and forget about it.

We rented a little house, but the winters were harsh in northern Ohio, and we were both homesick. After a year and a half, we returned to Kentucky. We settled in Ashland, and kept trying to have a baby. In the meantime, we took in foster kids and loved them as our own, only to have them taken away after a few months. Our first foster child was Sandy.* She was a beautiful two-year old with curly black hair, who had been cruelly abused. She'd had both legs broken, at separate times, and a head injury that left her with brain damage, so that she was more like a two-month old than two years. She could not sit alone or turn over in bed, and most of her food was given through a bottle because she didn't know how to chew solid food. She cried a lot and slept only an hour or so at a time. I spent most of my time holding her, rocking her, trying to reassure her that no one would hurt her again as long as Danny and I could protect her.

Three months after Sandy came to live with us, I became pregnant. It was an ectopic pregnancy. The doctor who performed the surgery said I had waited too long after the bleeding started to get to the hospital, and the tube had ruptured. He removed the tube and ovary, and afterwards we just assumed I would never be able to get pregnant again. It was so painful to lose my baby. The social worker had come the day I went into the hospital and taken Sandy to another foster home. We never knew what became of her after that.

A few months later, the social worker called about a newborn who needed a home immediately. Though I hadn't fully recovered from the emotional loss of both my baby and

Sandy, I could not turn down the opportunity for another child. Brent was tiny, only five days old. I'd sit and hold him in the rocking chair, falling more and more deeply in love each hour. He was so perfect, so beautiful, such a balm for my bruised heart. We applied to adopt Brent after three months, but the social worker said we probably wouldn't be considered because there were other families who had been on the list longer than we had. We argued that we had taken care of him from birth and he knew us as parents, that they should be finding suitable parents for babies, not babies for parents. We took in other foster children while we waited.

We were not rich, but we knew that wealth was not a requirement for adopting a child, so we wrote to the State Department for Human Resources and also to our congressman, Carl Perkins, asking for any help or advice they could give us. We got letters from both and a call from the social worker in the same week. The adoption would proceed.

The papers were signed, and we left the courthouse with our son tightly in our arms and forever in our hearts. We celebrated with ice cream, then took him home. Brent was always a sweet and loving child, but we worried about his reaction to being adopted as he grew old enough to understand what it meant. We always knew we'd tell him one day. He was four years old when I became pregnant again. As my belly began to protrude, I explained to him that his little brother or sister was growing in there.

He asked, "Did I make your tummy big, too, Mommy?"

I said, "No, Sweetie, you didn't grow in my tummy. Another lady let your grow in hers and then she gave you to us because we loved you so much."

He thought for a bit, then said, "I'm glad she gave me to you, Mommy." Brent is now twenty-four years old, and he has never been anything but our real son to us.

Our son Joseph was born by caesarean-section after twelve hours of unproductive labor. He was a sickly baby, born with chemical pneumonia. He was in the ICU nursery for three days before I was allowed to see him and hold him to my breast. He'd been tube and bottle fed, and had no interest in nursing, but he looked into my eyes and seemed to know who it was who held him and wiped her own tears from his tiny face. He soon recovered from his traumatic birth experience, and became a beautiful, intelligent little boy.

Our third son, David, was born also by caesarean-section, and by that time I was over thirty-seven. During my fifth month, I'd had an episode of fainting and some spotting, and the doctor found that the placenta had broken away from the wall of the uterus and was laying across the birth canal. The ultrasound had shown that we were having another little boy, and we prayed he would be okay after the ordeal with the placenta. I went into the hospital the night before his birth as scheduled. Around midnight, the nurse came in and gave me a shot to help me sleep. I picked up the novel I'd brought. The next I knew, the lights were on and there were the orderlies ready to wheel me to delivery.

I was able to remain awake for the procedure. In what seemed like minutes, I heard this small human protest, just a squeal, and the nurses and doctors present began smiling. A tiny little miracle was soon laid on my chest and he seemed to look right into my eyes. He blinked in the bright light and turned his mouth toward my face as if to kiss my cheek. His head was covered with dark hair still damp from his ordeal, and his hands seemed to be reaching for some elusive reality. As I put my finger into his tiny palm, he closed his own wrinkled fingers tightly around it as though he feared he might float away if he let go.

I had gone back to work at Ashland Oil when Brent was around two and my mother helped by keeping him during the day. She continued to help me when my other children were born. Although I longed to be with my little ones, we needed my income to help us get by. Teachers in Kentucky were paid so little that, unless the spouse worked, they easily qualified for food stamps. Danny was working on his principalship by going to evening classes in Morehead, and working weekends for extra cash doing painting and roofing jobs.

157

When David was eight months old, my mother's old back problems returned and she was unable to lift him onto her lap. I was unwilling to trust anyone else with my children, so Danny and I decided we could live on his income if we were careful. I would rather be a family without money, than a poor parent. I stayed home with the boys for the next eight years. Then, at the age of forty, I was pregnant again.

It was wonderful to think we would have at least one more child, hopefully a girl this time. I woke up one morning and found I was bleeding. Danny had already left for school, and I didn't want to alarm him, so my mother took me to the emergency room. I told the lady at the desk I might be having a miscarriage. She rushed me into the emergency section and put me to bed. After being in the emergency room for several hours, the doctor told me he thought it was another ectopic pregnancy, and he wanted to do surgery before it ruptured as the first one had done. I prayed they were wrong and we could be blessed with just one more child. The doctor came in and sat on the bed, wiped my tears and said, "You're forty years old. You should not be having a baby."

I was angry at that statement and lashed back, "Well, somebody forgot to tell God!"

The nurse came in to check my vital signs and to do an electrocardiogram in preparation for the surgery. She said I needed to settle down and stop crying for her to get an accurate reading on my heart rate. I told her she needn't waste her time, because my heart was already broken.

The surgery was over soon, and I was given some kind of pain medication that caused me to hallucinate: *I was walking on a beach, near the waves, with my baby wrapped in a pink blanket in my arms. As I watched, the baby with its blanket was lifted gently from my arms and floated into the sky. I saw her become smaller and smaller, then disappear to become a twinkling star. I felt then that I had to let her go and that she'd wait for me.*

When Joey was seven and David was five, they wanted to take karate classes. I joined the club with them. It was hard work, but in two years I lost 30 pounds and, at forty-three years of age, I earned my first degree black belt in Kung Fu. Two years later, I earned my second degree belt. I taught karate at the YWCA in Ashland for eight years, and learned as much as I taught. It was good for me and the kids, though Danny did not seem to wholly approve of my choice of physical fitness exercise. He didn't consider it a feminine sport. At first, my parents seemed proud of me, but later they thought I spent too much time working out, running and teaching classes.

I took a yoga class at the YMCA and later became a vegetarian. The instructor was a vegetarian who challenged us to try to avoid meat. I had no problem giving up meat. I didn't try to convince my family to give up meat, and eventually they learned that I would stick to my vow, although they told me I could not "live by bread alone," and that "meat was made for the body." I'm happy to live without it. I believe I'm healthier.

My father died of cancer in 1990. He had been diagnosed a year and a half before, and was taking chemotherapy treatments. I spent most of my time during those 18 months with him. Dad and I had long ago silently agreed not to discuss our religious differences, and we had become very close. He knew I would not back down from my own beliefs, and seemed content that I was living a decent life.

During his illness, I would see Dad each evening and massage his feet. The chemotherapy he was taking was causing his nails to become very thin and brittle and his skin to lose some of its elasticity. I would massage lotion into his hands and feet and then use a vibrator to stimulate the circulation. It seemed to make him feel better, and he said he always slept better after I had "worked on his feet."

A couple of weeks before Dad died, I was sleeping on the couch in their family room, and my brother Bob woke me and said, "Dad wants to talk to you." I went into his room and sat down on the side of his hospital bed. I put my arm around him and he quietly asked me, "Do you still believe in that church you joined all those years ago?"

I loved him so much right then, and had no desire to hurt him, but I could not lie to him, so I told him, "Yes, Daddy, I still believe in that church."

He said, "I just wanted to know. It's okay. You'll do the right thing, I know you will." Then he turned his head and fell peacefully to sleep.

In the days that followed, hospice personnel were constantly at the house and they kept an IV going to keep Dad comfortable. His colon cancer had progressed to the point he was unable to eat and every day it seemed a little of his will to live was gone. I had been in this situation for so long, I was becoming dazed. One day I got in my van and drove to the cemetery. I sat there in my vehicle and knew I needed to let go. I began to cry and cried until it seemed there were no tears left, then I went home and cleaned myself up and went back to sit with Dad. My mother cried a lot, too. She would be losing her companion of fifty-two years. She was not a healthy person, and I worried about her as well.

Dad passed away quietly in the afternoon on Sunday before Labor Day. I tried to remain calm for Mom and the others, relying on the meditation training I'd learned in karate and yoga. It worked well, so well that once the funeral was over, I could barely recall the events of those three days. I couldn't remember who was there, what sermons were preached, the trip to the cemetery, or what I'd worn. I stayed several nights with Mom after the funeral was over. She began to withdraw and became so depressed she wouldn't eat. She mostly locked herself away in a bedroom at the opposite end of the house from where she'd shared a room with Dad. She seemed to shrink a little every day, as though she were trying to disappear from the world of grief. I found that the more time I spent with her, the more I became depressed as well. Eventually, she collapsed and I called an ambulance to take her to the hospital. She was diagnosed as clinically depressed. She ultimately published a beautiful story about Dad called "Ambassador for Jesus."

I was having my own difficulty with grief. Many times I could feel Dad's presence and hear him ask that question in his frail voice, "Do you still believe . . .?"

And I would have to answer, "I'd never want to hurt you, Dad, but yes, I do still believe."

I spent more time alone. It was September and the boys were in school, Danny was back to teaching, my mother was doing well, but I was feeling the need to escape the grief. Every morning I would take the boys to school, then go to the cemetery and sit by the grave of my father, alone, lost, wondering where to go from there. I read, contemplated, worried about Mom, worried that my children would sense my withdrawal from life. I jogged five miles at a time. It seemed I wasn't getting anywhere. Something had to change, and Danny knew it as well. He urged me to go back to work. I was hired by a law firm.

It was June, three years after my dad's death, and I was getting ready to go to the YWCA to teach my karate class when the phone rang and my mother said, "Johnny is having chest pains. Can you come up right away?"

Johnny, my oldest brother, was overweight and not in very good health. His wife and two youngest children had gone to Michigan to visit relatives, and he was alone. I ran all the way up the hill and found John sitting on the front steps of his mobile home, sweating, and breathing with difficulty. His face was pale and he was having trouble talking.

I ran to the service station next door to call an ambulance. By the time the ambulance arrived, John was clutching his chest and practically collapsing with pain. The paramedics examined him, put in an IV and rushed him to the hospital. John was taken to ICU, and Mom and I waited. We heard an announcement on the intercom, "code blue," and we heard the sound of running feet. Shortly, a nurse came out and said, "We are doing everything we can for him."

After a half hour or so, two doctors came in and sat down with us. They told us John had an aneurysm near his heart and had died while they were talking with him about surgery.

We went through another funeral, and it was almost a repeat of the three years before. The grief and numbness, and having to help my mother was so like the days when Dad had died. By the time the funeral was over, I was certain my mother would have another breakdown. She said she couldn't stand the hour of three o'clock anymore because that was when John always came by to visit her. Finally, Mom decided she wanted to sell her place and move away.

When I got back into the swing of working and keeping house and rearing children, I realized that, while I had learned a lot of lessons in life, my scholastic education had been sadly neglected. Even then, it took me seven years to decide to do something about it. In the fall of 1997, I started taking classes at Ashland Community College to earn my paralegal degree. The first semester I took 12 hours, and it was grueling. I had been away from school so long, I'd forgotten how to study, and found I could read the assignments and sit through classes, but not retain much of what I was there to learn. I worked hard, though, and finally finished the semester with two As and two Bs.

During that first semester, at Thanksgiving break, my sister and I were jogging with her two miniature schnauzers, when suddenly one of the pups decided to change course and I tripped over his leash. I fell to the ground and heard a profound snap. It was the fibula in my left leg. As I sat on the ground with the cold breeze blowing my hair into my face, I thought I was going to vomit; the pain was so intense. My sister ran about half a mile to get the car. I was taken to the hospital and came away with a cast and a heavy heart, wondering how I could manage to work at the law firm and finish the semester on crutches.

The next morning I found I had also injured my shoulder and crutches were not an option. The pain from my leg and shoulder kept me awake for three nights before I was able to see the orthopedist, who replaced the heavy cast with a soft bandage and a cumbersome boot which I would wear for the next two months. A friend donated a wheelchair and once I learned to maneuver it, I was able to accomplish much more than I'd thought.

The first week or so, my husband drove me to school, and one or the other of my sons would push my chair from class to class, then wait in the student lounge area until my classes were over. Once I recovered from my shoulder pain, I was able to drive myself to class, park the car, remove the wheelchair from the back seat, and take myself to classes. I took a lap desk with me, hooked my backpack over the wheelchair arms, and was able to attend all my classes and complete the finals in relative comfort. The professors were very understanding and accommodating, and the students were always helpful and sympathetic.

I began my third year at ACC in the fall of 1999, and I've never missed a class. Every semester I've taken a full load despite my full-time job, and have also taken a class during each of the summer sessions. The only class I've failed so far is college algebra during a short summer class. I took it again in the fall and somehow made a B.

My paralegal degree should land me a better paying position, and more importantly, it will give me the knowledge and education I've put off for so long. Though sometimes it's difficult to work all day, then go straight to school, I'm enjoying the process for the most part. I've met so many wonderful students and professors. Most of the time I'm the oldest student in the class, and sometimes I'm even older than the professor! I got most of my earlier education in the "school of hard knocks." Adversity is strength training, and you could never know how happy you are unless you have some sadness and disappointment to compare it with. My life to date has often presented a challenge, but with someone you love you can weather any storm. Danny and I have been married for 34 years. He's a wonderful, intelligent, hardworking, humble man whose real value may never be known.

He quietly goes about his day, doing what he feels is right and proper, giving advice to me and our sons, endeavoring to teach us to look out for ourselves in case he's not around someday. We disagree on many points, but we don't fight about it. He wonders sometimes why I pursue the things I pursue; for example, why I want to get a degree this close to retirement age. He sometimes gives the impression he's holding his breath wondering what I'll think of next.

My scholastic education is just beginning. I'm fifty-four years old now, and it will be another year or so before I can graduate from college with my hard-earned degree. I want to keep on learning, with no limit, as if my life would never end. At the same time, I want to live each day fully as though it were my last.

– Marti Knipp

Drought

Thirty-nine days
is a long time to go
without rain –
or speaking.
Trees once proud and straight,
droop under the stress
of nothingness.
Hardened brown spikes
piece tender feet,
bared.
Why do we remove our shoes
when we know our feet are so tender?

– Trish Lindsey Jaggers

Teresa

My name is Teresa McAlister. I was born in Columbus, Ohio, but I was reared a little bit everywhere. My mom and my real father got divorced when I was about seven years old, because he sexually molested me. I had a sister, two and a half years younger than me, and a brother, two and a half years younger than her. All of us had the same father. When he went to court on the molestation charges, they made me testify. It was supposed to be done in a separate room, video taped, so I wouldn't have the pressure of seeing him and all the people. My grandparents, his parents, bought our lawyer off and, at the last minute, they put me in the big room. I froze up and was unable to testify. They let him go.

Then, my mother met another man who became my stepfather. He didn't sexually molest me, but he physically hurt me. He was abusive and we went from sexual to physical abuse. My mother never had any goals. She never did anything for herself. All she cared about was making her husband happy, serving him hand and foot.

We moved around a lot. We were really poor and often homeless. We went from campground, to campground, living in a truck and trying to find motels that we could afford. Then we found an abandoned school bus, with half the windows knocked out, and moved into it. It was a short school bus, not a long one, and we were incredibly crowded. I don't know why, but my mother and stepfather figured they didn't have enough mouths to feed. They had to have seventy animals in the school bus with us, including a lot of birds that were constantly squawking.

I was eight then. My brother and sister and I just stuck together, trying to survive. There was no communication with my stepfather. When he was home, all of us would hide, trying to stay away from him. I read, sometimes eight books a day,

trying to escape from my home life. But my little brother got it worse, I guess because he was a boy. He got abused the worst, plus he was hyperactive.

So, we lived in the bus with all the animals in it. Our neighbors lived in a trailer, and when the regular school bus dropped us off, we wouldn't go to our bus, we'd act like we lived in the trailer until the regular bus was out of sight. We were ashamed. Then, we finally got one of those little, silver, Spartan trailers and graduated to that. We didn't have running water for a long time. We had to go to the bathroom in a bucket and take turns dumping it. When we were younger, my parents spent a lot of their money on drugs. We'd do without. We'd eat beans. We'd eat rice, sugar, and milk for breakfast, then we'd eat rice and beans for lunch and dinner. I remember them sending us to bed early, seven o'clock, and we thought we were being punished for something. I didn't know until I was fifteen or sixteen that it was because my mother didn't want us to get hungry, so she just went ahead and put us to bed. But they kept the animals.

It was hard to sleep with all the animals. They had birds, lizards, snakes and rats. We lived in a small trailer, but once we had a big rat cage that took up half of our living room. It had two hundred rats in it. They were trying to sell them for money to pet shops or people that had snakes to feed. My stepfather didn't work much. Most of the time he was unemployed. He was in the welder's union, so we had to travel a lot, and it was hard for him to find work. Then we got stuck in Louisiana and there weren't any jobs there for him, so he just went unemployed for awhile.

When I turned eleven, my mother and stepfather turned Pentecostal, really strict Pentecostal. They went from one extreme to the other. From not caring what we did, passing a joint to us, having us separate the seeds from their marijuana leaves and telling us to not tell our friends, to telling us we couldn't do this; we couldn't do that. My sister and I weren't allowed to wear pants. We had to wear dresses. We weren't allowed to cut our hair. It was hard being different in school. I didn't have any self-esteem because I had to be so different. We couldn't listen to music or watch television. That's probably why I read so much, because we had no television or music, and we lived way out in the country. All I did was go to school, come home, go to church. This was from the time I was eleven until I was fifteen.

But, when they'd get mad they'd cuss. They'd say it was okay because they could repent, because they had the Holy Ghost. It was so hypocritical. My sister and I were best friends, but we felt sorry for my little brother, because he was getting the worst of it. In a way, though, we were glad it was him because that meant it wasn't us. It's sad, but we couldn't help him because he was so out of control; he was so hyper. They had a wooden boat oar they'd hang by the front door, and it was used as a paddle. They would write our name on it whenever we got a whipping. It was a record of who got the most whippings. They broke it over my little brother. It split in half. Then we didn't have to worry about that anymore.

I left home when I was fifteen. I'd run away about five times, and each time I'd stay a day longer. The last time I'd run away, they'd taken me to a counselor. I talked about everything except the real problem because I knew I would get in trouble if I said anything bad about my parents. But, the last day I went, I told them what my mom and stepfather were doing and said that I couldn't deal with it. The counselor said they could bring my mom in, but I said, "If my stepdad finds out I'm gonna get beat." And sure enough, they called her and said they were going to have a meeting with my stepdad. They told her not to tell my stepdad, but she went right home and told him. She was the type that if we did anything, she thought it was directed toward her. She thought we were doing it to hurt her or prove something. She was so sensitive. Then, when my stepdad would get home, she would exaggerate, trying to get us in trouble, telling on us even though she had already disciplined us. So, she went home and told him and he threatened me. He said, "The next time I have to deal with you, I'm going to blow your brains out, and when the police find you in a ditch with your head blown off, I'll blame it on temporary insanity."

He had this shotgun. My mom was standing right beside him, and she didn't say a word. My mom chose him over her children. That was on a Tuesday. I started hiding, even at church. I was trying to stay away from him, because any little thing could set him off. I knew I had until Friday to leave home because I wouldn't make it through the weekend, staying at home with him, with no school to go to. I tried to hide that whole week. Then I found the right time and left, but it wasn't the best ride out of town.

I felt bad for my little sister when I left home, because I was leaving her in an abusive situation, but I couldn't take her out to the street, to be homeless or hungry. I didn't know where I was going. I didn't know if I would be able to take care of her. We were living in Benton, Louisiana at the time, so I went to Sulphur, Louisiana. I lived on the streets for about six months, here and there, stealing candy bars to eat. Then I got caught and went to a bunch of foster homes and juvenile hall a few times. They tried to stick me back with my parents. It was considered contempt of court if a person ran away from a foster home, so I finally told them I would stay in a foster home if they would just send me to a family, any other family, just not back home.

When they finally made that deal with me, I stayed in a foster home. They went through the usual red tape and decided to put me in my aunt's custody. My stepfather and mother tried to come get me from court. He said, "You ain't even met the Devil yet. Wait until you get home." He threatened me like that, yet my mom brought a Bible to the courthouse. She was trying to quote Scriptures to the officials, but they went ahead and put me with my aunt (my mother's sister) in Columbus, Ohio.

I was making bad grades in school when I was living at home, but at my aunt's house, I was on the honor roll. When I was moved to my aunt's custody, I saw she was the opposite of my mother. She was independent. She's never been married. If something didn't get done, she'd do it herself. She was a perfectionist. Things had to be right the first time. That's who I wanted to be like.

I met my real father again when I was sixteen, after not seeing him since I was seven. The whole time I was growing up, I thought my mom was wrong about him. I thought people change, and he must be sorry for what he did. I thought my real father must be a good person. So, I met him when I was sixteen and we were good friends for about a year while I was in high school. I spent time with him every now and then, visiting him in Ohio. When spring break came, I went to spend a couple of days with him. He had rum and coke and he got me drunk, saying it was a celebration for the spring holiday. I passed out and he took advantage of me; he raped me. That blew my mind because my whole life I had faith in people changing, and I thought he regretted what happened in the past and had changed. The next morning I asked him why he raped me, and he said it was because I looked like my mom. He said it was my fault because he loved my mom, he loved me and I looked like her. Then he proposed to me! He said if I loved him, I would leave my family and marry him. It was crazy. I began hyper-ventilating. I had him take me home. I couldn't believe it had happened. I asked him why he'd molested me when I was young. He said it was because I came and hugged up beside him on the couch. I said I should be allowed to show my father love without him thinking that way, but he said it was my fault and my mother's fault because she wasn't giving him any affection. He said he turned to the person he loved second best. My father figure was taken away. I stopped talking to him and seeing him. He tried to bribe me, but I didn't call him back. I don't hate him. I feel sorry for him.

I did well in my last year of high school, and I graduated in June 1992. I got married to someone I met in school. I was pregnant before we got married, which was the reason we got married. I was young, straight out of high school, and I was only married for seven months, then I was divorced. I had my child, a son, with me until he was a year old, but when we got the divorce I lost custody.

My ex-husband's mother was a paralegal, and I didn't stand a chance. He got everything we had. Before our divorce, when we were living at his mother's house, she would try to take my son and put him in her room to sleep. After the divorce, I was working really hard at a drugstore and trying to take care of my son and myself. I worked and my roommate watched my son. I had no furniture; all I had was one bed. I didn't have a car. I had nothing. I'd lost everything. I was running out of food. I was trying to work, trying to survive and things just got crazy for me, trying to take care of my son. I lost our apartment because my roommate didn't pay enough of the rent on time, and I lost my job from trying to take care of my son when I didn't have a baby sitter.

My ex-husband's mother began acting really sweet and said, "Go ahead and sign over temporary custody of the child until you get on your feet." So, I let her take custody of my son and I had a nervous breakdown. I was freaking out. I couldn't take all the stress, so I said I was going down and visit my family, to see my mom. I hadn't seen them in a long time. I went down to visit them for two weeks, but things were awkward. I stayed with my sister who was living with someone else. Then I went back up to Ohio to find that my ex-husband's mother had arranged a hearing while I was gone. They charged me with "abandonment" since I went out of state. So she set me up and the court gave her permanent custody of my son. She wouldn't even let her own son have my child. He and I would talk, and say we could get back together and be roommates. Even though we weren't right for each other, we could be roommates and get our son back. His mother wouldn't go for it. He was willing for us to live together so we could have our son, but his mother had permanent custody. They were middle class and I didn't have any family. I didn't have anyone to talk to or help me.

I felt like there wasn't a lot I could do. I didn't know the law. I didn't have any money. I didn't have any family. So, I buried it for a year. I'd developed OCD (obsessive/compulsive disorder) during my childhood, and it began getting worse, taking the form of perfectionism. I'd also suffered from Tourette's syndrome, bulimia, anorexia. I had bulimia until I got pregnant with the child I have now. I overcame that. But, my ex-husband's mother still has my son. I tried to visit him on the weekends, but after a while, they wouldn't tell him I was his mother. It was very hard on both of us when I went to visit him because he didn't remember me. I didn't want to make it harder on him. I know they give him everything he wants. He has a good home. I lost him when he was one year old. By the time he was three I realized he had been in the same place for so long that, even if I could fight for him, it would be unfair to him. I didn't understand how the justice system could do that to me. I didn't know my legal rights, and I didn't have any support, so I just buried it and accepted it.

I started going to the bars and nightclubs a lot, drinking a lot, doing a lot of drugs. And I stayed busy. I was busy, busy, busy so I wouldn't have any time to think about my son. I was working for a while, then lost my apartment and became homeless and stayed homeless off and on. I sold a lot of blood, drifted from here and there to here and there. Then, I met my second husband. I met my second husband in a bar when I was doing the bar scene. He was doing drugs and I was doing drugs. I'd lived on the streets for about two years before I met him, just going from place to place. He was really funny and we had a lot in common. His family was Pentecostal also.

We went to Louisiana for him to meet my family. My mother had said, "Come down and we will meet your new husband." But when we got there, she said my stepdad didn't want us around so we were stranded down there, homeless. We got stuck down there for six months, homeless, in New Orleans. We were sleeping on park benches, really living rough.

Life at home was harder than life on the street. With life on the street, all we had to do was worry about our next meal and where we were going to sleep. Pretty much we just loafed around all day, being silly. The other people on the street were kind of a family, but not a family we could trust. There were homeless shelters we could go to during the day and take a bath and get a lunch – soup lines and stuff like that. But, we would have to break into abandoned houses to sleep, and sleep on dirty mats with scalies on them. We had to worry about getting diseases and food poisoning because we would eat out of the trash cans, old food, or leftovers people would give us. We would steal bread from in front of the bakery. It was just however we could eat or drink. My husband pulled scams all the time trying to get us money. It was like constant worrying my whole life. Not having security at home has taught me about it, so now I strive for security.

His family lives here in Kentucky and I have a grandmother here. We came here to Kentucky so I could meet his parents. We were living in Ohio when I got pregnant, but we got evicted because he spent the rent money. We came to his parents here in Kentucky with a three month old baby, and I've been here since. The marriage didn't work out. He was abusive, physically and mentally. He's got a really bad temper. Also, he put us at risk with his behavior, but even more serious, he put our daughter at risk. I thought, *Nobody is going to take her from me ... nobody is going to take my daughter from me ... he is not going to put my daughter at risk.*

I went to a shelter for women who were victims of domestic violence or homeless, and stayed there for about three months, then got out on my own. I divorced him on August 4, 1998. My daughter was away from her father and grandparents for about four months when I got the divorce. I felt really bad about that, but I wanted that divorce really bad, and I didn't want him to contest it. I came back and stayed in Kentucky so he could see his child and his parents could see her.

We got back together after the divorce for about two months, then he started getting physical and I left him, but I found I was pregnant again. My second child by him, a boy, was born on December 26, 1999. It will be hard, but at least my daughter and son will be full brother and sister. With my daughter, I prayed to God to let me get pregnant, after losing custody of my first son. I prayed to get pregnant and have another chance, and I am a better mom now, although I was a good mom with my first son. But this second chance makes me able to show her more love, more security. I've never replaced him with her, but I am glad I've had a second chance. And now a third, my son, but this is the last. I want to stop with them because I only have so much time and money.

My ex-husband calls me, harasses me, beats on my door. I would like to move away, but I've got so much going for me here that I'm stuck in the situation. Last week, I was supposed to put a restraining order on him, but I didn't because he threatened me and said if I put him in jail, I was going to pay for it. I'm afraid of him if I do something like that, but I'm not afraid of him otherwise. Now I say, "If you threaten to kill me, I'm not going to live in fear that you're going to kill me. You might as well go ahead and do it because I'm not going to be afraid of you all the time. I'm not going to do what you want just because you're threatening me." The only reason he bugs me so much is because I don't let him do what he wants to do and he doesn't have control over me. I think it drives him crazy. But his parents are good people, and I want my ex-husband and them to be able to see the children.

I'm twenty-five now. He's twenty-four, and he won't grow up. He's taking risks, like everything's easy, like it's just supposed to be that quick. But he's not always going to be lucky. He's going to go to jail, and my kids aren't going to have a dad. But I don't have to worry about him risking us anymore.

I live on my own now. Everything I own I've gotten on my own. Nothing is his. I have my own apartment, in my name; I don't have to worry about losing it as long as I don't have him in my house, taking risks. If we were together and he took risks, with my children there, I could lose them. That's a big hang up of mine, the fear of losing my children, because I love them, and because of what happened before. It feels good to be on my own, my own house, no one threatening it or risking it. After so many years of moving around and not having security, I just want to be able to have some degree of control.

It feels really good to finally be in a classroom, where I've always wanted to be. For four years, I studied on my own at home, because every time I got accepted for a Pell Grant (a student financial aide grant), we'd get evicted or we had to leave. My ex-husband kept messing things up for me, so I just started keeping scrapbooks. I wanted to go to school and study alternative medicine, or natural medicine. I started studying on my own and collecting information, and teaching myself.

I got interested in alternative medicine because my whole family was into it. There is a lot of voodoo in Louisiana, with the herbs and everything. My grandparents were really into it and so is my mom now, so I was exposed to it a little bit when I was growing up.

My interest really started with my obsessive-compulsive disorder (OCD). I was trying to find self-help for myself. I didn't want to be on anti-depressants. When I was bulimic I decided that I wasn't going to feel guilty for eating food anymore. I wasn't going to throw it up, because when I threw up, it was like throwing up my problems and washing my hands of them. So, I decided that when I ate, it was going to be like eating medicine. There was no reason to get rid of it because it wasn't bad. It was doing me good, not doing me bad. So, every time I ate, I said, "This does good for me, it's good for my skin or it has a vitamin in it that is good for me." So, I didn't eat any bad foods to where I'd feel guilty. I did that for about two years, until I overcame the food complex, and I only ate stuff that was good for me. Then I got to where I could eat about anything, and I had the will power to not overdo it. After studying to overcome my bulimia, studying so much about the supplements that are needed for deficiencies that cause bulimia or OCD, I just started getting really interested in it. I like to know the answer to things. I like knowing why my body does something, how I can stop it, how I can help it. I just like to know.

I'm on a welfare program now. I either work or I go to school, and they pay me and provide day care. There's a day care at the college and I've finished my second semester in school now. I got As my first semester and I'm getting As this semester. I'm trying for a scholarship because the federal program only lets me have so many months, then I'm going to have to be able to work to take care of my two kids. I know there is no way I can do that, so I figure if I get straight As and get a scholarship, I won't have to worry about when my months run out.

I'm in continuing education classes where they tutor me on subjects where I need tutoring. I've taken parenting classes; I've taken self-management classes. Whatever I can take, I'm taking it. It's hard to go home and find time to do my homework. I'm a full-time student and it's hard to spend so much time on my studies, but I can do it after my children go to bed or when they take a nap. My daughter's grandparents take her on the weekends, every other weekend, so I spend my weekends at the college library, studying all weekend. I know I can get a degree.

They made me choose a two-year degree, to get federal aid, so I just chose general business management, because right now there is no degree in alternative medicine. There are only four colleges in the United States that have it. But things are changing in that field right now so I figure that, by the time I get done with the basic classes that are required, something will have changed. I figure if I get a general business management degree, I can always open up a natural medicine store. If alternative medicine doesn't work out, medicine in general is an option.It would take a lot more years of study, but I love medicine. It's going to be hard, but I'll go back to school when the baby is six months old – five months from now. I'm going to get my education slowly, but surely.

Now, the only thing I care about is making my babies and me happy. That's how it should be, because it is all focused on me and my children. When I was homeless, after I lost my apartment, I used to always worry about taking care of everything I owned, owning stuff, taking care of it, cleaning. I was overly clean, but when I got homeless, I got rid of whatever else I owned, gave it away, burned it, whatever. I said, "This is what I'm going to do for my OCD and for myself. I am going to find happiness without owning anything, find happiness in myself." It took me a couple of years, but I finally became happy with myself, making myself a better person, not looking better or living better or having more. I found happiness with myself, and now, as long as I am bettering myself in this way or that way, I think that is what happiness is.

My mom lives in Kansas now and is divorced. When I was eighteen or nineteen, I hated my mother and I held a lot of stuff against her. But, when I got a couple of years older, the hate turned to pity, I guess from getting older and realizing she is human. I started feeling sorry for her. All she had in life was my stepfather to make her feel good. I think she might have had a breakdown or something. She talks kind of slow and she's real distant sometimes. She calls me. We're talking now, but things are still awkward. She calls me and asks me about my sister. My sister tells my mom, "We was a dysfunctional family," and that hurts my mom's feelings. I'm trying to make my mom feel better; trying to make it seem not as bad because I don't want my mom to feel bad for choosing her happiness over us. And, it's in the past. You can't keep bringing up the past. She still doesn't have a goal. She stays home. She's afraid to be on her own, afraid to be independent. That's one thing I don't want to be, like her, with no self-esteem.

My sister left home at sixteen for the same reason I left. My stepdad threatened to kill her in front of my mom and she left home and went into the custody of a guardian, a friend's mother. Then my brother left home at seventeen, into the custody of some woman. So, all three of us left home in state custody.

I realized I was the only one who could change what they did to me when I was a child by realizing I could only change myself. But, as long as I love myself, and as long as I set an example for my children, where they see their mom isn't afraid to go to school, isn't afraid to do everything on her own, then they can be proud of me, and my daughter will know that she doesn't have to depend on anyone.

When I'm thirty-five, I'm going to have a home that my son and my daughter can know won't be taken away tomorrow. And they're not going to have to go to bed early, hungry, like we did when I was young. I'm not going to be like my parents and spend all my money on drugs. I'm just going to make sure that my children have what they need.

– *Teresa McAlister*

The Braiding

I taught him to braid
my hair,
how to manipulate the strands
between four large fingers
and a thumb
that interfered.
I taught him to braid,
but I did not show him how.
This he took upon himself –
skipping the comb through
my unruly mess,
trying to make a sense
out of me.
Each shock stings
a wound I didn't know
existed –
until he throws the comb
to the floor,
right away, twisting
his three strands:
My right,
My left,
My center
into such a tight
rope
only he can walk it.

– Trish Lindsey Jaggers

Chiquita

I am a 38-year old African-American, single parent with two sons and a disabled mother. I am also a full-time student. Previously, I was a full-time employee of a local, well-established financial institution in Bowling Green, Kentucky. My life was financially stable for the eleven years I was employed there.

In May 1998, the bank officials announced, in a conference call, that we were being bought out by the Bank of Cincinnati (Ohio). We were given approximately ninety consecutive days to work. Each and every day I went into the work place, I experienced anger, hurt, and depression. My fellow employees suffered in the same way. Everything I had was being taken away from me. I found myself crying a lot those days because I didn't know how I would pay my bills or support my sons and mother. A lot of the other employees had husbands to support them, but I didn't have that advantage. I couldn't leave the job early to look for another position because I'd lose all the benefits that were due to me: vacation pay, severance pay, my employment savings plan retirement. So I stayed, and worried, until August 21, 1998, which was my last day of employment.

In June, I was told that if I wished to obtain a two-year college degree, the dislocated worker program would pay for my tuition, books, and supplies, plus pay me ten dollars per day for school attendance. I could also draw unemployment and severance pay at the same time. That sounded like a good decision, so I did just that. I applied in July through the Employment Office in Bowling Green. I went through a lot of procedures, took tests, filled out forms, and finally registered to become a full-time community college student. The more I thought about it, the more I became enthused. I started to feel better about myself because, although I was losing my job, I was going back to school after nineteen years, and that was a once-in-a-lifetime opportunity. As the time of

my release date drew closer and closer, I was really excited about going to school and pursuing a management information systems/business technology degree. I knew once I have that degree, no one could take that away from me.

My graduation date will be December 2000. I have a 3.6 grade point average. I am quite proud of myself. I know that when God closes a door, He also opens a window, and that's what He's done for me. I know I can't make it without the grace of God. I am still striving to achieve as high as I can possibly go with this degree, and I am working part-time at another financial institution on the university campus as a teller (savings associate). I work every other Saturday. I am not sure where I'm going, and what I'll be doing, but I feel very strongly it will be better than before.

During the eleven years my work life was stable, my personal life was very difficult. First of all, I dated a guy that I thought was very nice person but, instead, he turned out to be a raging lunatic. He had a very serious drug addition and did cocaine, or any other drug he could get his hands on. He had mood swings and personality changes. We'd started to date in 1988. Then he moved in with me and we lived together for three long, miserable years. He had no respect for me nor his own mother. He wasn't a "business attire" type of man, and he drank every single day. For three years I was unhappy. He was so ornery and vulgar that I was constantly miserable. One day I told him he had to go. I was tired of him and his drinking, his smoking, his staying out all hours of the night. I was tired of him bringing strange people to my house, people I didn't care to associate with. We split up for nine months, after living together for three years. I was so happy to not have him around making me miserable.

He returned in April of 1994, asking me to go back with him. I had a son by him who was two years and seven months old. We decided to go back together. He convinced me that he had changed, and said he was going to do right if I took him back. I will never forget what my mother told me. She said, "If you take him back it's gonna be worst than the first time." I thought I knew more than she did, so I didn't listen. I've always been told a "bought" lesson is better than a "told" one. I let him move back into the house with my sons and my mother. We began missing items from our house: new VHS movies we'd just received in the mail, a new bumper jack that had never been opened, tools, a tool box, a chain saw. Things were coming up missing one after another. My mother asked me about the items, and I told her I didn't know what happened to them. At the time, we both worked and were gone from the house all day. My sons were in school or day care.

When I asked him what happened to the missing items, he insisted he didn't know. The next thing I knew, he had taken my debit/ATM card and had gone to work on my checking account and it was overdrawn. I'd also signed for him get a 1990 red Chevrolet sports car. He refused to pay for it, so I told him to take it back to the dealer. I later found out he'd been riding around with other women in that car. One day, I looked under my bed for something and found a plate with a white powder substance and a razor blade. I scraped it off the plate and flushed it down the commode. I confronted him and, of course, he denied it and said it wasn't his; it was his nephew's.

I told him, "Well, he needs to be doing that at his own house not mine. I better not ever see or catch this stuff in my house again. I don't do it. I don't like it, and I don't appreciate it being around my sons."

He got mad and stormed out of the house. One time he disappeared for three days, and nobody knew where he was. Another time, he was in some apartments across town. I went there and he looked like he was in a heavy daze. I tried to talk to him but he wouldn't respond. He looked spaced – a zombie. He was glassy eyed and his lips were white. He hadn't bathed in days. When he finally came down, he didn't remember anything. Prior to this disappearance, he had started acting crazy, paranoid, looking out the window constantly and putting his shoe in front of the door. I didn't tell anybody about how scared I was because he'd begun mistreating me, throwing me up against a wall, smacking me, pulling my hair. He even went as far as to choke me. I thought he was going to kill me one night. He was 6' 5" and weighed about 230 pounds. I am 5'4" and weigh 127 pounds. I didn't tell anybody about the miserable life I was living in my own home. He always told me, "I'll kill you if you leave me." I was scared, frightened, unhappy, depressed.

We'd been together nearly three months, the second time, when one night of holy terror came to my front door. I'd seen these things on television and in the movies, but not in real life. A drive-by shooting took place at my home. They were shooting at my house, trying to get him, because he had stolen some cocaine or rocks from some young guys. They either wanted their drugs or they wanted to kill him. My mother was standing in the doorway, my oldest son was standing in the living room, and I was in the bedroom with my little son. I was terrified that night. They came up into our yard and shot high, midway and low into our house. The police found eight bullet slugs from a nine millimeter. They took a report but, we couldn't identify any of the cars or the people that drove by our house. He wasn't going to identify any of them because he was scared himself. Our windows were boarded up, the lamp in front of the window was broken, the entertainment center had bullet holes in it and there were bullet holes in the walls. It was a total mess.

When the shooting took place, in July 1994, it was the last straw – he had to go. I packed all his belongings the next day and took them to his brother's house. My mother and I changed the locks on the front, back and side door. We had new living room windows put in, hired an electrician to fix our outlets, replaced the damaged items, had our phone number changed and had sensor lights put up around our house. As we swept up glass, I felt so bad because I hadn't listened when my mother advised me not to go back with him. I'd gone back because I thought I loved him and because he was the father of my son. I thought he had changed, and I gave him the benefit of the doubt, thinking that he was going to do right. I was wrong – totally wrong.

He was gone for a little over two weeks, then he came by my job on August 5, around 3:00 in the afternoon. He handed me $140.00 for the jack that had been taken from us and pawned for cocaine. I didn't get off work until 5:00 p.m. When I got home, he came by and wanted me to give him back the money he had just given to me two hours before. I thought he'd already spent his pay check with the dopeman, so I gave him $80.00 and he left. I had promised my sons I'd take them to the Southern Fair in the park, and take them out to eat. He came back and wanted the rest of the money, $60.00.

I told him,"I'm not giving you anything."

We had harsh words and he left again. In the meantime, my sons and I left just as I planned. Mom also left to go out to a golf club at about 7:00 p.m.

My sons and I returned to our house at 11:45 p.m. I drove around to the back of the house, and my back door was standing wide open. I opened the front door with my key in one hand and a baseball bat in the other. I was really frightened because I was by myself with two young youths at my side. I didn't know if he still in the house of not, but I wasn't going to take any chance of letting him get the grabs on me or my sons because he was crazy. I knew he was strung out so bad he didn't know if he was coming or going. He surely didn't care about me or anything else, all he wanted was to get high, and he would do anything to achieve it. As I walked in the front door, I smelled motor oil and bleach. I went into the kitchen. The kitchen chair was turned over. I walked down the hallway and looked into my sons' bedroom. It was torn up. The living room furniture was sticky. I walked over to the entertainment center, looked at the VCR, and it also had something sticky poured into it. I felt it and knew it was syrup. When I went into my bedroom, it looked as if a tornado had hit it. He had cut up some of my clothes and thrown the rest all over the floor. He'd torn up my bed and even went so far as to stab the mattress with three butcher knives; they were sticking straight up in the middle of my bed.

I went to my walk-in closet. He had pulled some of my clothes down from the closet bar and poured motor oil from one end of my closet to the other. What he hadn't cut up with a knife, or oiled, he'd destroyed with clorox bleach. I walked into my mother's bedroom and saw he'd pulled her belongings out of drawers and scattered them around the room. He'd even cut the telephone wires in the kitchen and bedroom. The cordless phone was taken off the base and we couldn't find it. But, thank God, there was no sign of him inside the house.

I got in my car and drove down to the Golf Club to see if I could find my mother, but she wasn't there. It was about 1:00 a.m. I was tired, scared, frustrated and angry. So I drove back to the house and found two police cars in my driveway. My mother and her friend were standing outside. I told the officers I had been there about 15 or 20 minutes earlier and it wasn't a forced entry. The officer wanted to know if anything was taken. I said I could not tell as of yet, but I knew who did it – my ex-boyfriend who was strung out on cocaine.

The next day he came over to my aunt's house, where my mother, my sons and I were staying. He was acting crazy, ranting and raving and wanting me to go outside and talk to him. I refused, so he finally left. When I did go outside, I saw he'd keyed my Honda Accord from the front to the back on the passenger side. He'd done $650.00 damage to my car and $2,500.00 damage to my house. Again, we got the locks changed, our phone number changed, and requested a police patrol around our house and the neighborhood. We didn't feel safe in our own home for a very long time, although, after the last incident, I got an emergency protective order (restraining order) stating he was to stay away from me and my family. I went to court twice in August of 1994, but he failed to appear. The sheriff's office issued a subpoena once in September 1994, but his mother said he had moved to Oregon, which was a lie.

For a very long time I was afraid to go anywhere by myself. I used to watch over my shoulder constantly. I was very scared because I knew I couldn't trust him. I made up my mind I would never get involved with another man. I was determined to stay by myself from that day forward. I knew that I could have lost everything that was so dear to me – my mother and my two sons – in the blink of an eye, but God spared them and me. I realized I should had been closer to the Lord during that time but I wasn't. I wasn't praying hard enough to ask Him to help me get past that bad relationship. Later, I did ask Him to help me to go forward and not turn back. A word of advice: If you are in a similar situation to mine, please get out for your own sake as well as the sake of your children. If you know someone else who is in a dangerous situation, urge them to seek help.

I had no interest in meeting another man, but when I was in court for the restraining order that August, I sat next to a man, and we began to have a conversation while we waited to be called up to the stand by the judge. We talked as if we had known each other a lifetime, although we had just met. His name was Anthony and he was car salesman at a dealership. I told him I worked at a financial institution. He was a very attractive, clean-cut, well-dressed businessman. We learned we both had relatives living in Nashville, Tennessee. We talked about why we were both in court. We exchanged business cards. My case was called before his. I left and went back to work. Later that same month, Anthony asked me out to dinner. I asked if I could take a rain check. I'd just gotten out of a bad relationship and I wasn't interested. I didn't see or hear from Anthony until October when I had occasion to be at the dealership. I talked to Anthony very briefly, and he asked me to call him. With the state my life was in, I had no desire to call him or anybody else. On December 14, I went to pay my car insurance and ran into Anthony at the insurance company. He was with a woman. I called him later and teased him about the woman. He explained to me that she was a customer of his; she'd bought a car from him. Then, I went on to ask him was he married. He told me "yes," but he was going through a divorce. My understanding of "going through a divorce" is that the couple has been to court and procedures have taken place. I thought that was the case with Anthony. I told him I wasn't looking for a relationship. He said, "Okay, let the chips fall where they may."

On Thursday, December 15, Anthony came by my job. He was dressed in a suit, looked handsome, and bought me three peach carnations in a vase with a card that read, "Something to Brighten Up Your Day and It Gets Brighter."

I told him, "That's so nice, but it wasn't necessary."

He said, "I know, but I wanted to." I told him I was very surprised to see him. I felt like crying but I didn't. I took the carnations and he said, "I went to every bank trying to find you."

I told him, "Well, you found me." We just stood and looked at each other for a while and then he said, "I'll let you get back to work."

On December 16, Anthony called to say "hello" and he asked me if I was going to be at work. He came by my job with a Christmas bear and a box of Russell Stover candy. It brought tears to my eyes because he was so sweet to me. I sat at my desk and wondered about this man I just met. Was it legitimate or was he just trying to impress me? Later that night he called me and asked me out to dinner. We went to a seafood restaurant and had a very pleasant conversation. He was wonderful company, even though I was a little nervous because I didn't know him. After dinner Anthony drove me home, walked me to my door and kissed me on the cheek. After that, we had several more lunch and dinner dates.

As Christmas neared, I made a remark to Anthony that we weren't going to exchange Christmas gifts with each other. A couple of days before Christmas, Anthony came to my house with a dress and a pants outfit. I told him I thought we weren't going to buy anything for each other. He said, "I know what you told me." From that day forward, we really started to see a lot of each other. Anthony would stop by the house after work or we would leave my house to go somewhere private, just the two of us. In January of 1995, Anthony came by my house and brought me an ice-cream cake and a bottle of champagne. We called and saw each other almost every day. Anthony was constantly doing something for me, buying me presents, giving me money for bills, putting gas in my car, having my car cleaned. He did things for my sons, like picking them up from practices or ball games.

Anthony gave me a gold chain and a ring the day before Valentine's Day. The next day, he came by work and hand delivered a dozen red roses to me. When I was in bed, sick, in March he brought me a bouquet of red and white carnations. As the months went by, we grew closer and closer. In December 1995, we had been dating one year, and we talked on the phone every day. We were inseparable. Anthony was everything I'd ever wanted in a man: caring, faithful, loyal, understanding, intelligent, thoughtful, loving. I'd made up my mind that I wasn't going to give him up for anything or anybody; he was my all-in-all. Although after my last relationship I'd quit looking for a man and decided I was going to be by myself, when Anthony came into my life, I realized he was legitimate and I could love again.

It was while I was with Anthony that I lost my brother, Wayne, whom I loved dearly. I was the oldest of the three children with two younger brothers. One passed away when I was four years old. That left just Wayne and me, growing up. Wayne moved to Nashville in 1982, but we remained very close. We talked on the phone often and saw each other on holidays and weekends. On May 3, 1997, Wayne came home to show us his new motorcycle. He was on his way back to Nashville after attending the Kentucky Derby. He came to visit again on Mother's Day. His last visit was on July 5, a Saturday, and he stayed until Sunday night. On July 20, I answered the phone and a Dr. Blume, from Nashville's Vanderbilt Hospital's trauma unit, was calling. He told me that they had a Dwayne Sparks in ICU. He'd had a motorcycle accident. I screamed at the top my lungs and I could hear mom, on the other phone, hollering and crying. He told me that my brother wasn't going to make it.

My cousin and I went to Nashville. I needed to satisfy my curiosity of what happened to my dear brother. He had hit two parked cars. When he hit the first car, he broke his neck, then went airborne and came down and hit the second car. When the police found him he was already brain dead. His neck was broken, his ribs were broken, and his lungs were punctured; his hands were dangling like a puppets on a string. Anthony came and stayed with me during and after the loss of my brother. I can remember crying every day, every morning, every night before he was laid to rest. I couldn't sleep. All I could do was think about him and all the special times we shared. His time was limited to 33 years, six months and one day. The whole time I was in mourning, Anthony was right there by my side. I really needed him.

In August 1997, three years had passed since Anthony and I began dating. Anthony and I were closer than ever; we were deeply in love with each other. I knew that Anthony was the man I wanted to spend my life with. I remember telling him that I didn't want to grow old by myself; I wanted him in my life forever. On August 26, Anthony told me something had been bothering him for a long time, but he couldn't tell what it was because he didn't know himself. It upset me because I wanted to know what it was and he couldn't tell me. Anthony started to slack off seeing me. I wondered what was going on. He told me it wasn't me; he just needed to be by himself, to deal with whatever was bothering him. He would go fishing to spend time by himself. I was scared and confused.

In January 1998, we were starting our fourth year together. We still dated and we were more in love than ever. I just knew we would always be together because our relationship was so good and strong, and we were so close to each other. But, you can't take anything or anybody for granted. Anthony came to my house on February 7, a Sunday, and told me he had accepted his calling to become a Baptist preacher. Now I knew what he was toiling with. I could tell he had been crying. He sat on the bed, I hugged him, and I told him I was happy for him, but he didn't hug me back. He didn't say much of anything. He was really quiet and stayed for about fifteen minutes, the shortest time he'd ever stayed at my house. He left to see my pastor. It's hard to describe, but he looked so different, as if he had a glow about him I'd never seen before. I think Anthony had been touched by God. After Anthony left, the reality really hit me. *We wouldn't be seeing each other anymore.* It was like losing a loved one to death; it's the same feeling because the relationship dies, and it's hard to bear losing someone you love.

He couldn't be a Baptist preacher and see me at the same time. When we met, Anthony told me he was going through a divorce. I found out later he and his wife were just separated, but by then I was deeply in love with him. It wouldn't do for a married preacher, even if he had been separated from his wife for years, to be involved with another woman. On February 8, Anthony came by my house after work. We talked and cried together. He held me, but I couldn't feel any desire for him at all.

I told him, "We have to do this right."

He didn't stay long at all. I cried all night, and the next day, and the day after that. My life was torn apart in every way. On Tuesday, I got down on my knees and prayed to God to help me get through it; I prayed so hard. On Wednesday, I woke up and tried to think of Anthony and recall my feelings for him, but I couldn't. My feelings and desires were gone and so were my tears – they were wiped away from me totally. It was as if Anthony never existed in my life. I called Anthony and told him how I felt. Anthony said God was working with me and to let Him work.

On Thursday, I called Anthony and told him I wanted him to come by my house. We talked and Anthony loaded up all his belongings. He cried.

I told him again, "This is something we have to do, and it has to be done right. It's going to be fine."

I told Anthony we were good for each other, but God was better for both of us. While I was telling Anthony all these things, I wasn't crying at all. God had taken the pain from me so

I could be strong and persuade Anthony to forget about me, to go on and do God's will. We hugged each other and he left. We continued to have phone conversations just to hear each other's voice – to tell each other how much we loved one another and how much we missed one another.

It has been a year since he accepted his calling to the ministry. I've been busy with studies, my job, my two sons, and caring for my mom. Anthony is busy working and doing his ministry; eventually he will attend a Baptist seminary. We still keep in touch with each other, but we don't talk every day like we used to. The distance between us has become accepted. We have adjusted and adapted to our new lifestyles. If it's in Gods plan, we will be reunited someday.

Today, my oldest son, Asa, is eighteen. Khalin, my youngest, is eight. I am taking care of my mother, Marie, who has been disabled since September of 1998, and is no longer able to work. She is dear to me and the best friend I've ever had on this earth. I have been a single parent for eighteen years without a real father figure in the household. I've been blessed by not having to rely on welfare, being able to provide for my sons and myself. I carry the household expenses. I live mostly on financial aid at this point, but I know I have to pay the loans back.

I'm proud of my sons, mainly my oldest son. He is a very mannerly and a respectable young man. He goes to church every Tuesday for prayer meeting and Bible study teachers' meetings. He has been writing spiritual poetry, and, hopefully, someday he will publish. My sons attend the Boys and Girls Club of America after school every day. Asa is a role model for many members at the club. He is focusing on enlisting in the Air Force.

Khalin, my younger son, is following in Asa's footsteps. He looks up to Asa, and I feel he will make the same strides and good decisions as Asa. I am indeed blessed to have two wonderful sons that do not hang out in the streets, do drugs, drink nor smoke.

I've made a personal promise to myself that my happiness means the world to me. Some people would rather have money. I'd rather have God and my happiness. Without those two things I'm nothing, and I know that as long as I keep God in my life, I'm always going to be happy. May God bless each of you.

– *Chiquita Sparks*

Kept

She ran one fist
through the wall
of silence
which wept dry
tears like dust webs
in the corners
where the ceiling meets –
three surfaces
facing off at knife points,
and no one backs down
or the walls would fall,
the ceiling would come crashing,
and complacence would grab
the fist, twisting
the arm from its socket,
erasing the scream
with an explosion of dust.

– Trish Lindsey Jaggers

Michelle

I hurriedly scribble down some thoughts in my journal:

In darkness I sit, consumed by the coals which burn deep within my soul.

Bound by chains of the past, I find myself a prisoner, trying to recall the ways of a simple life. I thought I could ignore the bitter winds that hardened my heart to stone; yet, somehow I can't let go, so I am faced with a world of uncertainty, in which I am in constant battle.

I never knew living could hurt so deep, but if you can't see the proof of battle on my face, you will surely find it in my heart, for it is there that you will find the struggles that go on with every mountain I climb and every step I gain.

A child grows up and learns to hide by molding a face that smiles a lot and could seemingly last forever; but, in spite of the ideal, this face has wept and tasted many tears.

My life is being dictated by a sense of fear and doubt, leaving my spirits drained and my faith very fragile. There are times I think I can't go on and I begin to question, "What happened? Why me? Why now? When will all this end?" And death seems to be the only way to leave all my struggles far behind, but somehow I muster up enough strength to carry on – for one more day.

It seems as though my life is moving backward; the crowds consistently pass me by. I'm running in the wrong direction.

My eyes are always fixed upon the answer, but I'm constantly blinded by haunting memories of pain and of loss.

Instead of living and growing in the light, I have been uprooted and replanted in the darkness, where my entity is craving the life-giving water called Hope.

Rather than turning to people for comfort, I often seek solace in my solitude through self-destructive behavior.

The tension can be so tremendous that I feel as though I will explode. My mind races; my body trembles. Then the blade of contentment is exposed, cutting below the surface of my hardened skin. Somehow the blood still flows freely, and for once, I feel relieved.

Physical pain is so much easier to endure than the emotional anguish I suffer. The cuts run deep. They can't be taken at face value. It's not so black and white.

Each one of us has a song to sing, but I need more than a melody to free me from this dreary lyric. I need more than a spark to lead me out of this darkness.

There is a proverb that states that our friends know us in prosperity and we know our friends in adversity. I have come to see the truth in this. There are a few people who have stood by me through the blood, the painful memories, the cries – both silent and voiced, the long sleepless hours, and the daily conflicts. To you, I dedicate my life because you are in fact the source of my motivation to live.

Many times we must break things down in order to build them better – old bridges, houses, and relationships. I have been "pressed down, but not crushed... persecuted, but not abandoned... perplexed but not in despair... TORN, BUT NOT BROKEN."

I offer you this, my story, in hope that you, too, can mend. Those words are the cathartic remnants of silenced pain. Too often our mouths are sealed shut by fear, guilt and embarrassment, but our hearts refuse to be quieted. This is the innate gift of survival.

Consider a little girl lying in bed, cold with fear. The only sound is that of a heartbeat, pounding aloud; commotion in the other room is a distant blur. Then suddenly the door squeaks open and a shadow becomes larger as the steps become louder. She gasps with fright as a hand reaches out. She tries to yell; no one can hear. The hand reaches down, slowly but intently. The covers are yanked out of the girl's tight grasp and laid aside. The crying girl shivers in the chill of the moment. Towering over supple flesh, the shadow's darkness is revealed. He grabs her and tosses her like a doll onto a mattress on the concrete floor. On the musty and damp padding, the girl crawls in a fetal position. Then her legs are stretched to their limits and the shadow's smoky breath envelops her as he leans down. With a few thrusts and moans of success, the shadow returns to his knees and stands up. He tidies himself and nonchalantly exits the room. While the marijuana makes the other room seem like heaven, this bedroom is hell. Weeping in the silence, the little girl crawls into the corner and shakes uncontrollably.

The next morning the girl awakens by the sunlight beaming in through her uncovered window. She looks around her. Though the sun lights the room, it still feels dark and scary. She makes her way into the bathroom and cleans up the bloody, remaining evidence of the previous night of terror. After getting dressed, she wanders into the living room, only to find her mother passed out on the couch after a night of ecstasy. Men lay like dirty laundry around the apartment. Weaving in between their sprawled legs, the little girl makes her way to the door and walks to school. Silenced by fear, she tells no one.

A teen-age girl goes to a relative's house to visit. After a long day of school, she and the relative unwind by playing Nintendo. She is enjoying herself and actually winning at the video game. This seemingly innocent game turns into a nightmare. The relative approaches the adolescent from behind and places his hands on her shoulders. A massage would be great. But with the firm hands still on her shoulders, he leans down and begins kissing her neck.

Laughing, she pushes him away and directs her attention back to the game. But he does not stop. Standing behind her chair, he slides his hands down the front of her shirt and kneads her breasts. He continues to talk seductively as they do in the movies. He tells her he wants to have oral sex. She denies his request. The boy doesn't approve of her response and pushes her onto the waterbed. She tries to sit up but is unable to due to the rocking of the mattress and the power of the male. He straddles her body and unzips her jeans. Then he continues to rip off her clothes and pin her spread legs against the bed by wedging them between the bed frame, desk and a chair. While tears are steaming down her white face, the teen achieves his goal and smiles with delight. His mission is accomplished. He asks the girl if she liked it. She says nothing, and hurriedly gets dressed and walks out. Silenced by guilt, she tells no one.

A graduate student sits in her vehicle contemplating the meaning of life, and the lack thereof. The tears have dried up over the years; there is nothing visible of her pain. Distraught, she drives around the city and ends up at a park overlooking the river. The only lights are those of trolling boats. She reviews her life as a mini-series in which the main character dies at the end of the story. With her decision in mind, she heads back to her apartment and spends the next three days compiling her last words to dearest friends and relatives, even down to her own funeral arrangements. Others seem oblivious to her intent since she greets them with a smile. There is solace in the realization that the pain will soon end. The last straw is drawn and the moment is near. Few friends realize the imminent crisis will be the last they see of her. Authorities are notified while the woman meets with a dear confidant. During their meeting, she is focused and non-emotional. Her friend understands her state of mind and cries in distress. Without having answers, the friend continues to ask the questions. The woman stands in contentment, knowing her impending relief is near. After a few hours of discussion, she heads back to her apartment and lies in her bed. Suddenly, there is a banging on the door and the telephone is ringing. Shaking with fear, she jumps up and runs to the door. Through the peephole, she sees a uniformed policeman. Quickly, she returns to her bedroom and grabs her loaded gun. She yanks the pillows from the bed and stacks them on the floor. She takes the top one and leans over, putting it over her head to silence the gunshot. The safety lock is taken off; the gun is pressed against her covered skull. Her whole life flashes before her in the seconds that pass. She remembers her promise to the confidant – that she will see her tomorrow. Times passes, and the woman thinks she can escape, but the police stop her. She spends the next week in the psychiatric unit. Silenced by embarrassment, she tells no one.

Despite having just passed my twenty-fifth birthday, I have lived through a great deal. Until age eighteen, I hid behind my smile and immersed myself in school, church and sports. But the silence took its toll, and the lock of secrecy broke. In return, I broke down, physically and emotionally. Paralyzed by depression, I spent a year or more of college in a daze. Attempts to repress memories proved futile. Even though my mouth was closed, my heart was speaking volumes. Somehow I found a few, dear people who became my lifelines. Guided by their unending support, I survived.

Journaling has been a vital outlet for me. Through triumph, tragedy, and in between, my pen has helped me safely express my frustration, guilt, embarrassment, desire and rage. It has been beneficial in enabling me to better understand my feelings, and, in return, has become a tangible report of progress.

Perhaps more than anything else, breaking down the wall of protection and allowing myself to become vulnerable has propelled me into triumph. After years of hurt, we become hardened and seemingly unbreakable. And this is our protection that has served us well for years. The irony in this is that before healing can begin, we must unarm ourselves and be willing to hurt again. Dealing with events and repressed emotions is no easy task: it takes hard work and courage. Many people never get to that point. I may not have either if I were not so blessed with extraordinary support.

Since I have a bachelor's degree in psychology and have nearly completed my master's degree in social work, I feel compelled to include the benefits of therapy. This is a link in my support system as well. Tough? Absolutely. But I have yet to find something worthwhile that I haven't had to work toward. No matter where we find support on the outside, it is necessary to get us through the trenches until we can find some support within.

I must give credit to a dear friend of mine. Without her ceaseless support, undying patience and skills for listening, I would not have been able to see the triumph in my story. Through the tears, silence, laughter and rage, she has stood strong. It is with great honor that I consider her my engine – the one that keeps me going even when I am ready to give up.

– *Michelle Wallace*

In Reverse

smoke
falls
and the night
rises
to the occasion
a farce
intended
for those
who believe
all good things go up
all evil rests with props below stage
under
the devine feet
of the god
knowing all
have nothing to lose
by believing
in childhood
by being short
and looking up
to what
we will become
if we only
lose our fear
of heights
or falling

– Trish Lindsey Jaggers

Works Cited

Kentucky Women, Governor's Commission on the Status of Women
Kentucky State Government, Frankfort, Kentucky:
May 12, 1966.

The Merck Manual, 16th edition, Merck Research Laboratories, Merck & Co., Inc., Rathway,
NJ, 1992, 1369-70

Yahoo.Health/Diseases.com

Smith-Mello, Michal, et.al.
The Context of Change: Trends, Innovations, and Forces Affecting Kentucky's Future
The Kentucky Long-Term
Policy Research Center, Frankfort, Kentucky: 1994.

www.ingramcontent.com/pod-product-compliance
Lightning Source LLC
Chambersburg PA
CBHW031547260326
41914CB00002B/315